Chambers

BOOK OF CINEMA FACTS

SWAYAM GANGULY

hachette INDIA

First published in 2024 by Hachette India
(Registered name: Hachette Book Publishing India Pvt. Ltd)
An Hachette UK company
www.hachetteindia.com

Cover Image Credit: Camera Image: Freepik.com.
This cover has been designed using assets from Freepik.com.

ISBN 978-93-5731-569-2

Hachette Book Publishing India Pvt. Ltd
4th & 5th Floors, Corporate Centre,
Plot No. 94, Sector 44, Gurugram 122003, India

Typest in Cambria 10.5/13, Open Sans 13/13
by Avishek Bhattacharya

FSC
www.fsc.org
MIX
Paper | Supporting responsible forestry
FSC® C010615

Printed and bound in India
by Thomson Press India Ltd.

Contents

Preface *v*

Chapter 1
LET THERE BE LIGHTS, CAMERA, ACTION! 1

Chapter 2
WORLD CINEMA 17

Chapter 3
TINSELTOWN 71

Chapter 4
INDIAN CINEMA 173

Chapter 5
BLOODLINE 267

Preface

Welcome to the enthralling world of cinema on the page, where facts unfold like scenes in a meticulously scripted film. This book is not a collection of narratives but a fact-driven journey through the expansive landscape of film-making that has shaped our understanding of the seventh art.

As you navigate through these pages, prepare to be immersed in the rich tapestry of cinema from around the world, where every frame tells a story of cultural convergence and cinematic brilliance. Discover intriguing anecdotes and behind-the-scenes insights that illuminate the creative processes behind some of the most iconic films from the US, Europe, Asia, Africa, and beyond.

Bollywood, with its kaleidoscope of colours and melodies, also takes the stage as we delve into the facts that have defined its journey. From the inception of the industry to the lesser-known stories of legendary films, explore the fascinating details that make Bollywood an integral part of global cinematic history.

Venture also into the diverse realms of Indian regional cinema, where every snippet contributes to the mosaic of storytelling. From the origins of regional film industries to the remarkable achievements and challenges they faced, uncover the layers that define the unique narratives of each corner of India.

Hollywood's captivating narrative unfolds with a focus on facts and figures that have marked its evolution. Learn about the historical milestones, technological innovations, and the intriguing behind-the-camera dynamics that have shaped the powerhouse of the global film industry – not forgetting the stars of course.

This is not just a journey through time; it's a deep dive into the technical intricacies of film-making. Uncover facts about cinematography, camera angles, and the evolution of cinematic techniques that have shaped the visual language of films. From the ingenuity of the silent era to the technological marvels of today, we explore the facts that underpin the art and science of film-making.

As you flip through these fact-filled pages, may you gain a profound appreciation for the real stories behind the reel magic. Whether you are a seasoned cinephile or a curious novice, this cinematic odyssey is a treasure trove of verified information, captivating anecdotes, and astonishing revelations.

Lights, camera, action – let the journey through the corridors of cinema begin!

1

LET THERE BE LIGHTS, CAMERA, ACTION!

CINEMA WAS NOT INVENTED BY A SINGLE PERSON. IN 1891, A SUCCESSFUL DEMONSTRATION OF A PROTOTYPE OF THE KINETOSCOPE BY THE EDISON COMPANY MADE IT POSSIBLE FOR ONE PERSON AT A TIME TO VIEW MOVING PICTURES. THE KINETOSCOPE WAS SUCCESSFUL COMMERCIALLY, AND PUBLIC PARLOURS WERE SET UP ACROSS THE WORLD.

The First Moving Picture

The first moving picture happened as early as 1888. The *Roundhay Garden Scene* (1888) was a two-second, silent, short clip filmed by French inventor Louis Le Prince showing his family dancing around in a circle. This innovation eventually led to film cameras and motion pictures.

The First Motion-Picture Film Camera

The Kinetoscope was the first motion-picture film camera and was invented by Thomas Edison and William Kennedy Dickson. The camera permitted one person to view a film through a peephole window at the top of the device.

The First Motion-Picture Film Camera
The Kinetoscope was the first motion-picture film camera and was invented by Thomas Edison and William Kennedy Dickson. The camera permitted one person to view a film through a peephole window at the top of the device.

The Lumière Brothers

In December 1895, the Lumière Brothers are believed to be the first to show moving pictures to a paying audience in Paris, France. They used a device they had invented called the Cinématographe, which was a camera, a projector, and a film printer, all rolled into one.

The First Short Films

The first short films were somewhat boring by today's high standards. They had just one silent scene, which was a minute long. To compensate for the lack of sound, a band would sometimes play live music in the theatre as the movie was aired.

Themes of First Short Films

The first short films were aired at music halls, fairgrounds, or any location where a screen could be set up and a room darkened. The topics ranged from local scenes and activities, glimpses of foreign lands, short comedies, and newsworthy events.

Adding Colour

Colour arrived! Colour was added through hand colouring, tinting, toning, and stencilling. In 1906, the principles of colour separation were applied with the British Kinemacolor process to create 'natural colour' moving images. This was first presented to audiences in 1909. Invented by George Albert Smith, it was used commercially till 1914.

The Cinema Lumière

The period from 1903 to 1909 witnessed the beginning of the Italian film industry after the first public presentation by the Lumière brothers in Paris. The Lumières brought the new art form to Italy in 1896. As the first movies arrived, the first Italian movie theatre, the Cinema Lumière, was built in Pisa in 1899.

The Rise of Italian Cinema

By 1910, the Italian film industry was thriving in Rome, Turin, Milan, and Naples. Later, cities like Venice, Genoa, Catania, and Palermo were added to the list. Just before World War I, Italian cinema received worldwide adulation and screenings in the United States.

Documentaries as the First Italian Films

The first Italian films were documentaries, lasting just for a few seconds. They recorded facts and eminent people of their times, like royals and popes. The apparatus used was a simple, crank-operated camera.

The First Italian Film

The first Italian movie *La Presa di Roma* directed by Filoteo

Alberini was released on 18 September 1905. The movie highlights the last moments of Rome in the hands of the pope in 1870. The film recorded the important event of the capture of Rome by the newly formed Italian army.

The First Italian Movie with Sound

The first Italian movie with sound was shown on 19 October 1906 at the Cinema Lumière in Pisa by Professor Pietro Pierini. This oldest Italian theatre is still operational.

The Aspect Ratio

In the Kinetoscope, Thomas Edison had used perforated 35mm film. In 1909, this was accepted as the worldwide industry standard in film-making. The width-to-height relationship of the picture is known as the aspect ratio. The aspect ratio is 4:3 or 1.33:1. The first number denotes the width of the screen, and the second refers to the height. Hence, for every four centimetres in width, there will be three centimetres in height.

Kinemacolor

The British Kinemacolor process was used mainly to create documentaries like the epic *With Our King and Queen through India* or *The Delhi Durbar,* which was released in 1912 and was over two hours long.

By 1914, several national film industries were established in Europe, Russia, and Scandinavia. The industries thrived here initially as films expanded in length and as narrative or storytelling became the all-important form of film expression.

The Three-Colour Process

The year 1915 saw innovative Technicolor processes but these were tiresome and expensive. It all changed when the three-colour process was introduced in 1932. The process was used in the UK in *A Matter of Life and Death* (1946) and *Gone with the Wind* (1939), and *The Wizard of Oz* (1939) in Hollywood.

The Academy Ratio

After the introduction of optical sound in film, the aspect ratio was adjusted to 1.37:1. This is called the 'Academy ratio' simply because it was officially approved in 1932 by the Academy of Motion Picture Arts and Sciences (the folks giving away the Oscars).

Adding Sound to Cinema

The addition of synchronized sound to projected pictures was first attempted using phonographic cylinders or discs. But the first movie that successfully incorporated synchronized dialogues in Hollywood was *The Jazz Singer* (1927). The Warner Brothers' Vitaphone system was used, having a separate record disc with each reel of film.

Innovation in Sound

The Vitaphone system was however not that effective and later made way for an optical, variable-density soundtrack recorded photographically along the edge of the film. This was created originally for newsreels like Movietone but was used in cinema instead.

Singin' in the Rain (1952) is considered by many as the greatest Hollywood musical ever made. The narrative template involves the use of romantic comedy along with the musical genre. Music, songs, dance, and dialogue have been wonderfully fused to depict the era in Hollywood when the transition was made from silent film to talkies.

Animation

Animation was first used in cinema before 1900. In December

1899, a British film producer created a stop-motion short film titled *Matches: An Appeal*. Through this film, viewers were urged to send matches to British forces fighting in the Boer War.

The Growth of Cinema

The first thirty years of cinema witnessed the growth of an industrial base, narrative form, and technology. People paid more money to watch movies. The production, distribution, and exhibition budgets went up too as large studios and cinema halls were built.

Dogme 95

A united effort to launch a European film movement was made by the formation of a film-makers' collective in Denmark, called Dogme 95, with Lars von Trier and Thomas Vinterberg as its founding members. The first Dogme 95 film, *The Celebration*, won the Jury Prize at the 1998 Cannes Film Festival. This manifesto had ten rules that favoured realism in film content and style instead of technological gadgetry.

The Horse in Motion

English photographer Eadweard Muybridge created a stop-motion technique in 1878 used for the first moving picture. He arranged twelve cameras around a horse-racing track. As the horse passed, it triggered each camera, and twelve photos were taken in quick succession. This technique was known as 'The Horse in Motion'.

The First Fiction Film

The first fiction film was produced in 1895. It was only a minute in length, and the subject of the film was a practical joke. Louis Lumière's *L'Arroseur Arrosé* had a boy standing on a gardener's water pipe, and when he stepped off, the gardener was drenched in water.

The Panorama Shot

Before 1987, cameras were stationary and to derive any movement while filming, you had to move the entire camera and tripod. But the invention of the panorama shot or pan shot transformed film-making and revolutionized cinematography.

Early Camera Shooting Techniques

The first cameras used a shooting speed of sixteen frames per second (fps), which was pretty slow. Today, modern 35mm camera films use twenty-five fps. But thirteen fps is the bare minimum speed a human brain requires to process consecutive images as movement. That's why old movies look unnatural.

The First Feature-Length Film

The first feature-length film was *The Story of the Kelly Gang* (1906). This iconic Australian film was an hour long and was almost destroyed over time. Thankfully, a few pieces were discovered in 1975 and at least some of it was restored and preserved.

The First Movie Theatres

The first movies were a part of carnivals or shown in traditional theatres. Only after the creation of the first movie theatres in 1907 did movies become the main attraction for audiences.

Digital Light Processing (DLP)

Today most modern theatres use digital video projectors using the technology called digital light processing. Films are projected digitally instead of transporting vast reels of film to theatres, thus saving time and money. The videos are sent via hard drive, internet, or satellite.

The First Public Movie Screening

Paris witnessed the first public movie screening on 28 December 1895. The Lumière brothers presented the black-

and-white film *La sortie des ouvriers de l'usine Lumière (Workers Leaving the Lumière Factory).* The black-and-white film was just fifty seconds long, showing what the title promised – workers leaving the factory.

Britain's First Cinema Theatre

The Regent Street Cinema in London was officially Britain's first cinema theatre. It began operations on 21 February 1896.

The First Film Kiss

The first kiss on camera happened in 1896. An aptly titled thirty-second film called *The Kiss* captured the first kiss on film between Broadway stars May Irwin and John Rice. The film was produced by Thomas Edison's company.

The First Narrative Film

The 1903 film *The Great Train Robbery* is considered the first narrative fiction film in Hollywood as it's the first film that told a proper story. The film was under twelve minutes long and was shot in Edison's New York City studio and at outdoor locations in New Jersey.

The First Public Movie Theatre

The first public movie theatre in America opened on 19 June 1905. After the opening of the Nickelodeon theatre, a dozen Nickelodeon theatres sprang up in Pittsburgh in the space of a few months. The next two years saw more than eight thousand theatres launched.

First Nude Scene

The year 1915 saw the first film to feature a fully naked woman in *Hypocrites* directed by female director Lois Weber. The first fully naked man on film arrived late as usual – fifty-four years later. Ken Russell's 1969 film *Women in Love,* adapted from the D.H. Lawrence novel of the same title, won an Oscar.

The Hays Code

The Motion Picture Producers and Distributors of America (MPPDA) was formed in 1922 as a measure of industry unification. The Hays Code, named after the then MPPDA President Will H. Hays, was created to censor inappropriateness in American cinema in its early years.

The Hays Code included a 1927 list of 'Don'ts' including profanity, nudity, use of illegal drugs, and sexual perversion. The code also included several 'Be Carefuls', which did not ban behaviours but simply warned against them.

The First Drive-In Theatre

The first drive-in movie theatre opened in Camden, New Jersey, on 6 June 1933. Drivers watched the British comedy *Wives Beware* (1932) with tickets priced at twenty-five cents per car. The popularity of drive-in has nosedived today, but 321 theatres were still operational in the United States as of June 2020.

Use of Multiple Shots

The early films were all composed of a single shot. The film that changed all that and used multiple shots was a French film on the life of Jesus Christ.

Innovation in the Silent Era

Films were produced without sound in the silent era. American film-makers innovated to attract audiences to the theatres by introducing 'intertitles' (similar to PowerPoint slides used today). These enlightened audiences with details and dialogues.

Popcorn in Theatres

Initially, any kind of food was frowned upon in theatres as cinema was serious business. But the Great Depression changed everything, including prudish mindsets. Sound was added to film, which became increasingly popular. Snacks like popcorn were introduced in theatres to satiate the appetite of this growing clientele.

The First Movie Stuntman

Frank Hanaway holds the distinction of being the first movie stuntman. He was cast in the film *The Great Train Robbery* in the year 1903. Hanaway was an ex-cavalryman in the US Army and best known for falling off a running horse without injuring himself.

The Western

The Western is a popular genre in cinema not only in America but across the world. Mostly associated with folklores from the American West, the genre is set in the American West of the late 18th and 19th centuries, usually featuring cowboys, settlers, and outlaws, exploring the frontier. The most popular Western hero in real life to have been portrayed in cinema is Buffalo Bill Cody. He's followed closely by Billy the Kid.

The First British Talkies

The first director to bring sound to British cinema was Alfred Hitchcock. *Blackmail,* which released in 1929, was Hitchcock's first hit and also the first talkie film to be released in Britain.

The Motion Picture Rating System

The year 1968 witnessed the beginning of the motion picture rating system with G, PG, R, and X. But two years before that, the first film to have a stipulation that no one under the age of eighteen was allowed to watch it was *Who's Afraid of Virginia Woolf?.*

The First European Movie Studio

Georges Méliès built the first movie studio in Europe. He constructed Studio A in the vegetable garden of his property on the outskirts of Paris. This building was made totally of glass walls, and a shed sufficed as a dressing room.

Pioneer of Film Techniques

French film-maker Georges Méliès is the pioneer of three film techniques still used today. The first is the 'double exposure' used in *The Cave of the Demons* (1898). The second is the 'split screen' used in *Four Heads Are Better Than One* (1898). The third is the 'dissolve' used in *Cinderella* (1899).

The First Black Oscar Winner

Hattie McDaniel became the first Black actor to win an Oscar in 1940 for her portrayal of Mammy in *Gone with the Wind* (1939). Oscars then were designed as plaques instead of statuettes.

FILM BASICS

Five Main Types of Modern (or Method) Acting

Stanislavski Method

This systematic acting training technique was developed by Konstantin Stanislavski of the erstwhile Soviet Union, known for authoring the famous book *An Actor Prepares*, originally published in 1936. The objective of this method is to bring a sense of realism to one's performance by breaking down the role according to the circumstances faced by the character.

Method Acting Technique

Lee Strasberg, American director, actor, and acting teacher, developed the popular method acting technique inspired by the Stanislavski method. The aim is to keep the performance emotionally realistic. Actors are encouraged to use personal experiences from their past to extract a strong emotion and blend it into the performance.

Meisner Technique

This acting technique was developed by the American actor Sanford Meisner, also influenced by the Stanislavski method. The objective is to be more instinctive and in the moment during the performance. Improvisation and imagination are encouraged to bring out emotion rather than be reliant on memory.

Five Main Types of Modern (or Method) Acting

Chekhov Technique
Stanislavski's student Michael Chekhov, Russian-American actor and director, pioneered this technique that taps into the subconscious mind and demonstrates more physicality to transform an internal need into a gesture rather than use emotion in the performance.

Practical Aesthetics Acting Technique
David Mamet, American playwright and film-maker, made this technique popular by combining the teachings of Stanislavski and Meisner with the methods of the Greek philosopher Epictetus. The actors get into character by using a four-step analysis to break down a scene that includes:

- The literal
- The want
- The essential action
- The 'as if'

Types of Cuts Used in Editing Films

Standard Cut
A standard cut or hard cut is the basic cut in editing where one clip is cut to another.

Jump Cut
A jump cut helps the scene jump forward in time. It is the most

famous editing cut where the continuous sequential shot of the subject is cut in two parts to give the viewers an illusion of the future.

L Cut

The L cut shows the action in one clip where the sound is coming from the previous shot to bring about a natural flow of the scene.

J Cut

The J cut is the opposite of the L cut, where the sound of the next shot overlaps the video from the present shot. This audio provides the lead-in to the next scene as the audio is heard before we jump to the next shot.

Montage Cut

The montage cut uses a series of rapid images that are in sequence with each other to add to the context of the narrative of the film across genres.

Cross-Cut

The cross-cut is used to add suspense and mystery to the scene by cutting between two scenes that are happening at the same time but in different locations. This cut is also called parallel editing and is used to tell two stories simultaneously.

Camera Angles for Different Types of Shots

Eye-Level Shot

The eye-level shot keeps the subject at the eye-level giving a neutral perspective, where the subject is neither inferior nor superior. The eye-level shot symbolizes how we see real people in real life.

Low-Angle Shot
The subject is framed from below their eyeline in a low-angle shot and is made to feel superior or powerful in a particular scene or to evoke fear or dread.

High/Top-Angle Shot
The camera points down at the subject in a high-angle shot making the subject look inferior, vulnerable, or weak. But this shot is used to depict other situations as well, like a stylized shot for example.

Hip-Level Shot
In this shot, also known as the cowboy shot, the camera is placed waist-high. This shot is often used when one subject is standing and the other is seated. It is commonly used in cowboy movies or Westerns when someone is reaching for a gun in a holster at the hip.

Knee-Level Shot
The knee-level shot is when the camera is placed as low as the subject's knees and is used to communicate a character's walk, creep, or crawl.

Ground-Level Shot
In a ground-level shot, the camera's height is on ground level with the subject. This camera angle is used to feature the character walking without showing the face.

Shoulder-Level Shot
This camera angle is as high as the subject's shoulder and makes the subject look shorter than they actually are by reducing their head room.

Dutch-Angle or Dutch-Tilt Shot
The camera is slanted to one side in the Dutch-angle to increase

tension in the scene or create a sense of disorientation or a destabilized mental state of the subject.

Overhead Shot or Bird's-Eye View

An overhead shot is taken from ninety degrees above – that is, vertically above, and looks down on the subject. Anything less than ninety degrees becomes a high-angle shot. It is also known as neutral or divine point of view.

Aerial Shot

An aerial shot is taken from much higher up in the air, usually from a drone or a helicopter.

What Does a Film Producer Do?

A film producer is someone who supervises the entire process of film production from its inception to the finished product, including aspects of pre-production activities like script selection, writing, selection of actors, locations, and technicians, and also aspects of production like direction and logistics to post-production elements like editing, animation, and dubbing, to name a few. By and large, arranging funds to finance the film is the major role played by the producer. Another important function is to ensure that the production process is smooth and the film is completed within the stipulated time without exceeding the budget.

Casting Whodunit?

Casting for films is a pre-production process which involves a collaborative effort among various members of the team. Primarily, casting directors, tasked with finding the right talent, play a pivotal role. They work closely with film-makers to scout actors, reviewing portfolios, holding auditions, and conducting screen tests to assess the actors' suitability for specific roles. In many cases, casting directors or their teams actively approach actors or their representatives, inviting them to audition or submit their work for consideration.

Directors and producers also play integral roles in the casting process. The director, as the creative visionary, actively participates in selecting actors who align with the artistic vision of the film. Producers often work alongside casting directors and directors, contributing to decisions that balance artistic vision with commercial viability, taking into consideration marketability, budget constraints, and the broader commercial appeal of the chosen cast. Collaboration between these key stakeholders ensures the assembly of a cast that not only fits the story but also resonates with the audience.

Alternatives in casting methods have emerged over time. While traditional auditions remain prevalent, the digital age has facilitated virtual casting calls, allowing actors to submit video auditions online, broadening the scope for discovering talent from across the globe. Additionally, some directors opt for unconventional methods, such as street casting, scouting non-professional actors who might bring authenticity to the roles.

2

WORLD CINEMA

WHEN BONG JOON-HO, THE SOUTH KOREAN DIRECTOR OF *PARASITE* (2019), ACCEPTED THE GOLDEN GLOBE AWARD 2020 FOR BEST FOREIGN LANGUAGE FILM, HE FAMOUSLY SAID, 'ONCE YOU OVERCOME THE ONE-INCH-TALL BARRIER OF SUBTITLES, YOU WILL BE INTRODUCED TO SO MANY MORE AMAZING FILMS.' WORLD CINEMA IS A MORE PLURALISTIC OUTLOOK TOWARDS THE ART OF CINEMA, WHERE AUDIENCES ARE EXPOSED TO MOVIES FROM AROUND THE GLOBE. THIS HAS ESPECIALLY GAINED MOMENTUM WITH THE ADVENT OF TECHNOLOGICAL SUPPORT, MAKING GLOBAL CONTENT MORE ACCESSIBLE TO PEOPLE.

The Contribution of European Cinema

European cinema has been at the helm of artistic and experimental film-making, thanks to film movements like the French New Wave, Italian Neorealism, German Expressionism, and the Danish Dogme 95. European cinema has also shaped the language and grammar of film-making with the invention of jump cuts, non-linear narratives, and handheld camera techniques.

SWEDISH CINEMA

Light Dedication

To prepare for the filming of *Winter Light* (1963), Swedish director Ingmar Bergman and his cinematographer Sven Nykvist would sit for hours every day in a church in northern Sweden. This was done only because they wanted to see how the light changed between 11 a.m. and 2 p.m. each day.

Notorious Affair

Great Swedish actress Ingrid Bergman (not to be confused with the great Swedish director Ingmar Bergman) tasted success with movies like *Casablanca* (1942) and *Notorious* (1956). But it was her notorious affair with acclaimed Italian director Roberto Rossellini that caused quite a scandal.

Leaving Sweden

In 1976, the great Swedish director Ingmar Bergman was charged and arrested for income tax evasion. He was proved innocent later. But this act broke Bergman's heart, and he decided not to work in Sweden anymore. Bergman moved to America and made films there.

Bergman's Devilish Streak

The Swedish film-maker Ingmar Bergman once became so angry because of a dispute over censorship that he decided to get even by putting many obscene pictures in the front credits of his film *Persona* (1966).

DANISH CINEMA

Before World War I

One of the oldest but still-running film studios in the world, Nordisk Film, was established in 1906 in Valby, Denmark. The Danish cinema business was one of the most active and productive in the world during the silent film era, and Danish performers and films were well-known all over the world.

First to Legalize Porn

Denmark was the first nation to legalize pornography in the late 1960s, which sparked the creation of several raunchy movies. Because of this, the Danish film industry developed a reputation for being free, controversial, and unrestrained.

The Big Bier of Danish Cinema

Danish director Susanne Bier has a distinguished career and filmography. She earned an Academy Award for *Hævnen (In a Better World)* in 2010, solidifying her place among the most well-known Danish film-makers in the global arena. She also holds the record for being the first woman ever to take home an Academy Award, a Golden Globe, a Primetime Emmy, and a European Film Award.

Mads Mikkelsen and Thomas Vinterberg

Mads Mikkelsen

Mads Mikkelsen and Thomas Vinterberg are two of the Danish personalities representing Danish cinema on the global stage. While the former is a talented and versatile actor and one of the most renowned Hollywood stars from Denmark – having played everything from a

Bond movie villain to a psychopath cannibal killer; the latter is a famous director and one of the founding 'brothers' of the Dogme 95 Movement.

Collaborations between Mikkelsen and film-maker Thomas Vinterberg include *Jagten* or *The Hunt* (2012) and *Druk* or *Another Round* (2020), which received the Academy Award for Best International Feature Film.

SPANISH CINEMA

Open Your Eyes for a Vanilla Sky

Spanish director Alejandro Amenábar's 1997 film *Abre los ojos (Open Your Eyes)* was remade in Hollywood by Cameron Crowe in 2001 as *Vanilla Sky*. Beautiful and talented Spanish actress Penelope Cruz played the character of the enigmatic Sofia in both films.

Pedro's Obsession with Cinema

Pedro Almodóvar's parents sent him to a religious boarding school when he was eight years old so that he would become a priest. But Pedro wanted to become a film-maker and moved to Madrid later. When the Spanish dictator Francisco Franco closed down the National School of Cinema in Madrid, the determined Almodóvar decided to be self-taught.

Almodóvar's Struggle

As a young man, Spanish director Pedro Almodóvar supported himself with jobs like selling used items in the Madrid flea market El Rastro and working as an administrative assistant with the phone company Telefónica for twelve years. He worked only up to 3 p.m., pursuing his film-making after that.

Pedro's Shorts

Almodóvar bought his first camera when he was twenty-two. He purchased a Super-8 with his first pay cheque from Telefónica and started making short films with his handheld camera. In 1974, he made his first short film, and by the end of the 1970s, his shorts were aired in Madrid and Barcelona's night circuit.

First Oscars for Spaniards

Javier Bardem became the first Spanish actor ever to bring home an Academy Award. He received the Oscar for Best Actor in a Supporting Role for his work in the movie *No Country for Old Men* (2007).

Penelope Cruz became the first Spanish actress to win an Oscar for Best Actress in a Supporting Role for her work as Mara Elena in the movie *Vicky Cristina Barcelona* (2008), which also starred her husband Javier Bardem, just one year after Bardem made history as the first actor from Spain to get the honour.

Zorro's Rise to Fame

Antonio Banderas

Antonio Banderas is an international star who hails from Málaga, Spain, and can be credited for paving the way for the Latino community in Hollywood, being the first Spaniard to taste such international success at home as well as in Hollywood, in both theatre and the films. He credits his rise to international fame to his iconic character Zorro, which he played twice, in *The Mask of Zorro* (1998) and *The Legend of Zorro* (2005). His other iconic works include *Desperado* (1995), the *Spy Kids* series (2001–2003), *La piel que habito* or *The Skin I Live In* (2011), *Dolor y gloria* or *Pain and Glory* (2019), etc.

GERMAN CINEMA

Werner Herzog Eats His Shoe

German director Werner Herzog promised fellow documentary maker Errol Morris he would eat his shoe if Morris completed his film on pet cemeteries. Morris finished his film, and Herzog publicly cooked and ate his shoe. Herzog also made a short film on the subject aptly called *Werner Herzog Eats His Shoe* (1980).

The Anti-Nazi Director

Director Fritz Lang shocked and awed the audience with the themes in his movies. But he must have felt like a character in his movies when Hitler asked him to oversee German propaganda movies. The Jewish director fled to Hollywood, where he made anti-Nazi thrillers and dramas about persecuted Jews.

Stealing Your Own Film

German auteur film-maker Rainer Werner Fassbinder once applied to a film school where he was rejected. But the authorities refused to return the short film Fassbinder had submitted with his application. This made Fassbinder so angry that he reportedly broke into the film school and stole his own short film.

Stranger than Paradise

When German film-maker Wim Wenders gave American director Jim Jarmusch his 16mm black-and-white leftovers, Jarmusch included the material in his half-hour short film *Stranger than Paradise* (1984). Later, this short turned into a famous feature film after a producer watched it and came on board.

Wings of Improvisation

The same German director Wim Wenders shot *Wings of Desire* (1987) without a script. Suddenly, Wenders realized a character was missing and called Peter Falk to play a former angel who had become a human. The film won the Best Director Award at Cannes, and Hollywood bought the rights to remake it as *City of Angels* (1998).

Tenacious Tykwer

German film-maker Tom Tykwer has directed iconic films like *Run Lola Run* (1998) and *Heaven* (2002). After being rejected by all the German and French film schools, Tykwer refused to give up. He started working at an independent movie theatre in Berlin, where he met his future cinematographer Frank Griebe, employed there as a film projectionist. Together, their journey began.

Short Sharp Stock

German/Turkish film-maker Fatih Akin wrote the script for his first feature film *Short Sharp Shock* (1998) while he was in school. He handed over the script he had written in his school books to a production company in Hamburg, who thankfully recognized his talent and gave him two short films to direct.

The Unconventional Film-Maker

German director Werner Herzog has a reputation of being an extremely unconventional film-maker. He has been known to take on challenges bordering on the extreme while making his films. Once he dragged a 320-tonne steamship over a hill for his film *Fitzcarraldo* (1982).

Blood Red Sky

One of the most popular German movies ever on Netflix is the vampire horror thriller *Blood Red Sky* (2021). Yet surprisingly, the film-maker Peter Thorwarth spent years trying to get funding and even struggled to find a local distributor.

Animation in German Films

With the influence of avant-garde artistic movements like Bauhaus and Dada, Germany developed into an incubator for animated films in the 1920s, with artists who dared to make 'absolute film' experimenting with colour, tone, geometry, and shadow. Numerous new animated films resulted from this increased artistic flexibility. *The Adventures of Prince Achmed* (1926), directed by paper silhouette expert Charlotte 'Lotte' Reiniger, was the first full-length animated film made in Europe. She drew her ideas and motivations from the collection of Arabic folktales known as the *Arabian Nights*.

POLISH CINEMA

Third-Time Lucky

Krzysztof Kieślowski is the most influential Polish film-maker. But he was rejected twice after applying to the Łódź Film School, which had film-makers like Roman Polanski and Andrzej Wajda among its alumni. The determined Kieślowski applied for the third time and was accepted in the school's directing department in 1964.

Three Colours

The commercial success of his film *The Double Life of Veronique* (1991) helped Polish director Krzysztof Kieślowski fund his ambitious final film *Three Colours (Blue, White, Red)* (1993–1994). This trilogy was based on the virtues that the three colours of the French flag symbolized.

Saving the Best for the Last

The trilogy *Three Colours* (1993–1994) is hailed as Krzysztof Kieślowski's best cinematic work. It received three Academy Award nominations, the Golden Lion for Best Film at the Venice Film Festival, and the Silver Bear for Best Director at the Berlin Film Festival.

Working on *Three Colours* in One Day

Krzysztof Kieślowski was in such a rush to finish his *Three Colours* trilogy (1993–94) that he once worked on all three movies of his famous trilogy – *Blue, White,* and *Red* – simultaneously. He wrote *Red* in the morning, shot *White* during the day, and edited *Blue* at night. That's colourful!

FRENCH CINEMA

The Golden Age of French Cinema

The 1930s and '40s are considered the golden age of French cinema. The greatest French movies were made by the best French directors – Jean Renoir, Marcel Carné, and François Truffaut, among others.

The French New Wave

The French New Wave or Nouvelle Vague was a popular film movement of the 1950s begun by French film-makers to reject and transform traditional film-making. French cinema was also called the seventh art after the six prominent arts, namely, music, poetry, architecture, painting, sculpture, and dance. Exponents of this movement included Claude Chabrol, Jean-Luc Godard, Alain Resnais, and François Truffaut.

Characteristics of the French New Wave

- Many of the methods utilized in the French New Wave films were novel at the time, including fragmented, discontinuous editing and lengthy takes that let performers explore a scene.
- The French New Wave's fusion of reality, subjectivity, and critique allowed for ambiguous characters, goals, and even less-than-clear-cut conclusions.

- The French New Wave movies were renowned for utilizing amateur actors and for shooting in actual locations as opposed to soundstages and sets.

End of the French New Wave

In the early 1970s, the French New Wave movement came to an end. The movement peaked in the late 1950s and early 1960s, but by the end of the 1960s, it had started to lose momentum. By the early 1970s, many of the important personalities connected with the New Wave had either passed away or retired, and the movement as a whole started to fade. The New Wave didn't end with a single, decisive event, but rather with a gradual loss of power and significance.

Most Watched French Film

The comedy *Bienvenue chez les Ch'tis (Welcome to the Sticks)* (2008), directed by Dany Boon, is the most viewed French film, having sold around twenty million tickets. The theme of the film focuses on a man who is transferred to a small town in the north of France and must learn to cope with the local people and culture.

Comedy is King!

Most people who are unaware of French cinematic tastes consider cinema to be a very serious lot, but for French audiences, comedy is the most significant and favoured film genre. The French are recognized for their sophisticated sense of humour and like comedic and thought-provoking movies. Additionally, they value movies that present fresh perspectives on reality and pose intellectual challenges.

The Rules of the Game

Jean Renoir's 1939 film *The Rules of the Game* was banned twice in France. The first time was before World War II as it was considered demoralizing. The second time was when the Nazis banned it after occupying France. The film was only available for viewing in 1956.

Godard the Construction Worker

Famous French director Jean-Luc Godard was obsessed with cinema from an impressionable age, and this resulted in his failure to excel in academics. In 1952, Godard found employment as a construction worker at a dam construction site and immediately saw the possibility of making a documentary film on the dam.

Godard's First Film

After his contract as a construction worker ended, Godard took the job of a telephone switchboard operator to spend more time at the dam. Some Swiss friends rented him a 35mm film camera with which he shot his documentary. Godard's employers bought the film and used it for publicity.

Godard's Golden Era

After the documentary on the dam, Godard focused on his passion. His most celebrated phase as a film director began from 1960 when his first feature *Breathless* was released. It lasted till 1967 when *Weekend* was released.

A Man Escaped (1956)

Great French director Robert Bresson won Best Director at Cannes for *A Man Escaped*. This film was based on an autobiographical account of a French prisoner of war who escaped from the dreaded Gestapo. Bresson's personal experiences in a German war camp helped him direct this masterpiece.

Truffaut's English Woes

French director François Truffaut loved American cinema but never made an effort to learn English. This proved to be problematic when Truffaut started filming his only English film *Fahrenheit 451* (1966), adapted from Ray Bradbury's novel. Truffaut was much more pleased when he dubbed the film into French.

Breathless (1960)

The script for Jean-Luc Godard's famous movie *À bout de souffle (Breathless)* was written by another famous French director. François Truffaut had earlier written this as a short story before he turned it into a film script.

Godard's Wheelchair Innovation

French director Jean-Luc Godard couldn't afford a proper dolly track for his film *Breathless.* So he decided to effectively improvise by having the cinematorgrapher Raoul Coutard to sit a on wheelchair with his handheld camera and being pushed around for moving shots.

Collaboration of Dreams

The idea of Luis Buñuel's 1929 debut film *Un Chien Andalou (An Andalusian Dog)* originated from a conversation between him and painter Salvador Dali about dreams. Buñuel's dream had a long tapering cloud slicing the moon in half like a razor blade slicing, through an eye. Dali's dream featured a hand crawling with ants.

Amazing Facts about *Un Chien Andalou* (1929)

- *Un Chien Andalou*, the debut film of Spanish film-maker Luis Buñuel in collaboration with Spanish artist Salvador Dali, is considered the gateway to surrealism. The main purpose of this scandalous short film was to shock and awe the audience.

- Buñuel was aware that no production company would back such a scandalous and provocative film. So, he got his unsuspecting mother to finance the movie. Then, after he had squandered away half the budget of the film in nightclubs, Buñuel woke up and finally started filming.

- The most notorious scene in the film was the shocking slitting of an eye. Thankfully, it wasn't the eye of a human being but that of a dead calf. This was shot with the help of strong lighting and was the first scene ever to be shot by Buñuel.

- The premiere of *Un Chien Andalou* was held at Studio des Ursulines, Paris, and was witnessed by renowned artists like Pablo Picasso, Le Corbusier, Jean Cocteau, Christian Bérard, and Georges Auric, apart from the entire surrealist group.

- A visibly nervous Buñuel hid behind the screen with stones in his pocket. He was ready to throw them at the audience in case they booed the film. Thankfully, for both director and audience, the stones remained in Buñuel's pocket as the film received lengthy applause.

- The grand success of the premiere resulted in *Un Chien Andalou* being bought by Mauclaire of Studio 28. The film ran successfully for almost eight months, making Buñuel richer by eight thousand francs. But the film was criticized by both audiences and surrealists.

- Buñuel received countless threats and insults for his film's cruel and obscene imagery. The surrealist group dragged Buñuel to court for violating their terms. Buñuel was fed up and threatened to burn the negatives of his film. But it surprised everyone how such a scandalous movie became a commercial success.

- It all ended on a tragic note when both the lead actors of Buñuel's debut film committed suicide. Pierre Batcheff died of an overdose of veronal in 1932, and Simone Mareuil burnt herself to death in a public square in 1954.

Buñuel declines MGM offer

Luis Buñuel was offered a directing contract by the film company Metro-Goldwyn-Mayer (MGM) early on in his film-making career. But Buñuel turned down the lucrative offer after visiting Hollywood in 1930.

Cannes and the Big Five

The Cannes Film Festival, formerly known as the International Film Festival (*Le Festival International du Film*) till 2003, is an annual film event in Cannes, France, that showcases fresh films from all over the globe, including documentaries. The invitation-only event was established in 1946 and takes place yearly (often in May) in the Palais des Festivals et des Congrès. In 1951, the International Federation of Film Producers Associations (FIAPF) formally recognized the event.

It is one of the 'Big Three' important European film festivals, along with the Venice Film Festival in Italy and the Berlin International Film Festival in Germany. It is also one of the 'Big Five' significant international film festivals, which include the three important European festivals, the Toronto International Film Festival in Toronto, Canada, and the Sundance Film Festival in Park City, Utah, United States.

French Global Movie Stars

In the 1960s, Brigitte Bardot was one of the most well-known French actresses. French cinema actors started to become well-known internationally in addition to being famous at home. Apart from Brigitte Bardot, other well-known performers from the era were Yves Montand, Alain Delon, Romy Schneider,

Catherine Deneuve, Jeanne Moreau, Simone Signoret, Jean-Paul Belmondo, and even Jean Gabin.

Character actors Michel Piccoli and Philippe Noiret, Annie Girardot, Jean-Louis Trintignant, Jean-Pierre Léaud, Claude Jade, Anny Duperey, Gérard Depardieu, Patrick Dewaere, Jean-Pierre Cassel, Miou-Miou, Brigitte Fossey, Stéphane Audran, and Isabelle Adjani have competed with them and followed them since the 1960s and the early 1970s. A new generation, which includes Sophie Marceau, Emmanuelle Béart, Jean-Hugues Anglade, Sabine Azéma, Juliette Binoche, and Daniel Auteuil, joined them throughout the 1980s.

BRITISH CINEMA

Charlie Chaplin Enters Show Business

Charlie Chaplin entered the world of show business when he was just five years old. Chaplin's parents were in the entertainment industry, and Chaplin replaced his mother, who was suffering from laryngitis, at a music-hall show. He sang his first song *Jack Jones* before a crowd of soldiers.

Motherhood Flops

The film *Motherhood* (2009), directed by Katherine Dieckmann, is one of the biggest flops in UK history. The Uma Thurman starrer earned only £88 on its opening weekend. On Sunday, there was just one person in the theatre. No, it wasn't Uma Thurman.

Charlie Chaplin

The Guest of Honour

Charlie Chaplin and Albert Einstein were a mutual admiration society. In fact, the great scientist was a guest of honour during the premiere of the great actor's movie *City Lights* in Los Angeles on 2 February 1931.

Refugee from Czechoslovakia

Karel Reisz was a popular director of the British New Wave. He arrived in the UK as a wartime refugee from Czechoslovakia and began his career as a critic for *Sight and Sound* magazine. Then he became the first programmer to be appointed at London's National Film Theatre.

Four Weddings and a Funeral

British screenwriter, director, and producer Richard Curtis got the idea for his movie *Four Weddings and a Funeral* (1994) after he went through his old diaries to discover that he had attended seventy-two weddings in recent years.

Fast Facts about the British Film Industry

- During 2003–10, only seven per cent of British films were profitable.

- *Skyfall* (2012), directed by Sam Mendes, grossed $200 million at the box office and is the most successful British film of all time.

- UK/Ireland box office generated £986 million over the year, with *Barbie* the biggest film of 2023 and *The Great Escaper* leading the UK independent chart.

- Fifty-five per cent of the UK film industry is based in London.

Books to Screenplays

Novels by UK writers have contributed to fifty per cent of the Top Twenty global box office hits in the past twelve years. Unfortunately, only one of these authors is still alive. J.K. Rowling has authored five, and J.R.R. Tolkien has written three. Lewis Carroll and Ian Fleming have authored one each.

Not Enough Scottish for Bond

Ian Fleming, the author of the James Bond series, was inspired to rewrite the backstory of the superspy after he watched the Bond movie *Dr. No* in 1962. He did this to make James Bond's character appear more Scottish. Now, that's a classic case of a screenplay inspiring a book.

Ambulances for *Atonement*

According to estimates, just eight UK military ambulances that were used in WWII remain in the world. All eight ambulances were featured in the film *Atonement* (2007), directed by Joe Wright, based on British author Ian McEwan's best-selling novel.

The Eyes Have It

British actor Benedict Cumberbatch has been blessed with unique eyes that change colour depending on the lights. This is because he has a rare condition called heterochromia iridis, which causes his eyes to appear blue sometimes and green sometimes.

Benedict Cumberbatch Fast Facts

- His actor parents Timothy Carlton and Wanda Ventham played his reel parents in the BBC series *Sherlock* (2010).
- He worked as an English professor in a monastery in Darjeeling, India, for a year after graduating.

- Cumberbatch is also an excellent painter. He went to the Harrow School on an art scholarship.

Kidnapped

Benedict Cumberbatch and his co-star Denise Black were kidnapped by six men while filming the BBC mini-series *To the Ends of the Earth* (2005). Thankfully, the actor managed to smooth-talk his way out of the situation. Elementary!

Hitchcock's Phobias

English director Alfred Hitchcock was scared of oval objects, police officers, egg yolks, and children. These fears had caused him childhood trauma and were featured by him in many of his films. Another strange phobia that Hitchcock had was that he feared watching his own films.

The Elusive Oscar

Alfred Hitchcock is one of the few great directors like – Stanley Kubrick, Orson Welles, Charlie Chaplin, and Ingmar Bergman – who never received an Oscar for Best Director. Although Hitchcock's film *Rebecca* (1940) won Best Picture and he was nominated several times for Best Director, the award always eluded him.

Sir Ridley Scott

English director Ridley Scott was knighted by Queen Elizabeth II in 2003 for his significant contribution to the film industry. He joined the ranks of eminent film-makers and actors who had received the knighthood earlier, like Richard Attenborough, Alfred Hitchcock, Sidney Poitier, and Sam Mendes.

The Chaplin Lookalike Contest

In 1975, Chaplin took part in a Charlie Chaplin lookalike contest in France as a lark. He was stunned when he didn't win the contest and secured the third position. Neither the judges nor the audience realized that he was the real Chaplin. That's how strange life can get!

The British Quentin Tarantino

Guy Ritchie has often been called the 'British Quentin Tarantino' because of the dark humour and memorable characters in his movies. Guy Ritchie would have perceived this as a compliment as he had once credited Tarantino as an inspiration for his work.

A Rare Director

Sam Mendes received an Academy Award and a Golden Globe for Best Director for his debut film *American Beauty* in 1999. But what makes Mendes special is that he doesn't devote his time fully to cinema. As he was a stage director before, he works on both stage plays and movies.

Guy Ritchie Fast Facts

- English film-maker Guy Ritchie is a descendant of King Edward I.
- He has a black belt in jiu-jitsu.
- He married Madonna in 2000 at Skibo Castle in Scotland. They were divorced in 2008.

BELGIAN CINEMA

Belgian Brothers: the Director Duo

Belgian director brothers Jean-Pierre Dardenne and Luc Dardenne used a raw, radical, and naturalistic filming style using a handheld camera that invaded the personal space of the main characters for *Rosetta* (1999) and *L'Enfant* (2005). They won the Palme d'Or at the Cannes Film Festival for both films.

The Van Damme Package

Jean-Claude Van Damme

One of the most celebrated stars from the 1980s and '90s era in Hollywood, Jean-Claude Van Damme, actually hails from Belgium. He is not only an actor but also a martial artist, fight/action choreographer and a film-maker, and was born Jean-Claude Camille François Van Varenberg. Owing to his impressive physique, brilliant martial arts skills, and manly charm, Van Damme became a popular action star with movies like *Bloodsport* (1988), *Cyborg* (1989), *Lionheart* (1990), *Double Impact* (1991), and *Street Fighter* (1994).

ITALIAN CINEMA

The Musical Director

Director Michelangelo Antonioni learned to play the violin at a very young age and played his first concert when he was only nine years old. He was also a great painter. Sadly, his musical and artistic career took a back seat as he became one of the greatest film-makers.

The Beginning of the Italian Industry

The years 1903–09 witnessed the beginning of the Italian film industry after the first public presentation by the Lumière brothers in Paris. The Lumières brought the new art form to Italy in 1896. Italy is often considered the birthplace of art cinema.

Neorealism Revolution

Italian cinema sparked a cinematic revolution with Neorealism in the post-World War II era. Film-makers like Vittorio De Sica and Roberto Rossellini pioneered a raw and authentic style, depicting the struggles of ordinary people. This movement significantly influenced global film-making, emphasizing real locations, minimal editing, documentary style, and non-professional actors.

Cinecittà Studios

Dubbed the 'Hollywood on the Tiber', Cinecittà Studios in Rome stands as a cinematic powerhouse. Established during Mussolini's era, it became a hub for legendary productions like *Ben-Hur* (1959) and *La Dolce Vita* (1960). The impact of the studio on Italian and international cinema remains profound, showcasing Italy's contribution to the global film industry.

Oscar Domination

Italy boasts a remarkable success at the Oscars, securing the most wins for Best Foreign Language Film. Federico Fellini alone won this award four times (most by any director in the history of the award). With renowned classics like *La Strada* (1954) and *Cinema Paradiso* (1988), Italian cinema left an indelible mark on the international stage.

Divorce Italian Style

The only Italian film to ever win the Academy Award for Best Original Screenplay is the 1961 dark comedy *Divorzio All'italiana (Divorce Italian Style)* directed by Pietro Germi.

Discovering Claudia Cardinale

Italian director Mario Monicelli discovered actress Claudia Cardinale when he cast her in a small role as the traditional Sicilian girl in his film *Big Deal on Madonna Street* (1958). But her few lines had to be dubbed into Italian as Claudia spoke only French then.

Blood Feud

Lina Wertmüller gives her movies ridiculously long titles. Her 1978 film called *Blood Feud* in English is known in Italy as *Un Fatto Di Sangue Nel Comune Di Siculiana Fra Due Uomini Per Causa Di Una Vedova. Si Sospettano Moventi Politici. Amore-Morte-Shimmy. Lugano Belle. Tarantelle. Tarallucci E Vino.* It's the longest movie title.

The Italian Job in English Colours

The three minis that were used in the climactic chase in *The Italian Job* (1969) were in the colours red, white, and blue in that order, signifying the colours of the Union Flag of Britain.

Sophia Loren's Achievement

The first actress to win the Academy Award for Best Actress for a foreign-language performance was Italian actress Sophia Loren. She received the Oscar in 1962 for her role as Cesira in director Vittorio De Sica's film *Two Women*.

The Strange Condition to Play Jesus Christ

For his movie *The Gospel According to St. Matthew* (1964), Italian director Pier Paolo Pasolini hired a non-actor named Enrique Irazoqui to play Jesus Christ. Irazoqui accepted on one condition that Pasolini would pledge support to his student Marxist organization, which Pasolini agreed to do. Well, stranger things have happened in cinema.

Origin of the 'Paparazzi'

Federico Fellini's 1960 film *La Dolce Vita* is a cinematic masterpiece. But the word *paparazzi* that is so popular today has been actually derived from the character of a photographer in this movie called *Paparazzo*, played by the actor Walter Santesso.

Blow-Up Rock

Italian director Michelangelo Antonioni's classic film *Blow-Up*

(1966) features a nightclub scene with a performance by the English rock band, the Yardbirds, and has the legendary rock guitarists Jimmy Page and Jeff Beck playing guitar.

The Adventurous Fellini

Director Federico Fellini's love affair with theatre began when he was a young boy. This dangerous affair led him to run away from home and join the circus when he was twelve years old. Before he became a film director, Fellini worked as a magazine cartoonist and radio scriptwriter.

The Actor–Director Collaboration

Director Federico Fellini began a lengthy collaboration with actor Marcello Mastroianni with the film *La Dolce Vita* that released in 1960. After that, the actor played Fellini's on-screen alter ego on a regular basis.

Felliniesque

The word *Felliniesque* is reflective of the fantastic and surreal style of Federico Fellini's later films. But there was extreme pressure on Fellini to replicate the success of *La Dolce Vita* and it resulted in writer's block.

Otto e mezzo (1963)

With the producers on his heels and a writer's block rendering him ineffective, Fellini responded to the deadline in classic Felliniesque style with the film *Otto e mezzo* or *8½*, which was a masterpiece, winning him his third Oscar for Best Foreign Film, out of the total Academy Awards that he won.

8½ (1963)

The film *8½* is about a director struggling to find a plot. Fellini had turned his dilemma into his film's subject – a director in creative paralysis. The film was named after the number of films Fellini had made till then (seven features and two shorts, one of which was incomplete).

Actor-Turned-Director

Italian director Vittorio De Sica began his career as a stage actor. He started acting in front of the camera in *The Clemenceau Affair (Il processo Clémenceau)* in 1917. But he acted mainly to fund his career as a director. In the 1940s, Vittorio De Sica turned to direction.

The Spaghetti Western

Sergio Leone is probably the most popular and commercially successful Italian director outside his home country. This influential director is famous for inventing an entire movie genre – the Spaghetti Western, which were nothing but Westerns (see also The Western on page 10) but with a low budget, often filmed in Europe and directed by Italian directors, and hence the 'spaghetti' connection. The term was coined by Spanish journalist Alfonso Sánchez.

The Dollars Trilogy

Sergio Leone is famous for his unofficial trilogies in the Spaghetti Western genre. The Dollars Trilogy comprise the movies *A Fistful of Dollars* (1964), *For a Few Dollars More* (1965), and *The Good, the Bad and the Ugly* (1966), with Clint Eastwood in the leading role in all the films.

Roberto Rossellini

The experimental and unconventional Italian director Roberto Rossellini is regarded as one of the most important directors of the Italian neorealist movement. French director François Truffaut considers him to be a major influence on French cinema, especially for inspiring the French New Wave movement.

First Female Director to Receive an Oscar Nomination

Lina Wertmüller is the most loved female director in Italian cinema. She began her career by working with Fellini and collaborated with actor Giancarlo Giannini to taste success as a director. She became the first woman to receive an Academy Award nomination for Best Director with *Seven Beauties* (1975).

Bicycle Thieves (1948)

When Italian director Vittorio De Sica was busy in the pre-production of his iconic film *Bicycle Thieves (Ladri di biciclette)*, Hollywood producer David O. Selznick displayed an interest in the project. But De Sica said no when Selznick wanted to cast Cary Grant in the lead instead of Lamberto Maggiorani.

The Italian Perfectionist

Michelangelo Antonioni ordered his production designers to paint the grass and tree leaves for the park scene in *Blow-Up* (1966) to make them look greener. The façades of a street of houses were also painted for a single shot to make them look colourful. Later, the houses were repainted to their original colour.

Cartoonist to Film-maker

Federico Fellini began his illustrious career by drawing comic strips. He was a talented cartoonist as a boy and made them for his friends, teachers, and family. His passion for cartoons continued as a young man when he worked as a cartoonist and journalist at the daily paper *Il Piccolo*.

RUSSIAN CINEMA

Russian Ark

Director Alexander Sokurov attempted a mind-blowing technical experiment with his 2002 film *Russian Ark*. This was a full-length feature film with a duration of ninety-six minutes that was filmed in just one take without a single cut. It's a landmark in digital film-making.

One-Take Shoot of Russian History

Russian Ark was filmed at the State Hermitage Museum in St. Petersburg. The camera travelled two kilometres in real time through thirty-three rooms to record the several segments of Russian history being recreated there. A cast of two thousand actors had to hit their marks on time for the one-take shoot to be a success.

War and Peace

Russian director Sergei Bondarchuk's film *War and Peace* (1966–67) based on Leo Tolstoy's famous novel is one of the longest and most expensive films to be ever made. The film stretched to a length of over seven hours and was made with a huge budget of $100 million adjusted for inflation.

Animated Eisenstein

Celebrated Russian director Sergei Eisenstein is hailed as the inventor of the cinematic montage. Strangely, Eisenstein strongly believed that the animated Walt Disney film *Snow White and the Seven Dwarfs* (1937) is the greatest work in the movies. To him, all other movies dwarf in comparison. Even Walt Disney would have been surprised.

Adversity at Work

Russian director Sergei Eisenstein made only seven films in his illustrious career because he faced a lot of adversity at work. In the USSR, his film *Alexander Nevsky* (1938), about a hero who saved Russia from the Germans, was withdrawn suddenly after the Soviets signed a non-aggression pact with Hitler.

Eisenstein in Hollywood

Hollywood was excited when Russian cinematic genius Sergei Eisenstein arrived in 1930 to direct the Hollywood film *An American Tragedy*. Unfortunately for his admirers, Eisenstein did not shoot the film due to creative differences and a fight with the Hollywood moguls. An American tragedy for sure!

Tarkovsky's Belief in the Paranormal

As a young boy, Andrei Tarkovsky had gone on a geological expedition. One night, as he slept in his hut, he heard a mysterious voice ordering him to go outside. He obeyed and watched an old pine tree fall and destroy the hut. After that, Tarkovsky started believing in signs, omens, and the paranormal, which are reflected in his films.

Tarkovsky's First and Only International Award

Russian director Andrei Tarkovsky earned international fame when he was thirty years old after winning the Golden Lion at the Venice Film Festival for his 1962 war drama *Ivan's Childhood*. Ironically, this remained Tarkovsky's first and only international award as Soviet officials stopped his films from participating in festival competitions.

Tarkovskian

Andrei Tarkovsky had a huge impact with his cinematic style, influencing not only Russian directors but also film-makers all over the world. The Oxford Dictionary also introduced the word *Tarkovskian* which means 'something in the spirit of Tarkovsky'.

The Two Masters

Andrei Tarkovsky's idol was the Swedish director Ingmar Bergman. The respect was mutual as Bergman once called Tarkovsky 'the greatest master of cinema'. Strangely, the two masters of cinema never met. Even though they once attended the same event at the House of Cinema in Stockholm, they missed meeting each other.

Obsessed with Bergman

For his last masterpiece *The Sacrifice* (1986), Tarkovsky hired his idol Bergman's team, right from the lead actor Erland Josephson to the office administrator. He wanted to shoot on the island of Fårö, where Bergman lived and made films but was denied permission because of a nearby military base. So Tarkovsky chose the neighbouring island of Gotland.

Andrei Rublev

When Russian director Andrei Tarkovsky made his classic *Andrei Rublev (Andrey Rublyov)* in 1966 on the life of the iconic fifteenth century Russian painter, he received great international acclaim. Sadly, the Soviet authorities restricted Tarkovsky's work for political reasons, and the master made just seven films in a twenty-five-year career.

Eisenstein's Paid Hollywood Holiday

When famous Russian director Sergei Eisenstein made a trip to Hollywood in 1930, film fans were disappointed when the movie he was supposed to direct was shelved. But Eisenstein had the time of his life playing tennis with Charlie Chaplin and becoming great friends with the anti-communist Walt Disney.

EASTERN CINEMA

The Epitome of Japanese Manliness

Japanese actor Toshiro Mifune collaborated in sixteen films with acclaimed director Akira Kurosawa and was considered the epitome of Japanese manliness by cinema buffs. As part of his method acting, he studied the movement of lions and emulated them to prepare for some of his legendary roles.

Inspired by the Hidden Fortress

Akira Kurosawa inspired numerous film-makers across the world. One of them was American director George Lucas, who studied the works of Kurosawa since childhood. In fact, it was Kurosawa's 1958 film *The Hidden Fortress* that inspired Lucas to make his famous *Star Wars* movies.

Seven Samurai

Seven Samurai (1954) is the story of a band of samurai warriors hired by farmers to protect their village from bandits. The Akira Kurosawa film is probably the most famous Japanese film and one of the greatest action films. In 1960, it was remade as the hit Western *The Magnificent Seven*, directed by John Sturges, which further went on to inspire Ramesh Sippy's *Sholay* (1975).

In the Mood for Love

Wong Kar-wai's film *In the Mood for Love* (2000) is on the list of the greatest films of all time. Wong shot more than thirty times the footage he used and finished editing the morning before the film's Cannes premiere. The movie received the Grand Prize of the Superior Technical Commission and Best Actor for Tony Leung.

Food and Desire

Food is an important element of Wong Kar-wai movies, which are often set in restaurants, fast food shops, or wanton roadside stalls. Wong explained the fascination with food similar to desire between men and women. He said he had always been interested in the connection between food and desire. Food for thought?

Longest Korean Movie Title

The 2000 Korean movie *Daehakro-eseo Maechunhadaga Tomaksalhaedanghan Yeogosaeng Ajik Daehakro-e Itta,* loosely translated as *Teenage Hooker Became Killing Machine,* is the Korean movie with the longest title with as many as twenty-seven Korean characters. We daresay that this title seems to be a synopsis of the movie by itself.

Korean Director with Most Films

According to the Korean film archive database, the director who has produced the maximum number of films in Korean film history is director Go Yeong-nam. He has an astonishing 110 films in his résumé as director. Keep going, Go!

The Not-So-Great Dictator

In 1978, Kim Jong-II, son of North Korean dictator Kim II-Sung did something unexpected. To strengthen movie production in North Korea, he arranged the successful kidnapping of top South Korean director Shin Sang-ok and his actress wife, forcing them to work in North Korea till they eventually escaped in 1986.

Anime

The Japanese film industry is popular for 'anime' or its animated films. Anime has gained worldwide popularity and has also won many Academy Awards.

The South Korean Film Industry

South Korean cinema is popular across the world for their dramas and thrillers. The South Korean film *Parasite* (2019) directed by Bong Joon-ho created history by becoming the first non-English-language film to win an Oscar for Best Picture.

Japanese Revolution in World Cinema

The Japanese film *Seven Samurai* (1954) was a revolutionary concept for Japanese cinema and world cinema as well. Akira Kurosawa described his masterpiece as 'a movie as rich as a buttered steak topped with grilled eel'.

The Astronomical Budget

When *Seven Samurai* was filmed, the average budget of Japanese movies was $70,000. But filming for a year escalated the budget to almost $500,000. When the producers stopped production, Kurosawa did not panick, he simply went fishing. He was confident because so much money had already been pumped into the film, it wouldn't be scrapped.

Shooting the Sun

A truism from the early days of film-making maintained that it was impossible for a video camera to physically film the sun. But a legendary Japanese director changed all that in his 1950 classic *Rashomon* when he became the first director to shoot the sun. His name is Akira Kurosawa.

A Japanese Tribute to Shakespeare

Akira Kurosawa was a huge Shakespeare fan and adapted the bard's plays into two great films. *Kumonosu-jô* or *Throne of Blood* (1957) was based on *Macbeth* and *Ran* (1985) was a retelling of *King Lear* set in Sengoku-era Japan. Both films reflect Kurosawa's unique style and are a worthy tribute to Shakespeare.

Wong Kar-wai's Hobby

Wong Kar-wai's interest in cinema was aroused by his mother, who introduced him to movies at an early age. She took her son to the cinemas, which exposed him to a wide range of films. Later, Wong said that his only hobby as a child had been watching movies.

Tokyo Story

Yasujirō Ozu was the inventor of the 'Tatami Shot'. Tatami is a flooring material used to style Japanese rooms. The tatami shot involved a low-lying camera angle of about two feet off the ground, the eye level of a kneeling person. Ozu used this technique in almost all his films.

The Army Film-Maker

Yasujirō Ozu was drafted into the Japanese army as a film-maker. In 1943, Ozu was sent to Singapore to make the documentary titled *Derii e, Derii e (To Delhi, To Delhi)* based on the life of the great Indian freedom fighter Subhas Chandra Bose, who defied the British rule in India.

Ozu Captured by the British

In August 1945, Ozu was detained as a civilian by British forces in a rubber plantation. He was forced to destroy all the footage and the script of the documentary on Subhas Chandra Bose that he had so painstakingly created.

Letter to Kurosawa

When Stanley Kubrick, the American film personality considered one of the greatest film-makers of all time, received a fan letter from legendary director Akira Kurosawa, he was thrilled. Kubrick mulled for months over his perfect reply. After creating several drafts over several months, he still wasn't satisfied, and the reply remained unsent. Sadly, Kurosawa died before Kubrick could reply.

Ozu's Masterpiece

Tokyo Story (1953) is considered Japanese director Yasujirō Ozu's masterpiece and a must-watch for all film buffs. In fact, in 2012, worldwide critics of the British monthly film magazine *Sight and Sound* voted it as the greatest film of all time.

The 50mm Lens

Ozu's primary aim while making a film was to ensure that the viewer felt they were part of the movie just like real life. That's why the 50mm filming lens was a constant, while he worked as it was the lens equated to human vision.

Asian of the Century

The cinema of Akira Kurosawa had a profound impact not only in Japan but also in other parts of the world. In 1995, the American magazine *Asian Week* named Kurosawa the 'Asian of the Century' in the 'Arts, Literature, and Culture, category.

Unconventional Director

Wong Kar-wai never gives his actors a complete script. They are just given a rough plot outline so that they can develop their characters on their own while the director guides them. Wong also does not permit rehearsals as he wants his actors to be natural and spontaneous on-screen.

Wong Kar-wai's Sunglasses

Wong Kar-wai made public appearances in sunglasses, which added to the mystery around him and his movies. He stated that his lenses were called 'true colour' and used by pilots who wished to see clearly but wanted to avoid strong sunlight. Wong's sunglasses have been compared to Chaplin's moustache, riding a line between life and work.

Parasite (2019)

South Korean film-maker Bong Joon-ho's films *The Host* (2006) and *Snowpiercer* (2013) are among the highest-grossing films of all time in South Korea. But his film *Parasite* is his highest grossing release, believed to have earned $115 million at the worldwide box office.

Director Bong Joon-ho with Kang-Ho Song, winner of the Palme d'Or award for his film Parasite *at the Cannes 2019*

First Korean Film to Win an Oscar

Parasite (2019) became the first

South Korean film to receive an Academy Award nomination in any category and also won Best Foreign Language Film at the seventy-seventh Golden Globe Awards. Bong Joon-ho became the first Korean director to win the Palme d'Or at the 2019 Cannes Film Festival for *Parasite*.

Kurosawa's Inspirations

Renowned Japanese director Akira Kurosawa has influenced countless film-makers over the years. But he was himself influenced by the works of the great Russian directors Sergei Eisenstein and Vsevolod Pudovkin.

First Director of Colour to Win the Oscar

Taiwanese film-maker Ang Lee won two Academy Awards for Best Director and was the first non-white to win the award for Best Director. In 2000, his martial-arts film *Crouching Tiger, Hidden Dragon* won the Oscar for Best Foreign Language Film and was the highest-grossing foreign film in the US.

Master of Animation

Japanese animator, manga artist, and film-maker Hayao Miyazaki is renowned for his imaginative and visually stunning animated films using manga art. His films often depict themes of nature, technology, and the relationship between humans and the environment. The co-founder of Studio Ghibli, Miyazaki is one of the most accomplished film-makers in animation history.

Kurosawa's Shooting Technique

For the battle climax in *Seven Samurai* (1954), Kurosawa could capture certain scenes on camera only once. So he set up three cameras at various points with telephoto lenses that made zooming in possible. When he edited the footage later, he created a new, dynamic film-making style that became his signature.

Raise the Red Lantern

Director Zhang Yimou's film *Raise the Red Lantern* (1991) was initially banned in China for its depiction of Chinese patriarchy. Strangely, a ballet that was adapted from the movie was produced by the National Ballet of China and taken on a world tour.

AFRICAN CINEMA

Key Themes of African Cinema

African cinema is well known for its strong political and social commentary. African films highlight key issues plaguing the continent like colonialism, post-colonial identity, poverty, corruption, and human rights.

Nollywood

The Nigerian film industry is known as Nollywood, a portmanteau word created by the fusion of *Nigeria* and *Hollywood*. It is the second largest film industry in the world in terms of the number of movies produced, second only to the Indian film industry.

Father of African Cinema

The Senegalese film-maker Ousmane Sembène is considered the Father of African cinema. His debut film, *Borom Sarret* (1963), won first prize at the Tours Film Festival in France.

First Film Produced in Africa

The first film to be produced in Africa was *Palaver* (1926), a silent film that was directed by British film-maker Geoffrey Barkas and filmed in Sierra Leone.

SOUTH AMERICAN AND MEXICAN CINEMA

El Apóstol

The first full-length animated movie titled *El Apóstol* (1917) was made in Argentina. The political satire was created twenty years before Walt Disney came up with *Snow White and the Seven Dwarfs* in 1937. *El Apóstol* had 58,000 drawings with a seventy-minute run-time.

Pinocchio in Mexico

Guillermo del Toro's *Pinocchio* (2022) was not allowed to release in his home country Mexico initially because the film-maker lamented the state of Mexican cinema and the Mexican government's lack of interest towards new film-makers and artists. The movie was finally granted a limited release in a few cinemas in Mexico.

Bernal takes a Risk

Gael García Bernal was the first Mexican to attend London's prestigious Central School of Speech and Drama where students aren't allowed to engage in professional work until their final year. When Bernal was offered a role in *Amores Perros* (2000) in his second year, he risked expulsion to be part of the Alejandro Gonzalez Iñárritu film.

South American Cinema

South American cinema has been influenced by several international film movements like Italian neorealism, French New Wave, and American independent cinema to name a few. Mexico has the largest film industry in South America and produces over three hundred films annually.

Key Themes of South American Cinema

South American cinema often has themes related to social and political injustice. Several film-makers use their films to fuel social activism. Another common theme is the use of magic realism, inspired by the continent's rich legacy of art and culture.

The Three Amigos

Mexican film-makers Alejandro Gonzalez Iñárritu, Alfonso Cuarón, and Guillermo del Toro are known as 'The Three Amigos' of the film industry and have all made important contributions to both Mexican cinema and Hollywood.

Iñárritu's Travels

Alejandro Gonzalez Iñárritu left home as a sailor on cargo ships to sail down the Mississippi River. He also visited Europe and Africa as a seventeen year old, and his travels influenced him as a film-maker. After his travels, he returned to Mexico City and majored in communications.

The First Honours for a Mexican Film-Maker

Alejandro Gonzalez Iñárritu is the first Mexican film-maker in Academy Award history to be nominated for director or producer, the first to win Best Original Screenplay and Best Picture, the first to receive the Best Director Award at Cannes, and the first to win a Directors Guild of America Award for Outstanding Directing.

Amazing Alfonso Cuarón Facts

- When Mexican director Alfonso Cuarón was in film school, he helped make a film in English for a project, which was supposed to be made in Spanish. For this act of disobedience, he was expelled from the Centro Universitario de Estudios Cinematográficos.

- Alfonso Cuarón directed an English film later

though. The third film in the Harry Potter franchise, *Harry Potter and the Prisoner of Azkaban* (2004), was directed by him. He had not read any of the Harry Potter books but did a great job although the film was darker because of his unique style of lighting.

- For his film *Roma* (2018), Cuarón tied the record with four Oscar nominations for one film. The nominations were for cinematography, originality in the screenplay, director, and producer. *Roma* also received the Best Foreign Language Film Award.

- Cuarón has received Oscar nominations for his other films as well. He is the first Latin American to receive the Academy Award for Best Director. He also has three Golden Globes, two Directors Guild of America Awards, and seven British Academy of Film and Television Arts (BAFTA) awards in his kitty.

- On the set of *Gravity* (2013), Cuarón had told Sandra Bullock that he would like to give her an earpiece. But his heavy accent made her hear it as 'herpes'. Cuarón apologized to actress Bullock because of this after receiving his Golden Globe award. The audience found it rather funny though.

Embrace of the Serpent

Colombian director Ciro Guerra's film *Embrace of the Serpent* (2015) was the first Colombian film to be nominated for an Academy Award for Best Foreign Language Film.

Don't Breathe (2016)

Uruguayan director Fede Alvarez made his cinematic debut with the horror flick *Don't Breathe.* It was favoured by the critics and was also a huge commercial success, grossing over $150 million worldwide.

Mexico's Pride

Mexican director Guillermo del Toro is famous for his visually striking and original films like *Pan's Labyrinth* (2006) and *The Shape of Water* (2017), which won four Oscars, including one for Best Director.

The Mexican Hollywood Star Salma Hayek

Salma Hayek's main role in the telenovela *Teresa* marked the start of her career in Mexico, and she received praise for the part. After that, she starred in the 1995 movie *El Callejón de los Milagros (Midaq Alley)*, for which she was nominated for the highest film award in Mexico, the Ariel Award. The critical acclaim for her performance in the movie helped to establish her Hollywood career, making her the star of iconic Hollywood movies of the 1990s, including *Desperado* (1995), *Dogma* (1999), and *Wild Wild West* (1999).

Salma Hayek

Unique Argentine Film-Maker

Argentine director Lucrecia Martel is a unique film-maker. Her films are renowned for their distinctive use of sound design and atmosphere. They boast of unconventional narrative structures and explore bold themes like colonialism and class.

AUSTRALIAN CINEMA

The Beginnings

First screenings: Australia saw its first public screenings of cinema in October 1896, within a year after the Lumière brothers' global premiere in Paris. Harry Rickards's Melbourne Opera House (later known as the Tivoli Theatre) organized paid public screenings of the first movies in Australia on 22 August 1896. The magician Carl Hertz's film, part of a variety act, also forms a significant milestone. This show led to Australian tours, where they used similar projection machines. Australia's first cinema theatre, the Salon Lumière, located at 237 Pitt Street in Sydney, was opened to the public on 27 October 1896. They screened the first Australian-produced short film.

First movie theatre: Beginning in the 1880s, the Athenaeum Hall on Collins Street, Melbourne, functioned as a dance hall and occasionally offered customers other forms of entertainment. After the French Lumière brothers' first public showing of a movie in Paris on 28 December 1895, it was screened at Athenaeum Hall for the first time in October 1896. The Athenaeum would keep showing movies, including *Life in Our Navy*, a 60,000-foot documentary on life on HMS *Jupiter*, which was shown on 26 January 1901 by G. H. Snazelle.

First newsreel/first sports films: In a first, Caulfield Cup and Melbourne Cup films were shown at the Melbourne Opera House on race evenings in 1897. This became a watershed moment in newsreel photography. The events were taken on film for W.C. Baxter and processed the same day by photographer Robert William Harvie and inventor Ernest J. Thwaites.

First wax recording from outdoors: Anthropologists Baldwin Spencer and F.J. Gillen captured footage of Aboriginal dancers in central Australia between 1900 and 1903 for some of the country's earliest motion films. They invented wax cylinder sound recording, and they captured their films in very challenging circumstances.

First Australian Film: *The Story of the Kelly Gang*

The Story of the Kelly Gang debuted at Melbourne's Athenaeum Theatre on Boxing Day 1906. It was the world's first multi-reel, full-length motion picture ever made. By depicting the Kelly gang in a sympathetic light, the movie sparked a debate.

The movie *The Story of the Kelly Gang* chronicled the antics of Australia's most ill-famed bushranger and his gang. It culminated with the well-known Glenrowan siege, during which Kelly's men were slain and Ned Kelly himself was transported to Melbourne to be executed.

The movie cost £1,000 to create, but the money was made up in the first week of screenings, thanks in part to Kelly's constructed armour, which was loaned for the filming from the Victorian Museum. The movie was a huge hit and toured the nation for nine years.

This film, often referred to as the first feature film and the first movie to last more than an hour, served as the catalyst for Australia's thriving film industry.

First Talkies

F.W. Thring founded the Efftee Studios in Melbourne in 1930 for producing talking pictures with the use of American optical sound machinery. The same studio made the first sound films in Australia, beginning in 1931, producing movies like *Diggers* (1931), *A Co-respondent's Course* (1931), *The Haunted Barn* (1931), and *The Sentimental Bloke* (1932). Efftee produced nine movies, more than eighty short films, and numerous stage works throughout the course of its five-year existence. C.J. Dennis, George Wallace, and Frank Harvey were notable collaborators. A protest over the Australian government's refusal to set Australian cinema quotas resulted in the end of film production in 1934, and Thring died a year after, in 1936.

First Colour Feature

Jedda (1955) was Australia's first-ever feature film in colour and also the first one to be featured at the Cannes. With a cast of non-professional Aboriginal actors, the movie was about a young Aboriginal girl growing up in a closed white community. This landmark film starred Ngarla Kunoth as the titular character and was produced and directed by Charles Chauvel.

The movie begins with a white mother who has just lost her own baby adopts Jedda when she is a little child. She is separated from her culture and her language as she is raised as a 'white girl' on a distant cattle ranch. When a roving A Boriginal worker, Marbuck, arrives at the property, Jedda gets smitten by him, everything changes and they flee together. Subsequently, Jedda realizes she does not belong in any of the two worlds.

First Global Superstar

Errol Flynn, a Tasmanian native, was given the lead role in the 1933 film, *In the Wake of the Bounty* by director Charles Chauvel. Flynn later went on to have a glorious Hollywood career and became a global icon with his heroic action films, including *The Adventures of Robin Hood* (1938), *Captain Blood* (1935), *Gentleman Jim* (1942), *They Died with Their Boots On* (1941), etc.

Errol Flynn on a postage stamp

First Oscar(s)

Kokoda Front Line! (1942) became the first Australian film to win an Oscar, being one of the four best documentary winners at the fifteenth Academy Awards. It was a full-length version of the 1942 Kokoda Track campaign-focused Australian newsreel,

Cinesound Review, produced by the Australian News and Information Bureau and Cinesound Productions Limited.

Australian war photographer Damien Parer is often considered among Australia's first Oscar winners because the documentary was shot by him. However, the award was actually in the name of Ken G. Hall, the director of the documentary. It is interesting to note that a significant amount of Parer's work was utilized in *The Road to Kokoda* (1942), a documentary produced by Movietone, a competing firm.

Peter Finch received a posthumous Academy Award for Best Actor in 1976 for his part in the American satire *Network*, thus making him the first Australian to receive the honours. The first Australian to receive the Oscar for Best Actress was Nicole Kidman for *The Hours* (2002).

Maxed Profits: Meet Mad Mel

Mad Max (1979) literally created a road for other Mad Max movies to follow, being the first one in the series of dystopian apocalyptic road chase movies with many accolades to its name. It not only made Mel Gibson a star in Australia and the world but also held the record for having the highest profit-to-cost ratio of a motion picture in *The Guinness Book of World Records* for twenty years, until it was taken over by *The Blair Witch Project* (1999). It was made by George Miller for a paltry AUD $380,000 and made $8 million in the US but $100 million worldwide. In 1979, it received three Australian Film Institute Awards.

'Mad' Max Rockatansky, played by Mel Gibson, sought vengeance amidst gritty scenes of high-speed car chases and totally damaged vehicles. Despite a shoestring budget for twelve-week filming and editing being done in Miller's kitchen, George Miller's *Mad Max* surprisingly managed to be a global success.

American distributors were worried about how an all-Australian picture, replete with Australian accents, would be received, perpetuating the 'cultural cringe' that was already ingrained in the Australian mindset. Except for one song sequence, the whole production was dubbed. Since Mel Gibson was regarded as an unknown, the US trailers only included part of the stunning car crash moments from the film. In the year 2000, Australian dialogue soundtrack released in the US on a limited scale.

In many US regions, the sequel was released first, then followed by the first movie, which was launched with the catch phrase 'Find out what made Max mad'.

The Ultimate ANZAC Day Movie

The quintessential Australian and New Zealand Army Corp (ANZAC) Day movie, *Gallipoli* (1981), directed by Peter Weir, with Mark Lee and Mel Gibson as protagonists, was centred around the Dardanelles attack of 1915, emphasizing the human cost of the fatal choice to strike.

In the movie, Archy Hamilton (Lee) and Frank Dunne (Gibson) provided the perspective of the ill-fated ANZAC campaign that cost so many lives. The lads meet while competing in a foot race and enlist in the Australian Imperial Force before being deployed to Turkey. While Archy is an infantryman, Frank is a message runner in the 'Sniper Alley', avoiding bullets. The suicide attack on 'The Nek', where the soldiers, including Major Barton (Bill Kerr), are slaughtered by machine guns, brings the movie to a close. After the English command makes a late decision to alter the plan, a distraught Frank arrives too late to stop the attack.

Though it had limited success overseas, the film was the recipient of eight Australian Film Industry awards including Best Film, Best Director, Best Actor, Best Supporting Actor, Best Screenplay, and Best Cinematography.

Down to the Weir

Based on Australian author Joan Lindsay's novel of the same title and directed by Peter Weir, *Picnic at Hanging Rock* (1975) was a horror film set in a country girls' school on St Valentine's

Day, following the story of some young students who go missing on a deadly school trip. What happened to the girls who scaled the rock remains a mystery that is never unveiled. Many people believed the story to be genuine and that the Macedon Ranges, in Victoria, where the movie was filmed, were haunted.

Before the *Hulk* There Was *Chopper*

Andrew Dominik's film *Chopper* (2000) is the life story of one of Australia's most infamous criminals, Mark 'Chopper' Read, recounting his life of crime, from his attempt to abduct a judge to publishing his own book. This film is considered Eric Bana's (who plays the lead role) finest work, and it was because of this movie that he was offered his role in Ridley Scott's *Black Hawk Down* (2001). It is fascinating, humorous, unsettling, and overall, quite amazing.

Eric began as a comedian, and subsequently, became well-known for his impersonations. In 1997, he received the Most Popular Comedy Personality Logie Award, Australia's equivalent of the Emmy. His comedy drama *The Castle* (1997), directed by Rob Sitch, became a massive hit in Australia, because it poked fun at how Australians see their place in contemporary Australian culture, focusing on themes like land rights, the Tasmanian Dam, Australian rights protected by the Constitution, which were intertwined with self-deprecating humour. Overseas, some of the particularly Australian themes were modified to more generic ones (Rissole became Meatloaf, Camira became Corolla), which is one of the reasons this success was not reproduced in the foreign market.

Aussie, Aussie, Aussie. Dundee, Dundee, Dundee.

In 1986, Mick 'Crocodile' Dundee dominated the streets of New York City with a beaming smile and a hefty knife, using the same panache he used to wrestle crocodiles or hypnotize buffalo in the Australian outback. This happened when the stereotypical Australian persona was reinvented in an Australian movie,

Fun Fact
Although they are a regular sight in the northern region of Australia, water buffaloes are an invasive species. It was a wild Asian water buffalo that acted as the water buffalo in the film.

Crocodile Dundee (1986), directed by Peter Faiman, that became a worldwide smash and introduced *g'day* to the movie-goers.

Paul Hogan, who played the main character, is also credited with penning the hilarious script, along with John Cornell. In it, Mick Dundee is persuaded by New York writer Sue Charlton to go back and show her how he survived the vicious crocodile that gave him his name. Linda Koslowski's persona bravely accompanied Mick into the desert and made it out alive. When she extended an invitation to him to return to New York, she turned the tables on him and he discovered that in order to survive there, he would need all the survival skills an Australian bushman would possess.

Desert Queens

In *The Adventures of Priscilla, Queen of the Desert* (1994), directed by Stephan Elliott, two drag queens and a transsexual drive a bus (Priscilla) to Alice Springs, an outback town in Australia, to take part in a cabaret act. Tim Chappel and Lizzy Gardiner won the 1995 Oscar for Best Costume Design thanks to the movie.

The Unconventional Three

The year 1994 witnessed three Australian movies that defied the commercial norm to play it safe and took on unusual or contentious themes.

Jack Thompson and Russell Crowe appeared in the Kevin Dowling–Geoff Burton film *The Sum of Us*, that chronicled the lives of a father (Thompson) and his son (Crowe), wherein the former was seeking a lady to be his life partner, all the while battling prejudice and discrimination from others and making a conscious attempt to accept the gay lifestyle of his son.

When it described the journey of two drag queens and an aged transsexual to a cabaret event in the middle of the desert, *The Adventures of Priscilla, Queen of the Desert* sliced through a sea of controversy. Hugo Weaving, Terence Stamp, and Guy Pearce gave such stellar performances that they seemed destined to wear ostrich plumes and high heels.

Muriel's Wedding by P.J. Hogan followed the life of a young woman as she changed from an unappealing and obese girl to a beautiful young woman whose life was all about getting married. In this fim, Toni Collette played the titular character, while Rachel Griffiths played her companion Rhonda. The movie also touched on several other topics, including mental health issues, abuse, cancer, and suicide. The most contentious topic, though, was Muriel's nuptials, one of convenience, as she gets married to a South African sports star in order to help him obtain residence in Australia.

By George!

Australian cinema has two directors with the same name – George Miller. Both Millers were born in 1945. The first became a doctor and achieved fame by creating the *Mad Max* (1979) and *Babe* (1995) series. The second directed films like *The Man from Snowy River* (1982) and *Les Patterson Saves the World* (1987).

Who the F*** is Alice?

Adapted from the novel with the same name, *A Town Like Alice* (1956), directed by Jack Lee, was written by Nevil Shute, who was also one of the screenwriters for the movie. Virginia McKenna, a British actress, and Peter Finch appeared in it. Before moving to Australia, where he attended school and began working as a copy boy at a Sydney newspaper, Peter Finch was born in England but lived for a while in France and

India. He was performing in a non-commercial theatre play in Sydney when Laurence Olivier, who was in Australia at the time, spotted him. He went to London in 1948 before coming back to Australia in the 1950s to star in the movies *The Shiralee* (1957) by Leslie Norman and *Robbery Under Arms* (1957) by Jack Lee.

The place referred to in the title of the film is Alice Springs, a town in Australia, and one would assume from the title that this is a stereotypically Australian film. But it was primarily filmed in Malaysia and Great Britain. It did, however, include an Australian actor who, for his role in *Network* (1976), was honoured with a posthumous Academy Award for Best Actor.

Another Australian actor, Heath Ledger, posthumously won the Academy Award for Best Supporting Actor for his work in the Christopher Nolan film *The Dark Knight* (2008).

When Pigs Have Wings

Chris Noonan's *Babe* (1995) was a pig that truly took off at the box office throughout the world. The storyline begins with a sheepdog who had to watch all of her babies being sold adopting a charming little pig named Babe, who later acquires award-winning sheep-herding skills.

Magda Szubanski and James Cromwell featured in George Miller's *Babe: Pig in the City* (1998), the sequel to the hugely popular *Babe*. It followed the young pig's life as he returned to Hoggett's farm following his success in sheep herding. Sadly, the farmer was sick, so Babe travelled to the city to try and rescue the farm. Many of the animals used in the film were kept on location in specialized facilities.

In terms of special effects and computer animation, *Babe* and its sequel were both groundbreaking works. The audience may be excused for thinking the animal performers genuinely spoke!

Highway to Hell Begins at the Cemetery?

Thunderstruck (2004) was shot at the Fremantle Cemetery, where the lead AC/DC singer from Perth, Bon Scott, is buried.

This was because the movie chronicles the tale of five lads who make a promise that in case of anyone's death from their group, the rest will bury him next to Bon Scott in the Fremantle Cemetery.

Finding the Stolen Generation

The 2002 movie *Rabbit-Proof Fence* by Phillip Noyce was a bold attempt to bring to light the theme of atrocities subjected upon the A boriginals, the negligence and ruthlessness of the government in their treatment, and the horrendous 'cleansing' practices of government agencies. This was a subject that had plagued Australia since long, and it was the courageous and accurate description of the same by Phillip Noyce, and stellar performances by anonymous Aboriginal girls in the film, that compelled the country to face this ugly reality, which makes it one of the most significant productions of the first hundred years of Australian cinema.

The movie, based on Doris Pilkington's book about her own mother Molly, analysed the brutality, abhorrence, and embarrassment faced by Australia's stolen generation, through the story of three young Aboriginal girls, who were in search of their families and their cultural roots. The story takes place in 1931, when Molly Craig (Everlyn Sampi), Daisy Kadibill (Tianna Sansbury), and Gracie Fields (Laura Monaghan) were forcefully separated from their families, and sent to a camp miles away, where they underwent training to become domestic help for white houses. The girls, denied any rights to a family or home of their own, were referred to as 'half-breeds'. Ultimately, to find a way home, Molly managed to get away and directed her younger sister and cousin to the rabbit-proof fence.

Aussie PM Acts in a Movie

An Australian election serves as the setting for the Bruce Beresford movie *Don's Party* (1976). It was 1969, and the Liberal prime minister was expected to lose his job in the next election. He managed to live, but a few years later, his own party abandoned him. In the film, the same prime minister John Gorton had a cameo. In the 1968 Liberal Party-County Party partnership, Gorton conquered leadership contest and narrowly won the general election in 1969. He left his post as PM in 1971.

With lots of drinking, nudity, and sexual antics, *Don's Party* was a notorious film. The majority of the guests at the 'party' were Labour supporters, and as the outcome became clearer, they grew rather astonished and upset. A number of Australian Film Industry (AFI) awards were given to the picture, which starred some of the biggest stars in Australian cinema such as Ray Barrett, Pat Bishop, Graham Kennedy, Graeme Blundell, and Jeanie Drynan.

The revival of cinema in the 1970s, however, may be attributed to John Gorton, who served as Australia's prime minister from 1968 to 1971. He was responsible for launching many government initiatives to encourage the arts and film, including the creation of the Australian Film Development Corporation.

Outback Gothic

The concept of survival in the harsh Australian terrain emerged as a key one in Australian movies throughout the 1970s. In the 1970s, *Wake in Fright* (1971), *Walkabout* (1971), *The Cars That Ate Paris* (1974), and *Picnic at Hanging Rock* (1975) were examples of 'outback gothic', a term used for thrillers and horror movies. *Razorback* (1984) and *Shame* (1987) came in the 1980s. By the turn of the millennium, *Japanese Story* (2003), *The Proposition* (2005), and *Wolf Creek* (2005) were the prime examples. These movies describe the Australian wilderness and its critters as fatally dangerous, and its inhabitants as outcasts and psychopaths. In the Mad Max series, these components merge with futuristic post-apocalyptic ideas.

A movie that launched David Gulpilil to global cinema and became the precursor to several Australian films themed upon indigeneity was the British film *Walkabout*. An award-winning period film directed by Fred Schepisi, *The Chant of Jimmie Blacksmith* (1978), revisited the grievous tale of an Aboriginal bushranger.

Book to Screen: From Australian Literature and Australian History

Throughout the 1970s and '80s, successful film adaptations based on timeless Australian literature and historical tales were being produced. One such movie was Gillian Armstrong's *My Brilliant Career* (1979), based on the 1901 novel of the same name by Miles Franklin, and it starred Judy Davis and Sam Neill in early lead roles. Based on a memoir by Jeannie Gunn, *We of the Never Never* (1982), directed by Igor Auzins, showcased the life in the Australian bush through female experience. Tom Burlinson and Sigrid Thornton starrer *The Man from Snowy River*, directed by George T. Miller, brought the classic Banjo Paterson poem of the same name to life on-screen and became one of the all-time box-office hits of the Australian cinema.

Apart from the popular historical movies of the 1970s, *The Adventures of Barry McKenzie* (1972), *Alvin Purple* (1973), and *Barry McKenzie Holds His Own* (1974), among others, were films praising and satirizing Australian popular culture over the decade. Barry Humphries, a performing artist and writer, worked with film-maker Bruce Beresford on the Barry McKenzie movies.

The contentious trial of an Australian soldier during the second Boer War of 1899–1902 was dramatized in the 1980 film *Breaker Morant*, directed by Bruce Beresford, starring Jack Thompson and Edward Woodward. This was followed by the 1981 film *Gallipoli*, which was directed by Peter Weir and starred Mel Gibson. Gibson also featured in *Tim* (1979), directed by Michael Pate, a movie based on Colleen McCollough's famous book. These films, which are now regarded as masterpieces of Australian cinema, used significant incidents from Australian history to examine contemporary Australian identity.

Blanchett's Oscars

Cate Blanchett is the first Australian actor to win two Academy Awards, for both Best Actress and Best Supporting Actress for the movies *The Aviator* (2004) and *Blue Jasmine* (2013), respectively. She is also the most nominated Australian, with eight nominations in the acting category.

The Rush to Awards

Geoffrey Rush is surely the king having won the 'Triple Crown of Acting' – an Academy Award, an Emmy Award, and a Tony Award. He is the youngest actor in the world to achieve this feat and the first and only Australian actor to have received the honours.

Australian Global Movie Stars

Actor	Known For
Abbie Cornish	*Somersault* (2004), *Sucker Punch* (2011)
Ben Mendelsohn	*Animal Kingdom* (2010), *Mississippi Grind* (2015)
Cate Blanchett	*The Aviator* (2004), *Blue Jasmine* (2013)
Chips Rafferty	*The Overlanders* (1946), *Wake in Fright* (1971)
Chris Hemsworth	*Thor* in Marvel Cinematic Universe (MCU) (2011–22), *Extraction* (2020)
Eric Bana	*Chopper* (2000), *Munich* (2005)
Errol Flynn	*Captain Blood* (1935), *The Adventures of Robin Hood* (1938)
Geoffrey Rush	*Shine* (1996), *Pirates of the Caribbean: The Curse of the Black Pearl* (2003), *The King's Speech* (2010)
Guy Pearce	*Memento* (2000), *The Rover* (2014)

Heath Ledger	*Brokeback Mountain* (2005), *The Dark Knight* (2008)
Hugh Jackman	*Logan* (2017), *Wolverine* in the *X-Men* series (2000–17)
Hugo Weaving	*The Matrix* (1999), *Captain America: The First Avenger* (2011)
Jacki Weaver	*Caddie* (1976), *Animal Kingdom* (2010)
Joel Edgerton	*Animal Kingdom* (2010), *Loving* (2016)
John Jarratt	*Wolf Creek* (2005), *Wolf Creek 2* (2013)
Judy Davis	*Husband and Wives* (1992), *The Dressmaker* (2015)
Margot Robbie	*The Wolf of Wall Street* (2013), *Suicide Squad* (2016), *Barbie* (2023)
Mel Gibson	*Mad Max* (1979), *The Year of Living Dangerously* (1982), *Braveheart* (1995)
Mia Wasikowska	*Alice in Wonderland* (2010), *The Kids Are All Right* (2010)
Naomi Watts	*Mulholland Drive* (2001), *King Kong* (2005)
Nicole Kidman	*Eyes Wide Shut* (1999), *Moulin Rouge!* (2001), *The Hours* (2002), *Being the Ricardos* (2021)
Peter Finch	*Network* (1976)
Rebel Wilson	*Pitch Perfect* (2012)
Rod Taylor	*The Birds* (1963), *The Time Machine* (1960), *Inglourious Basterds* (2009)
Russell Crowe	*Romper Stomper* (1992), *The Sum of Us* (1994), *Gladiator* (2000)
Sam Worthington	*Avatar* (2009), *The Shack* (2017)
Toni Collette	*Muriel's Wedding* (1994), *Little Miss Sunshine* (2006)

Facts about Classic American Directors of World Cinema

- American director Billy Wilder wrote several scenes for Berlin's silent-film industry when he was in his twenties. In his younger days, he was a skilled dancer and was a hired dance partner for older women to make a living.

- During his Berlin days, Billy Wilder spent time in the august company of prominent writers and artists like Thomas Mann, Bertolt Brecht, George Grosz, Fritz Lang, Hermann Hesse, and Erich Maria Remarque, whom he met every day at a celebrated bohemian hangout called the Romanisches Café.

- John Ford worked with the same group of technicians and actors throughout his career. Often, he was seen with a drink in one hand and a cigar in the other on set. He wore a black patch over one eye, which had been injured in an accident in the 1940s.

- Frank Capra was Hollywood's most sought-after director of the 1930s. He is credited for establishing the screwball comedy as a genre, but his later films focused on more serious social or historical issues, revolving around a formula where an honest hero prevailed over corrupt people.

- In 1942, William Wyler volunteered to make movies for the armed forces at the outbreak of WWII. As an army major and a lieutenant colonel, Wilder created two 16 mm colour films as the director and cinematographer on combat duty. He was rendered permanently deaf in one ear after the war as a result. revolving around a formula where an honest hero prevailed over corrupt people.

3

TINSELTOWN

BEFORE WORLD WAR I, ITALIAN CINEMA WAS THE MOST POPULAR SOURCE OF ENTERTAINMENT. BUT AFTER THE WAR, EUROPE WAS SO DEVASTATED THAT IT TOOK TIME TO RECUPERATE. HOLLYWOOD QUICKLY BECAME THE NEW EPICENTRE OF CINEMA AS THE AMERICANS TOOK THE BATON FROM THE ITALIANS.

The Naming of Hollywood

It is often believed that one night in 1886, H. J. Whitley, the 'Father of Hollywood', stood at the highest point of a slope overlooking the Cahuenga Valley when a Chinese man approached in a wagon. When Whitley asked the man what he was doing, the reply was, "I holly-wood", meaning 'hauling or pulling wood'. Whitley decided to name his new town Hollywood. Whitley was actually from Canada and became a US citizen only in the 1870s. Official records show Daeida Wilcox, wife of Harvey Wilcox, who owned the area, submitted a subdivision map to the Los Angeles county recorder's office in 1887. There she used that name.

Escape from New Jersey

Hollywood became the centre of film-making in America because most movie-making patents were held by Thomas Edison's company in New Jersey in the early years. Other film-makers were sued when they tried to produce anything. So, film-makers began migrating westwards, where such enforcement was not possible.

In Old California

The Count of Monte Cristo (1908) is acknowledged as the first film completed in Hollywood. But the first movie made there is *In Old California*. This seventeen-minute silent black-and-white movie about the Mexican era of California was shot in and around Los Angeles.

It was made by the legendary director D.W. Griffith, who was also responsible for the path-breaking film *The Birth of a Nation* (1915).

Nuclear Effects

The Conqueror (1956) was filmed perilously close to nuclear testing grounds in the Utah Desert with the assurance of the government that it was safe to shoot there. But years later, many of the cast and crew developed a type of cancer from radiation exposure. You can't trust the government!

The Hollywood Walk of Fame

Being the chosen one to have your own star on the Hollywood Walk of Fame is a big honour as it is the biggest sign of respect from the Academy of Motion Pictures. But the benefactor must also pay for the Walk of Fame. It costs a neat $75,000 sponsorship fee upon selection.

Work from Home Saves the Day!

Executives of the Pixar Animation Studios were shocked when a wrong command on the 'master machine' deleted most of the material of *Toy Story 2* (1999). There was no other copy of the work but, thankfully, the technical director was working from home that day on a copy and most of the animation was restored.

Hollywood's Golden Age

The 1930s saw feature-length movies produced in Hollywood with full colour and sound to bring about a cinematic revolution. The American film industry became the best in the world, and the 1930s and 1940s are termed the Golden Age of Hollywood as cinema became the main form of entertainment in America.

Classic Hollywood Facts

- The first movie made entirely in what is now identified as Hollywood was *The Squaw Man* (1914) by Cecil B. DeMille.
- The Warner Brothers studio in Hollywood was founded in 1918 by four brothers – Harry, Sam, Albert, and Jack – from Ohio.
- Forever Cemetery in Hollywood has many Hollywood stars buried there.
- The must-visit places are the Hollywood Walk of Fame, Universal Studios, the Chinese Theatre, Charlie Chaplin Studios, Madame Tussauds Hollywood, and Roosevelt Hotel.

The Hollywood Sign

The iconic 'Hollywood' sign sprang up in 1923, when a real estate agent named Harry Chandler advertised properties in

the area. The cost of the sign that read 'Hollywoodland' was $21,000 and was supposed to be there for eighteen months. Instead, it was later edited to 'Hollywood' and stayed forever.

My Big Fat Greek Wedding (2002)

The most profitable movie in the history of cinema is strangely *My Big Fat Greek Wedding*. That is because it cost just $5 million to make and grossed over $240 million. That's a big fat profit!

A Cafe with Quality

The Quality Café in Hollywood was renowned as one of the most recycled sets. In 2006, the cafe was shut down probably for the best as it became what it did best – a permanent movie set! *Gone in 60 Seconds* (2000), *Training Day* (2001), *Catch Me If You Can* (2002), *Million Dollar Baby* (2004), *Mr. & Mrs. Smith* (2005), *Sex and Death 101* (2007), *The Stepfather* (2009) are some of the movies filmed at The Quality Café.

The Hollywood Walk of Fame

The idea for the Hollywood Walk of Fame was first proposed in 1953 by E.M. Stuart, the Hollywood Chamber of Commerce's volunteer president. Since then the Walk of Fame has been an integral part of Hollywood. Today, the Hollywood Walk of Fame is a historic landmark. It comprises over 2,700 five-pointed terrazzo and brass stars embedded in the pavements of Hollywood Boulevard and Vine Street in Hollywood, California.

Orson Welles has two stars in the Hollywood Walk of Fame, unlike most others. The first star can be found on the 6,500 block of Hollywood Boulevard for his contribution to radio, and the second is for his contribution to film, which is on the 1,600 block of Vine Street.

Hollywood's Strange Move

In a strange and baffling move, Hollywood permitted the German government to censor their films that were not flattering towards Germany or the Nazis throughout the 1930s. Clearly, Hollywood head honchos did not want to antagonize Hitler and his Nazi party, which was dominating Europe then.

Hollywood Informer

Strange as it may sound, Ronald Reagan was an active Federal Bureau of Investigation (FBI) informer in Hollywood. He reported on other actors whom he suspected of subversive activities. This was before he became the president of course.

The Television Invasion

The year 1963 is regarded as the worst year for Hollywood movies in terms of production and profitability. A measly 120 films were released in 1963, and the figure is far lower than any year since the 1920s. The steep decline was because of television's rise in popularity.

Titanic Film Reels

The film *Titanic* was released in 1997 when film reels were still used to project a movie; unlike today, when everything is digital. *Titanic's* duration was three hours and fifteen minutes, and it used up 17.7 reels. That is about 17,700 feet of film, which was over 3 miles in length!

The Most Expensive Film

The most expensive film until 2022 was *Pirates of the Caribbean: On Stranger Tides* (2011) with a staggering budget of $379 million ($499 million when adjusted to inflation). The high cost was induced by inflation, several locations, expensive equipment like 3D cameras, and numerous special-effects companies. Despite the efforts, it was only the fourth highest-grossing film of 2011.

The Big Five

Only three films have won 'The Big Five' Oscars, meaning Best Actor, Best Actress, Best Director, Best Screenplay, and Best Film – the three in chronological order of production being *It Happened One Night* (1934), *One Flew over the Cuckoo's Nest* (1975), and *The Silence of the Lambs* (1991).

The Matrix Code

Remember the green symbols trailing down in the movies? They are called the Matrix code but aren't complicated algorithms as perceived by many. A production designer named Simon Whiteley scanned symbols from his wife's sushi cookbooks and manipulated them to create the iconic code when his initial idea was rejected.

Gone with the Wind

The record for the highest-grossing film of all time was held by the film *Gone with the Wind* from 1939 to 1965. This record was broken by the release of *The Sound of Music* in 1965. However, *Gone with the Wind* is the highest-grossing film ever, having earned a total gross of 3.44 billion dollars (adjusted to inflation).

Cursing in Hollywood

The first curse word appeared in film in 1929 two years after sound did. Swearing in films soon became fashionable in Hollywood. The film with the most use of the F-word is *The Wolf of Wall Street* (2013), directed by Martin Scorsese and starring Leonardo DiCaprio.

Earlier, Martin Scorsese's 1990s gangster classic *Casino* (1995) held the record for the most swear words. But it slipped down the charts in the next decade. Scorsese regained the title with *The Wolf of Wall Street* (2013) that has 715 cuss words. The F-word is spoken 569 times, and that is 3.16 F-words every minute. Wolfish!

Women Cinematographers

Only three women have won an Oscar for Best Director so far. No woman has yet won the Academy Award for Best Cinematographer but three women had been nominated. Rachel Morrison was nominated for *Mudbound* (2017), Ari Wegner for The *Power of the Dog* (2021) and Mandy Walker for *Elvis* (2022).

Not Giving a Damn

'Frankly, my dear, I don't give a damn,' was Rhett Butler's iconic line in the 1939 film *Gone with the Wind.* But this was almost edited because of the profanity factor. Twenty-two alternative versions were considered but were all rejected eventually as they couldn't match up to the original.

Schindler's (Costume) List

The costume designer of *Schindler's List* (1993), Anna Biedrzycka-Sheppard, needed costumes for 20,000 extras and decided to advertise for the same. Several people in Poland still had clothes from the 1930s and '40s that they exchanged for cash. Biedrzycka-Sheppard received an Oscar nomination for her work in this Steven Spielberg film.

Mating Sounds in the Park

Jurassic Park's sound designer Gary Rydstrom was the recipient of two Academy Awards for sound design and mixing for the film. He spent hours recording various animal sounds before freezing on the mating sounds of tortoises to depict the sound of dinosaurs in the movie.

Killer Ed

Notorious American serial killer Ed Gein from Plainfield, Wisconsin, inspired three fictional characters in Hollywood. Buffalo Bill from *The Silence of the Lambs,* Leatherface from *The Texas Chainsaw Massacre* (1974), and Norman Bates from *Psycho* (1960) were all inspired by Killer Ed, aka Butcher of Plainfield or the Plainfield Ghoul.

Wings

The first film that won the Academy Award for Best Picture was *Wings* (1927) in 1928. The silent romantic action-war movie directed by William A. Wellman also won the Academy Award for Best Engineering Effects.

The King of Hollywood

Author Stephen King is credited with being the living author with the most film adaptations, excluding the character adaptations of other authors like Sherlock Holmes. Fifty-three movies have been made so far based on King's works, according to his official website. It all began with *Carrie* in 1976 directed by Brian De Palma.

Butch Cassidy and the Sundance Kid (1969)

The original script title of William Goldman's classic Western was '*The Sundance Kid and Butch Cassidy*'. But after Hollywood star Paul Newman agreed to do the role of Butch Cassidy, the title was renamed *Butch Cassidy and the Sundance Kid.* No prizes for guessing why.

Taxi Driver (1976)

Paul Schrader wrote the screenplay of *Taxi Driver* in just five days. Rumours are that he kept a loaded gun on his desk to motivate and inspire him to write quickly. Don't try this at home!

A Dog Named Indiana

The name of the legendary character in the movie series, Indiana Jones, was given by George Lucas. But ever wonder how the name came about? Of course, Lucas had a dog named Indiana.

Jawed

The author of *Jaws,* Peter Benchley, played the role of a TV reporter in the movie when it was being filmed. But he was reportedly thrown off the set after he always argued with director Steven Spielberg about how the film should end. *Jaws* (1975) became the first movie to gross over $100 million.

Jackie

The biographical film *Jackie* (2016) was based on former US first lady Jacqueline Kennedy. Starring Natalie Portman and directed by Chilean director Pablo Larraín, the movie was critically acclaimed and earned an Academy Award nomination for Natalie Portman.

Bound by Contract

Back in the old days of Hollywood, it wasn't possible for actors and actresses to work for different studios as they do today. They had long contracts for five to seven years and sometimes even longer, where the talent was reined in by a particular studio for a long period.

Actor Out on Loan

In the early days of Hollywood, an actor could only work with another studio if they were loaned to them. Actress Elizabeth Taylor would often force her hand with her home studio Metro-Goldwyn-Mayer (MGM) to loan her to other studios to enable her to work on the films she wanted.

Take What You Get

Actors in old Hollywood did not have freedom of choice. They had to accept any role that was offered by the studio. Turning down a role also was not an option as that could kill one's career. Bette Davis realized this when Warner Brothers suspended her once for turning down roles.

Lethal Make-Up

At least two actors in *The Wizard of Oz* (1939) suffered because of make-up. Margaret Hamilton had to wear toxic paint to play the Wicked Witch, which almost killed her. The aluminium dust from his make-up put Buddy Ebsen, the original Tin Man, out of action. He suffered breathing issues all his life.

A Streetcar Named Desire

A Streetcar Named Desire (1951) was the first film to win three Academy Awards. Vivien Leigh won for Best Actress, Kim Hunter received the award for Best Supporting Actress, and Karl Malden was given the award for Best Supporting Actor.

Animal Models for Disney

Using real-life models is a common practice at Disney for the animators to nail the character perfectly. Disney brought a live reindeer into the studio for the animators to study for *Frozen* (2013). They also fetched a bear cub for *Brother Bear 2* (2003). Wonder what they did for *The Lion King* (1994)!

Frozen in Time

Frozen took seventy years to make considering that Walt Disney wanted to make it since the 1930s. But the script was not perfect until 2008 because of its dark tone and the Snow Queen's portrayal in the previous version. It was certainly worth waiting for seventy years as *Frozen* is one of Disney's most successful films, making over a billion dollars worldwide!

Frozen Sequel

Frozen's sequel turned out even better. It is the second most successful animated movie ever (after *The Lion King*). Both *Frozen* and *Frozen II* (2019) are some of the most successful films to be directed by a woman! Jennifer Lee was *Frozen's* co-director and also the first woman to direct for Disney.

Only British Actors Please!

Author J.K. Rowling sold the rights to the first four Harry Potter books to Warner Brothers for a reported US $2 million. However, she had a condition that only British and Irish actors would be cast in the *Harry Potter* films. But this condition was not always followed.

Rebel Without a Cause

Rebel Without a Cause (1955) had a tragic mystique surrounding it because of the early deaths of all the three stars. James Dean died in a car accident a month before the film's release. In 1976, Sal Mineo was stabbed to death, and Natalie Wood died in 1981 by drowning.

The First Adult Film

Who's Afraid of Virginia Woolf? (1966) went through a stormy legal battle before its release because of its adult subject. It became the first US film forbidden to anyone less than eighteen years of age. The movie was a blockbuster, raking in about $40 million on a budget less than $8 million.

Invitation in an Elevator

Charles Foster Kane's character in *Citizen Kane* (1941) was based on media mogul William Randolph Hearst. Hearst failed multiple attempts to stop the movie. Before the premiere, director Oscar Welles met Hearst accidentally in a hotel elevator. Welles's invitation to Hearst to attend the premiere was angrily declined.

Hearst Fooled by Welles

When William Randolph Hearst couldn't stop *Citizen Kane* from releasing, he arranged for a naked woman to hide in Orson Welles's hotel room and hired a photographer to click a picture of the two to create a scandal. But Welles heard about the scheme and simply checked into another hotel.

Bollywood Inspires Hollywood

The early Bollywood movies were inspired from the Hollywood musicals that were made in the 1920s. Life came a full circle when film-maker Baz Luhrmann said that his hit musical *Moulin Rouge!* (2001) was actually influenced by Bollywood musicals. Even Danny Boyle's *Slumdog Millionaire* (2008) was inspired by Bollywood movies.

Shawshank Redemption (1994)

Rob Reiner offered *Shawshank Redemption*'s writer/director Frank Darabont $2.5 million to sell him the rights so that he could rewrite and direct it with Tom Cruise as Andy and Harrison Ford as Red. Darabont refused, replying that this was his 'chance to do something really great'. He was spot on.

Sahara (2005)

The budget for *Sahara* skyrocketed from $80 million to $160 million because of problems like crew disputes, location problems, delays in shooting, and bribes to Moroccan government officials, among others. The movie earned only $119 million on its release, making it one of the biggest box -office duds ever.

Spartacus and JFK

When *Spartacus* released in 1960, anti-communist and right-wing groups picketed theatres that showed the movie because of the uproar it caused in society. But the controversy ended when newly elected US president John F. Kennedy crossed the picket line drawn by protestors to watch the movie.

Fast and Furious (2001)

Stars of the *Fast and Furious* film franchise, Jason Statham, Dwayne 'The Rock' Johnson, and Vin Diesel fought to have their contract demands met. They insisted their characters take fewer blows while filming. Vin Diesel also came up with a plan to track all the punches, kicks, and head-butts. Too much of fury to take?

Red Dawn

The script for the 2012 remake of *Red Dawn* featured the Chinese army as the invaders. To enter the Chinese market, the studio replaced the Chinese with North Koreans in all references in the movie. But even after all these precautions, the movie never released in China.

The Good, the Bad, and the Ugly

Strange as it may sound, the entire plot for *The Good, the Bad, and the Ugly* (1966) was created on the spot at a meeting between Italian director Sergio Leone and Hollywood producers when they met to discuss what kind of film to make. That's quick on the draw!

A Very Thin Red Line

The actors of *The Thin Red Line* (1998) were greatly disappointed when their parts in the movie were massively or totally edited from the final cut. Adrian Brody discovered that his entire part had been cut. None of Billy Bob Thornton's three hours of narration was used, and Mickey Rourke had been relegated to the DVD extras.

Psycho Music

Initially, Hitchcock did not intend to use music for his infamous shower scene in *Psycho* (1960). Composer Bernard Herrmann, who did the score of the movie, requested him to listen to the music he had created for the scene. Hitchcock was so pleased with the music, he doubled Herrmann's salary.

Superman

Before the makers froze on Christopher Reeve to play *Superman* (1978), they considered numerous actors for the role like Sylvester Stallone and Arnold Schwarzenegger. Surprisingly, they also considered Muhammad Ali and Elton John, who had never appeared in a movie before. Thankfully, better sense prevailed.

The Jazz Singer

Singer Neil Diamond was a fresh actor in *The Jazz Singer* (1980) and was having difficulty doing a scene where his character was supposed to be angry. Diamond ordered his band to play a Barry Manilow song to actually make him angry during the filming of the scene.

The First Full-Length 3D Film

The silent drama *The Power of Love* produced in 1922 is regarded as the first full-length 3D film. Sadly, the original silent movie and its 2D version that followed are both lost forever.

Apocalypse Now

After shooting nearly 1.5 million feet of film for the movie, Francis Ford Coppola accidentally discovered important scraps of film that had been discarded as waste material. The opening shot of *Apocalypse Now* (1979) was reconstructed from these. Coppola also used the rock band the Doors' song *The End* in this opening sequence for fun.

Creating Hollywood History

In Hollywood history, this is perhaps the only instance where a Nobel Prize–winning author adapted the book of another Nobel

Prize–winning author into a movie. Ernest Hemingway's *To Have and Have Not* was adapted for a movie in 1944 by author William Faulkner, who had ventured into screenwriting too.

Fantasia

Surround sound is something that is really common today. But Walt Disney's *Fantasia* (1940) was the first Hollywood film with a multi-channel sound format. The sound reproduction system was called Fantasound.

License to Kill

In 1989, the title of a James Bond movie had to bc changed. The name 'License Revoked' was changed to *License to Kill* in post-production after it was discovered that test audiences in America associated the word 'revoked' primarily with driver's licences. We're shaken not stirred!

Arachnophobia

The biggest spider in the film *Arachnophobia* (1990) was a bird-eating tarantula named Big Bob after actor Robert Zemekis. Interestingly, the crew used a hairdryer and some lemon-scented spray to control the little spiders that were used in the film.

Mickey Mouse

The creator of the most-loved cartoon mouse was actually scared of mice! Walt Disney, creator of Mickey Mouse, was in perpetual fear of these four-legged rodents. But creating Mickey Mouse was the best thing that Walt Disney did as it turned Disney into one of the biggest entertainment companies.

The White House Movie Theatre

The White House has an exclusive movie theatre, which has

forty-two seats to accommodate the first family and their guests. In 1942, when the East Wing of the White House was built, the East Terrace cloakroom was transformed into a movie theatre on President Franklin D. Roosevelt's instructions.

The First X Rating

The Motion Picture Association of America (MPAA) ratings in Hollywood began in November 1968. In December 1968, the Brian De Palma movie *Greetings,* starring Robert De Niro, was the chosen one to receive the first X rating for its sexually explicit content.

Classic Cost Cutting

In the 1939 classic *Gone with the Wind*, old sets that were discarded were burned to create a fire scene to depict Atlanta going down in flames. To save costs, old sets were gone with the wind.

And the Winner Is...

The Academy announced Oscar winners differently earlier. Their names were announced three months before the first Academy Awards ceremony held on 16 May 1929. The sealed-envelope system was begun in 1941 because the *Los Angeles Times* announced the names of the winners in its evening edition even before the ceremony took place in 1940.

Asbestos Used as Fake Snow in Films

In the scene in *The Wizard of Oz* (1939), a blanket of snow falls over Dorothy who is lying in a poppy field. This snow that was dumped on Dorothy was fake and toxic material. As in many other movies, asbestos was used as a substitute for snowflakes.

The carcinogenic mineral asbestos was used in film-making as a substitute for snow till a little after World War II. For *The Country Doctor* (1936), as much as 1,000 pounds of asbestos was used to portray the snowy landscapes of Quebec.

Insuring Betty Grable's Legs

In what was probably a Hollywood first, 20th Century Fox insured actress Betty Grable's legs with Lloyds of London for $1 million in the late 1940s.

Lawrence of Arabia (1962)

The epic film *Lawrence of Arabia* took more than two years for pre-production to complete and fourteen months to film. The several locations of the shoot ranged from Jordan, Spain, and Morocco, among others.

Honour for Grace Kelly

Hollywood actress Grace Kelly was the first actress ever to be featured on a US postage stamp. She received this honour in the year 1993.

The First Computer Graphics

Computer graphics have existed in Hollywood longer than one would imagine. The first Hollywood film to use computer graphics was Alfred Hitchcock's *Vertigo* as early as 1958. Although the use of graphics was limited to the introductory sequence of the movie, it was still an indication of the future.

No Excessive Kissing

From the 1930s to the mid-1960s, no one kissed on-screen for more than a few seconds. The Motion Picture Production Code banned 'excessive and lustful kissing'. No time limit was specified, and three seconds was the unofficial standard. So, if one wonders why the romantic leads in a classic keep pausing between kisses, one knows why.

To Make Children Cry

In the early days of Hollywood, strange ways and manipulative techniques were adopted to make children cry in emotional film scenes. They were sometimes bribed and sometimes compared with other child actors who cried better. It's a far cry from today, where children act just like adults.

Chaplin Partners with Disney

Walt Disney was sceptical when Disney released *Snow White and the Seven Dwarfs* in 1937. That's because it was the first feature-length animated movie. But Chaplin encouraged Disney that the movie would perform at the box office, and even became his business associate for the same. A visionary for sure! Chaplin was a visionary for sure!

The Scariest Mask

While filming *Halloween* (1978), the budget became tight. Rather than splurge on expensive props, a $1.98 mask of Captain Kirk of *Star Trek* was picked up for killer Michael Myers. The eyeholes were widened and the mask was spray-painted white. It's one of the scariest masks in Hollywood horror history.

No More Risky Business

The sunglasses company Ray-Ban was considering discontinuing their Wayfarers range of glasses as sales were not encouraging. Then magic happened when Tom Cruise wore them in *Risky Business* (1983). Sales of Ray-Ban Wayfarers skyrocketed after the movie released as the glasses became iconic.

The Top Men and Ray-Bans

In 1986, Tom Cruise was seen sporting the Ray-Ban Aviator Classic in *Top Gun*, which increased the sale of these sunglasses by 40 per cent.

Eleven years later, Ray-Ban sales skyrocketed again thanks to the Will Smith–Tommy Lee Jones starrer *Men in Black* (1997). The Predator 2

Will Smith

eyewear sported by the two stars suddenly became fashionable and tripled the sale of those glasses. The movie, made at a modest budget of $90 million, collected $589 million globally. That was much more than the Ray-Ban sales of course.

Regenerating Hollywood Using Generative AI

In the technology-driven world today, use of AI, or artificial intelligence, in Hollywood is not a far cry. While visual effects (VFX) and computer-generated imagery (CGI) have been there for quite some time in the showbiz, generative AI is a fairly recent phenomenon. Generative artificial intelligence is a type of software programme that creates new written and visual works on its own by learning from pre-existing text and visuals.

Over the years, several movies have integrated AI with CGI and VFX and have created customized software to de-age actors portraying younger roles on-screen. Prime examples include:

Brad Pitt in *The Curious Case of Benjamin Button* (2008)

- As the protagonist suffers from a mysterious disease that causes reverse ageing, around fifty-two minutes of Brad Pitt's on-screen appearance was 3D digitization and AI. The efforts certainly paid as the movie won an Academy Award for its visual effects!

- **Jeff Bridges in *Tron: Legacy* (2010)**
  This sci-fi classic was the first movie to feature sequences as long as fifteen minutes that were completely generated by CGI.

- **Michael Douglas in *Ant Man* (2015)**
  The opening scene of the movie is set in the 1980s and features a de-aged Michael Douglas up to a time span of thirty years.

- **Robert Downey Jr in *Captain America: Civil War* (2016)**
  Downey was made to look in his early twenties, when the audience got a glimpse of Tony Stark's past in a flashback sequence.

- **Johnny Depp in *Pirates of the Caribbean: Dead Men Tell No Tales* (2017)**
  Apart from the CGI-aided special effects, Johnny Depp was de-aged up to 25–30 years for flashback sequences in the movie.

- **Kurt Russell in *Guardians of the Galaxy Vol. 2* (2017)**
  Considered one of the best stints at de-ageing an actor, the movie featured Russell playing a godlike character, Ego, where he looked like the Russell from the 1980s in the sequence.

- **Will Smith in *Gemini Man* (2019)**
  This movie took generative AI to a whole new level because it features a younger, cloned

version of Will Smith alongside him for the entirety of the movie, and yet, it is convincingly real. It is played by Will Smith only, but its skin is completely CGI generated.

- **Carrie Fisher and Mark Hamill in various instalments of *Star Wars* (1977–2023)**
  This famous movie franchise adopted a hybrid approach to de-age Fisher and Hamill in various instalments of Star Wars, including the recent series *The Mandalorian* (2019). While CGI was used in some of the previous instalments, deepfake techniques have been employed in the recent ones, where the original actors were not used at all, and everything, from their appearance to their voice, was artificially created.

- **Al Pacino, Joe Pesci, and Robert De Niro in *The Irishman* (2019)**
  The movie created quite a buzz because of its whopping budget spent on tech. De-ageing technology was used to reduce up to forty years from the actors' real ages.

- **Harrison Ford in *Indiana Jones and the Dial of Destiny* (2023)**
  Harrison Ford, currently eighty, looks like the Ford from the 1980s for around twenty-five minutes in the movie. A tool called 'FaceSwap', built by VFX supervisors from Industrial Light & Magic (ILM), was used to de-age Ford in the film.

Warner Brothers Magic

Harry Potter and the Order of the Phoenix (2007) recorded a $167 million loss because of Hollywood accounting. Warner Brothers ensured that the movie lost money as it paid itself a $212 million distribution fee from the profits. Abracadabra!

Spanish Dracula

The 1931 film *Dracula* was filmed in English in the day and in Spanish at night. The Spanish-language version used the same set and script but was finished in half the time and earned better reviews than the English version. Maybe it had the nocturnal Count Dracula's blessings.

Potter Stunt Double

David Holmes was the stunt double for Daniel Radcliffe in the Harry Potter movies. However, an accident during a flying broomstick scene in the last movie had David paralysed from the neck below. Radcliffe organized a celebrity charity auction that paid the medical bills. Today, Holmes runs a production company.

The First Oscars

The Oscars or the Academy Awards were first held in 1929 at the Hollywood Roosevelt Hotel. Two hundred and seventy people attended this banquet and only thirteen different awards were presented on that night's award ceremony. But the awards had an after-party in true Hollywood style.

The First Oscar Winners

Best Actor	Emil Jannings
Best Actress	Janet Gaynor
Art Direction	William Cameron Menzies
Cinematography	Charles Rosher/Karl Struss
Directing (Comedy Picture)	Lewis Milestone for *Two Arabian Knights* (1927)
Directing (Dramatic Picture)	Frank Borzage for *7th Heaven* (1927)
Engineering Effects	Roy Pomeroy for *Wings* (1927)
Outstanding Picture	*Wings* (1927)
Special Award	*The Circus (1928)/The Jazz Singer* (1927)
Unique And Artistic Picture	*Sunrise : A Song of Two Humans* (1927)
Writing (Adaptation)	Benjamin Glazer For *7th Heaven* (1927)
Writing (Original Story)	Ben Hecht for *Underworld* (1927)
Writing (Title Writing)	Joseph W. Farnham

No Alcohol in Hollywood

In 1904, the voters of Hollywood decided, by a majority of 113 to 96, to banish the sale of alcohol in their town. Alcohol was supposed to be sold only for medicinal purposes. That's not the case today, of course!

The Hollywood Chickens

Since the 1970s, a population of freeway chickens has been residing under a highway in Hollywood. No one knows how they arrived there, and all human efforts to move them from there have resulted in failure. Hollywood is prime property after all!

Solution for Writer's Block

Hollywood producer Hal Roach had a crazy idea to get rid of writer's block. He would hire a 'wildie', mostly a drunk or crazy guy, who would be seated in the writer's room. Whenever Roach's writers suffered from writer's block, the 'wildie' was encouraged to come up with crazy ideas.

Escape of the Snakes

When *Indiana Jones and the Raiders of the Lost Ark* (1981) was being filmed in London, a few snakes that were imported to be used in the movie managed to escape. Legend has it that their descendants still reside on the grounds of the London film studio.

Swinging Sirens

During the casino scene in the *Swingers* (1996), one can hear sirens. Those sirens were actually the police on their way to the set to stop the film crew from shooting because they didn't have a permit.

The *Almost Famous* Band

The members of Stillwater wanted to look convincing as a rock band in the movie *Almost Famous* (2000). So they rehearsed for six weeks, four hours a night and five nights a week. That's too much professionalism for a rock band, surely!

The Weird Sisters

Four of the Weird Sisters in *Harry Potter and the Goblet of Fire*

(2005) were actually established rock stars. They included Radiohead's Jonny Greenwood and Phil Selway, and Pulp members Jarvis Cocker and Steve Mackey. It is easy to guess that the director is a hardcore Pulp and Radiohead fan.

Batman Collects

The Dark Knight (2008) collected more revenue in its first six days in the US than *Batman Begins* (2005) collected in its entire domestic run in the same country.

I Saw It Coming

Worldwide ticket sales for the *Saw* franchise indicated earnings that were just short of a billion dollars. This made it the highest-earning horror franchise globally. Wonder if they Saw that coming?

Armageddon (1998)

NASA airs the film *Armageddon* during their management training programme but not for entertainment purposes. New managers are asked to spot as many factual errors as possible in the film. So far, 168 errors have been discovered.

Interview with the Vampire: The Vampire Chronicles

The lengthy make-up process involved the vampire-playing actors in this 1994 film to hang upside down for thirty minutes during make-up. The blood in their bodies rushed to their heads and the blood vessels in their faces protruded. The make-up artists traced over these swollen veins to create the translucent-skinned vampire look. Scary!

Low-Budget Movie

The budget of the movie *Dallas Buyers Club* (2013) was so low that the make-up budget was only $250. Surprisingly, the film's Make-up and Hairstyling won an Oscar.

The Good and Ugly Bridge

The bridge blown up by the characters of Eli Wallach and Clint Eastwood in *The Good, the Bad and the Ugly* (1966) was erroneously detonated by a Spanish army crew member. When they realized this error, the bridge had to be rebuilt, only to be destroyed once again.

Artists vs. AI: Hollywood Protests against Generative AI

The increasing trend of generative artificial intelligence that mimics humans, can replace them for good, is what lies at the centre of the 2023 Hollywood strike, a historic one in forty-three years and the first time in sixty-three years that Hollywood actors and writers went on a strike simultaneously.

Hollywood actors, writers, and others, represented by the Screen Actors Guild-American Federation of Television and Radio Artists (SAG-AFTRA) declared a strike on 1 May, after failed negotiations with Alliance of Motion Pictures and Television Producers (AMPTP), and this historic event reached the 100-day mark on 9 August. Most of the actors stood in solidarity with it. SAG-AFTRA joined hands with the Writers Guild of America (WGA) early in July, and their demands included better compensation, staffing requirements, and protection from job interference by artificial intelligence, among others. The strike not only saw a stoppage of late-night programmes and productions for Netflix, but also the walk-out of *Oppenheimer's* (2023) cast from its UK premiere in its support.

While there are other issues too behind the strike, protection from AI is at the core of it. With increased access to advanced technologies, nothing seems to be impossible to be portrayed on-screen, and this is what raises several job-threatening and ethical issues. With numerous deepfake accounts/videos available these days on several platforms, the impact of generative AI is not only limited to a particular section but to the masses in general. The artists fear that not only does it hinder their creative input but also threatens their very jobs, especially the ones in the background. This is why the demands include 'informed consent' (if any artist's work is to be used/reproduced on the screen using AI) to be incorporated into future contracts.

The Irishman

The Irishman, starring Al Pacino and Robert De Niro, released in 2019. The film had a budget of $159 million and a major amount was spent to make the two actors look younger in the movie with the aid of computer technology. The digital de-ageing technology reportedly cost well over $100 million.

The Curious Case of Shirley Temple

As Shirley Temple became a famous child actor, people were suspicious about the existence of such a mature and talented child. It was also strange that she was never seen on-screen without missing baby teeth. Soon a rumour spread all across Europe that Temple was actually an adult dwarf.

The Vatican Investigates

The Vatican's newspaper decided to investigate the curious case of Shirley Temple and dispatched Father Silvio Massante for the mission. He was satisfied after his investigations that Temple was a child. The cause of the missing baby teeth was also determined. The film-makers had filled the holes with temporary dentures.

The Black Box

The black box would definitely be illegal today. If Shirley Temple or any other child actor in the early 1930s misbehaved on set, they would be shut in a cramped sound box that was cooled by a big ice block. That was the black box dreaded by child actors.

Django Unchained (2012)

Leonardo DiCaprio was shooting for *Django Unchained* when he accidentally crushed a glass in his palm and bled profusely. But he remained in character and finished the scene. Quentin Tarantino was so impressed that he used this take in his final edit. Leonardo DiCaprio was rewarded with a standing ovation.

Moulin Rouge! (2001)

Nicole Kidman wore a necklace made of real diamonds and white gold in this movie. This was the most expensive piece of jewellery ever made for a film. The Stefano Canturi 134 carats necklace had 1,308 diamonds and was worth US $1 million.

The Dark Knight of Method Acting

Heath Ledger isolated himself in a motel room for six weeks to prepare for his iconic role as the Joker in *The Dark Knight* (2008). He dived deep into the character's psychology, perfecting his voice, mannerisms, and sadistic laughter. Unfortunately, this was his last role, as he died soon after.

The Lord of the Rings: The Fellowship of the Ring (2001)

The cast had to fly by helicopter to remote locations during shooting. Sean Bean was afraid of flying and preferred to climb to the set on the mountaintop to avoid the chopper. He spent two hours every morning doing so dressed in character as Boromir.

The Hungry *Terminator*

While shooting for *The Terminator* (1984), Arnold Schwarzenegger visited a restaurant in downtown Los Angeles to grab some lunch. But he forgot to take off his Terminator make-up. The others must have lost their appetites seeing his missing eye, burned flesh, and exposed jawbone. We're pretty sure Arnie said, 'I'll be back!'

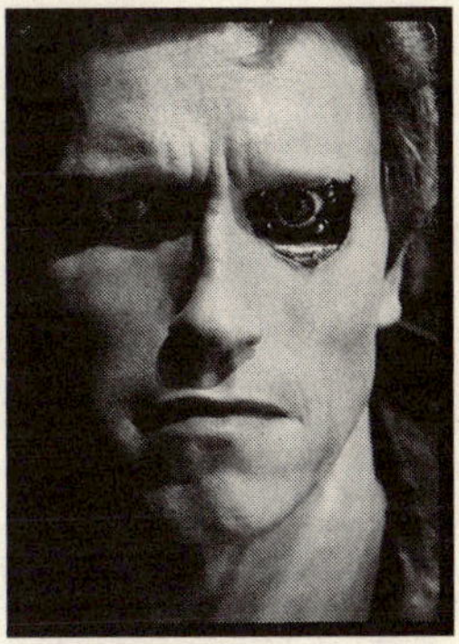

Arnold Schwarzenegger as Terminator

Leo's Oscar and *The Revenant* (2015)

While shooting for *The Revenant*, vegetarian Leonardo DiCaprio ate a raw slab of bison's liver, learned how to shoot a musket, build a fire, speak two Native American languages, and studied ancient healing techniques. DiCaprio calls it his toughest performance. Maybe that's also why it fetched him that elusive Oscar.

Leonardo DiCaprio received the Oscar for Best Actor, which had been elusive for many years, for *The Revenant* (2015). It took some special direction by Alejandro Gonzalez Iñárritu, a great performance by Leo, and a successful adaptation from the novel of the same name by Michael Punke for Leo to achieve his dream.

Rocky IV (1985)

To ensure that the boxing scenes looked realistic in *Rocky IV*, Sylvester Stallone asked Dolph Lundgren to actually hit him. Lundgren obliged, and the punch to the chest left Stallone in intensive care for nine days. Perfection doesn't pay always!

The Pianist (2002)

To prepare for his role in *The Pianist* and to connect with the feeling of loss experienced by his character, Adrien Body sold

I'll be back!
HASTA LA VISTA, BABY!
Put that cookie down, NOW!
My body, my choice!
Consider that a divorce.

INTER
CTURES
CHINE

his car and apartment. He also stopped watching television. Next time try acting, Adrien.

Casino Royale (2006)

When Daniel Craig was shooting the very first fight scene in this Bond movie in Prague, he lost his two front teeth. His dentist flew all the way from London to replace them. Craig was shaken but not stirred!

Star-Lord

Sometimes, stealing isn't actually stealing if it is for a good cause. Chris Pratt stole his Star-Lord costume from the Marvel movie, *Guardians of the Galaxy* (2014). But no one bore him any grudges as he did so to meet sick young fans in hospital who made requests to see Star-Lord.

Black Swan (2010)

For her role in *Black Swan,* actress Natalie Portman spent a year training as a dancer. But as the budget of the movie was rather small, Portman paid for the dance classes with her own money. With so much dedication, no surprises that she won an Oscar for this film.

The Departed (2006)

Jack Nicholson pulled a real gun on Leonardo DiCaprio while shooting a scene. This wasn't there in the script, and Nicholson decided to improvise to make the scene more intense. Leo was terrified and probably thinking about the movie title. The scene was natural and intense.

The Bald Bond

Sean Connery was one of the popular stars to have essayed the role of superspy James Bond on celluloid. But he wore a toupee in all the Bond films he starred in. This was because Sean Connery had started balding when he was only seventeen years old.

Pulp Friction

A famous shot in *Pulp Fiction* (1994) was filmed in reverse when John Travolta pulls the needle out of Uma Thurman's chest. This was to make it appear that the needle made contact with Thurman's skin, making it a safer shot and reducing the risk of Travolta puncturing Thurman.

Die Harder

Sometimes actors have to do their own stunts if it is unavoidable. Actor Alan Rickman was supposed to fall down from the Nakatomi Plaza in *Die Hard* (1988). He was dropped one second too early to evoke a natural reaction out of him.

Embarrassed Jack

During the filming of *Chinatown* (1974), actor Jack Nicholson was dating Anjelica Huston, the daughter of his screen nemesis John Huston. The day Anjelica visited the set, her father's character asked Nicholson's character Jake Gittes in a scene, 'Are you sleeping with my daughter?' It was an awkward scene for sure.

Les Misérables (2012)

To look the perfect prisoner, Hugh Jackman lost weight, grew a beard, and stayed without water for thirty-six hours to lose water weight around his eyes and cheeks. These scenes were shot first. Then, Jackman shaved and gained weight to play the wealthy Valjean. Victor Hugo would have been proud.

John Wick: Chapter 2 (2017)

Keanu Reeves decided to perform 95 per cent of the fight scenes himself in this movie. He trained for three months extensively to prepare for the role, learning judo, Brazilian jiu-jitsu, marksmanship, and driving. That's perfectionism!

Cast Away (2000)

The eternal perfectionist Tom Hanks stopped exercising to look

Bond. *James Bond.*

A martini, shaken not stirred.

I'm sorry, that last hand...nearly killed me.
What a helpful chap.
I never miss.

like an out-of-shape, podgy middle-aged man for *Cast Away*. Then, production was stopped for a year for Tom Hanks to lose weight to the extent of fifty pounds and grow his hair to look convincing as someone marooned for years on a deserted island.

Ambidextrous Arnold

To prepare for *The Terminator* (1984) Arnold Schwarzenegger practised with guns daily for a month. He learned how to dismantle and reassemble them blindfolded like a machine. Arnie also spent hours at the shooting range, firing with both hands without looking at the weapons while cocking or reloading.

Bridget Jones's Diary (2001)

Renée Zellweger gained twenty-five pounds and worked at a British publishing company under an alias for a month to prepare for her role in this movie. No one recognized her although her colleagues found it strange that she kept a framed picture of then boyfriend Jim Carrey on her desk.

Batman Returns (1992)

The Catwoman costume that Michelle Pfeiffer wore on this movie was vacuum-sealed once she was fitted into it. Hence, she had very little time to perform on a scene before the costume had to be opened or she would become unconscious. No retakes please!

Gone Girl (2014)

A huge Boston Celtics fan, Ben Affleck refused to wear a New York Yankees cap for a scene. Because of this, production was stalled for four days. Thankfully, a truce was reached before director David Fincher shouted Gone Ben! Affleck agreed to wear a Mets cap for the scene.

Moulin Rouge! (2001)

Filming for the movie was stopped for two weeks in November 1999 when Nicole Kidman suffered two fractured ribs and injured her knee during a dance rehearsal. Later, many scenes that filmed her from the chest up were shot with Kidman in a wheelchair.

Sunshine (2007)

For *Sunshine*, the *Peaky Blinders* star Cillian Murphy learned advanced physics from leading physicist Brian Cox to prepare for his role. He also toured the CERN facility in Switzerland and copied the mannerisms of physicists. The *Sunshine* physical experience also converted Murphy from an agnostic to an atheist.

Nightcrawler (2014)

Jake Gyllenhaal decided to get more intense than required in a scene where he was supposed to scream at his reflection in the mirror. The mirror cracked, and Jake cut his hand badly. He had to visit the hospital for forty-two stitches.

Pirates of the Caribbean: Dead Men Tell No Tales (2017)

Johnny Depp was in the midst of bitter divorce proceedings during this movie's production. He was always late, and sometimes, the shoot was stalled for hours. Then, a production assistant kept watch outside Depp's house and informed the crew he was awake when the lights came on in the bedroom.

My Left Foot (1989)

Daniel Day-Lewis remained in his hunched-over position in his wheelchair for weeks of filming for this movie. The result was two broken ribs. He also refused to come out of character even when the camera was not rolling, insisting that other people help him eat his food in the set canteen.

Low Budget *Taxi Driver*

Taxi Driver (1976) had a budget of only $1.9 million. Leads Robert De Niro and Cybill Shepherd received only $35K as remuneration while director Martin Scorsese received $65K. Despite the low budget, the film received as many as four nominations at the 1977 Academy Awards. That's a great taxi ride!

Home Sweet Home

When John Travolta arrived in Quentin Tarantino's apartment to discuss his role as Vincent in *Pulp Fiction* (1994), he discovered he felt very much at home. It was the same apartment that Travolta had rented when he was beginning his Hollywood career.

The Joker's Weight Loss Programme

For *Joker* (2019), Joaquin Phoenix lost fifty-two pounds to play the role of Arthur Fleck. He consulted with the same doctor who had helped him lose weight for *The Master* (2012). After the filming of *Joker* ended, Phoenix quickly gained twenty-five pounds.

A Strange Request

Actor Gene Wilder read the script for *Willy Wonka & the Chocolate Factory* (1971) and thought something was missing. He agreed to do the movie only if his character was allowed to limp out of the factory and then do a somersault. This request was granted.

Statham's Luck

Jason Statham almost drowned in the Black Sea while filming *The Expendables 3* (2014). Statham was driving a giant truck for a stunt when the brakes refused to work. The truck went over the edge of a cliff into the Black Sea. Luckily, Statham managed to escape through the open window.

Smart Tom

When the budgets for *Forrest Gump* (1994) escalated and Paramount refused to go over the agreed budget, Tom Hanks and director Robert Zemeckis rustled up the extra money, asking the studio for an increase in their profits. This was a sensible move as Hanks earned almost $65 million from the film.

The Talented Mr Chaney

Lon Chaney was one of the best make-up artists in the movies and also acted in over 150 films. He played the central characters in *The Hunchback of Notre Dame* (1923) and *The Phantom of the Opera* (1925) doing his own make-up for the roles.

After Twenty Years

Actor Chris Pratt's life came a full circle when he acted in *Jurassic World: Fallen Kingdom* (2018). The movie that made Pratt richer by $10 million was filmed in Oahu, Hawaii. Twenty years ago Pratt was living in a van in Maui, Hawaii.

Broken But Not Busted!

When Buster Keaton performed a stunt in *Sherlock Jr.* (1924), he fractured his neck. But strangely, he only realized this years later. The scene that caused this injury had a flood of water descend on Keaton from a water tower. The force was so strong that it led to the fracture.

Expensive Cleopatra

Cleopatra (1963) was one of the most expensive movies with an original budget of $5 million. It is interesting to compare it with the production budget of the recent Hollywood blockbuster *Avatar: The Way of Water* (2022), which amounted to $460 million.

But the movie *Cleopatra* was unfinished after two years and more money kept being pumped into it, over $370 million by today's standards. Thanks to *Cleopatra,* 20th Century Fox almost went bankrupt.

The Genie of the Lamp

The makers of *Aladdin* (1992) wanted Robin Williams to play the genie so badly that they even animated him as the character to coax him into accepting the role. Robin Williams obliged and the rest is cinematic history.

Scotch is Better than Water?

The actors on location for *The African Queen* (1951), including Katharine Hepburn, got dysentery from drinking contaminated water despite precautions taken by drinking bottled water that was also boiled and treated with water purifier tablets. Only Humphrey Bogart and director John Huston were unaffected as they drank only scotch on set.

Beauty and the Beast (1991)

The title track from *Beauty and the Beast* was recorded by Angela Lansbury in a single take. This was despite the fact that she had stayed up all night on a flight.

Move Over Darling!

On the sets of *Move Over Darling* (1963), the huge and over -enthusiastic James Garner accidentally broke two of Doris Day's ribs while picking her up from the ground. Doris Day had a good laugh about it even though it hurt to laugh as she shot that movie strapped with adhesive tape because she had immediately returned to work after the incident.

Carpenter Ford

Harrison Ford might look any part that he has to play but before joining the movies, he was a master carpenter. True to his original craft, Ford still does it in his free time as a hobby.

The Water Tattoo

Actress Jennifer Lawrence has an H^2O [sic] tattoo on her body which serves a strange purpose. It reminds her to drink more water. Well, isn't it easier to carry a water bottle, Jennifer?

The Firefighter

Actor Steve Buscemi was a firefighter before he made it in the movies. During 9/11, Buscemi was in New York City and immediately went to his old unit to help out when the tragedy struck. His offer was accepted, and he worked like a dog during the crisis. Steve was just eighteen when he first took the FDNY civil service test. Hats off, Steve!

Blame it on Leo

Do you know how Leonardo DiCaprio was named? Well, it so happened that his mother was staring at a Leonardo da Vinci painting in an Italian museum when Leo first kicked.

Overdose of Vitamin D

Actor Jonah Hill had to snort Vitamin D as a substitute for cocaine almost every day for as long as seven months during the production of *The Wolf of Wall Street* (2013). He had to eventually visit the hospital for bronchitis as a result.

Keanu contemplated A Name Change

Keanu Reeves confessed on the *Jimmy Fallon Show* that he was so frustrated at the direction his movie career was headed that he considered changing his name to Chuck Spadina or Templeton Paige Taylor to bring better luck. Thank god he didn't!

The Blonde Bond

Daniel Craig was the first blonde Bond. But he was also the only actor born after the Bond series began in 1962 on celluloid to play the iconic character of James Bond.

Dwayne 'The Rock' Johnson

The Rich Scorpion King

Dwayne Johnson made his entry into Hollywood and earned a staggering $5.5 million as remuneration for *The Scorpion King* (2002). Johnson entered the Guinness World Records for receiving the highest salary for a leading role by a debutant actor.

High Flier

Actor Morgan Freeman probably dreamt of flying high ever since he was a kid. To fulfil his childhood dream, he earned his private pilot's licence at the young age of sixty-five!

Daniel's Wands

Harry Potter star Daniel Radcliffe broke more than eighty wands during the production of the famous Harry Potter movies. That's because he used them as drumsticks when the cameras weren't rolling. Naughty Harry!

The Portman Papers

Natalie Portman's papers were published in two scientific journals. Her high school paper, 'A Simple Method to Demonstrate the Enzymatic Production of Hydrogen from Sugar', was published in the *Journal of Chemical Education*. She co-authored a study in Harvard called 'Frontal Lobe Activation during Object Permanence: Data from Near-Infrared Spectroscopy'.

Cuban Pete

Actor and comedian Jim Carrey was unpredictable since childhood. As a kid, he wore tap dancing shoes to bed just in case his parents needed some dance moves to cheer them up late at night.

Woody's Demons

We all have our inner demons that haunt us all our lives. Hollywood actor Woody Harrelson's father was a hitman and a member of the American mafia. Charles Voyde Harrelson was convicted of assassinating federal judge John H. Wood Jr. Woody did pretty well in life in comparison.

The Blue-Eyed Star

Because of the black-and-white cinema that he churned out, the people in the audience had always thought that Charlie Chaplin had brown eyes. But most people did not recognize Chaplin in real life as he had beautiful blue eyes!

Addicted to Junk

Robert Downey Jr claimed that Burger King saved him from his drug addiction. But the addiction to junk was not desirable as he hid snacks everywhere during the filming of *Avengers* (2012). He would pull these out when hungry and also offer them to his co-stars. Hungry like a wolf?

The Antique Guitar

On the sets of *The Hateful Eight* (2015), Kurt Russell accidentally smashed a 4-year-old antique guitar instead of the prop he was supposed to smash. This 1870 antique guitar was on loan from a museum that changed their policy after this incident, refusing to loan guitars to movies under any circumstances.

Hugh Jackman as Coco the Clown

Hugh Jackman's performance as Wolverine was a smash hit with the kids. Jackman always had a knack for entertaining children, though. Before he made it big in the movies, he used to perform at children's birthday parties as Coco the Clown!

Daniel's Waxed Butt

In an interview, Daniel Radcliffe confessed that the weirdest thing he ever had to do to prepare for a role was wax his butt. Well, that's a small price to pay when he is believed to have been worth about $110 million at 33 in 2022, eh?

Chaplin's Swiss Move

Charlie Chaplin refused to become a US citizen after living there for over forty years. Chaplin was branded as a communist sympathizer, and the US government revoked his permit, not allowing him to return from holiday in England. Chaplin moved to Switzerland, only returning to the US in 1972 to collect his honorary Oscar.

The Theory of Everything (2014)

Eminent physicist Stephen Hawking was very pleased about the way Eddie Redmayne had portrayed him in the movie and communicated the same in an email to director James Marsh. Hawking said that he felt that he was watching himself during some scenes in the film. The film even used his own synthesised voice.

The Mummy (1999)

Brendan Fraser, who's had a whale of a time recently, almost died when he was filming *The Mummy*. During a scene where his character is hanged, Fraser stopped breathing and had to be resuscitated.

Cruella Costumes

The period film *Cruella* (2021) had intricate costumes, and actress Emma Thompson found it particularly challenging as she needed a team of people to help her use the bathroom in between scenes. This was because of the heavy costumes and underwear she had to wear during filming.

Out of the Woods

Actress Meryl Streep was rehearsing for the movie *Into the*

Woods (2014) when she fell dangerously towards a concrete floor. Actor James Cordon and director Rob Marshall watched helplessly and in shock when a pregnant Emily Blunt saved the day. She rushed forward and caught Meryl Streep to save her life.

Toto's Remuneration

Toto was Dorothy's dog (a female brindle Cairn Terrier named Terry) in the movie *The Wizard of Oz* (1939). Surprisingly, Toto's remuneration in the film was more than the actors who played the Munchkins. The Munchkins received $50 a week, while Toto earned $125 a week. It's a dog's life!

Sugar Daddy

When actor Will Ferrell was filming for *Elf* (2003), he had to consume so much sugar that it gave him terrible headaches, sugar highs, and insomnia.

Why Sinatra was Offered *Die Hard* First

Die Hard (1988) is based on Roderick Thorp's 1979 novel, a sequel to his 1966 novel *The Detective,* which was adapted into a 1968 film starring Frank Sinatra. 20th Century Fox was contractually obligated to offer the sequel first to Sinatra. The seventy-three year-old refused, and Bruce Willis came into the picture.

Drive to Mulholland Drive

Laura Elena Harring was so excited on her way to audition for *Mulholland Drive* (2001) that she got into a car accident with another actor also on their way to an audition. Later, Harring realized that her character gets into a car accident in one of the first scenes. Life's a David Lynch movie!

Easy Money?

Arnold Schwarzenegger speaks just 700 words in *Terminator 2: Judgement Day* (1991). The Austrian Oak was paid $15 million

How do I look?

That is what we do. That is what people do. They stay alive for each other.

I have doubts…
I have such doubts.

If no one's in the kitchen, who's to see?

for his efforts. Quick maths reveals that he made $21,428 per spoken word. If that seems excessive, the studio certainly doesn't think so as the movie made $520 million worldwide. My word!

Mission Possible

In *Mission: Impossible – Fallout* (2018) Tom Cruise aka Ethan Hunt operated the helicopter like a pro. But Tom Cruise invested 2,000 hours of his valuable time before filming the chopper stunt to train and become a certified helicopter pilot. He made this mission possible too.

Everyone Wants to Play a Vampire

As many as 5,000 actors auditioned for the character of Edward Cullen in *Twilight* (2008). Robert Pattinson was shortlisted after such a mammoth audition list. Imagine so much interest to play a 108-year-old vampire!

Bale's Blues

Christian Bale received $15 million for playing Batman in *The Dark Knight Rises* (2012). In comparison, Anne Hathaway who had a nineteen-minute role in the same movie took home $7.5 million. That's half of what Bale earned playing Batman. The Joker's not the only one having a good laugh here.

The Cold-Faced Brando

Marlon Brando was known as the perfect actor. But his techniques to achieve perfection were extraordinary. In *The Godfather* (1972), Brando opted to read from cue cards rather than memorize his lines. This was intentional as Brando wanted to look natural and deliver his lines with a cold-faced look.

Jackie Chan's Many Roles

The film *Chinese Zodiac* (2012) was a first of sorts as it still holds the record for the most credits for an individual in a single movie. Jackie Chan had fifteen credits as he was the writer, director, producer, and also essayed eleven other roles in the film.

The Nickname Jackie

Jackie Chan's real name is Chan Kong-sang. He was given the nickname Jackie while working on an Australian construction site. A builder named Jack showed him the tricks of the trade, and he was called 'Little Jack' on the site. This name turned to Jackie and has stuck since then!

Al's got a Gun

Al Pacino worked as a janitor and assistant waiter to pay for his acting classes. Twenty-year-old Pacino was arrested and imprisoned after police officers discovered a gun in his car. It took the cops three days to realize the gun was a stage prop while Pacino remained in jail.

Lucky Dorothy

An actress called Dorothy Gibson was one of the lucky ones to survive the sinking of the *Titanic*. Later, she starred in a silent short film called *Saved from the Titanic* (1912) that released a month after the sinking and was based on the sinking. In the movie, Dorothy was wearing the same dress she had worn when she boarded the *Titanic*. Talk about detailing!

The Human Touch

Oscar-winning actress Emma Thompson had adopted a former child soldier from Rwanda without letting people know about it. She is a human rights activist. Good on you, Emma!

Lion Tamer to Movie Star

When he was sixteen years old, Hollywood movie star Christopher Walken used to work as an assistant lion tamer in a travelling circus for a living.

Don't Mess with the Bond

When actress Lana Turner was shooting with Sean Connery for *Another Time, Another Place* (1958), her jealous boyfriend, Johnny Stompanato, barged in to point a gun at Connery and threaten him. The actor quickly disarmed the intruder by twisting his arm and threw him to the ground. Never point a gun at someone who has played James Bond! Stompanato was later killed by Turner's daughter.

Downey Going Down

Actor Robert Downey Jr was once arrested for driving naked in his Porsche with cocaine, heroin, and a .357 Magnum in the car. We wonder who was more embarrassed, the actor or the cops who pulled him over.

Charlize Theron's Hollywood Break

Charlize Theron was broke after arriving in Los Angeles. When she tried to cash a cheque at the bank, the teller refused. Charlize began shouting, and her histrionics were noticed by a talent agent, in the queue. He introduced her to casting agents and the rest is history.

Banned from Japan

In 2008, when Robert Downey Jr arrived in Japan for the *Iron Man* premiere, he was detained at the airport for a history of criminal activity and interrogated for six hours. The Japanese authorities allowed him to attend the premiere, but he couldn't enter Japan ever again. 'But please, never come to Japan,' an official begged.

Stroke of Luck

Anna Paquin attended the audition for *The Piano* (1993) for a lack of better things to do. She was selected for the role from 5,000 candidates. Anna eventually received the 1993 Academy Award for Best Supporting Actress when she was eleven years old, making her the second-youngest winner in Oscar history.

Actor-Turned-President

Legend has it that the fortieth president of the United States, was an actor-turned-politician. It is said that in 1960, he had auditioned for the role of a president in a play titled *The Best Man* (1964). But he was rejected because he didn't look presidential enough. Many will argue that he was not presidential enough to be the fortieth president.

The Hitman

Once, a depressed Angelina Jolie hired a hitman to kill herself. She felt that murder would appear less scandalous than suicide on her family. The killer had a talk with Jolie and managed to convince her to change her decision by waiting for a month. Jolie is happy that she listened to him.

Christopher Consistent Walken

Actor Christopher Walken had a movie release every year from 1974 to 2009. The year 2010 was the first when he didn't appear in any of the movies that released. That is a mind-boggling consistency rate for thirty-six years. Wow!

Emily Blunt's Stutter

In her childhood, actress Emily Blunt had a stutter that refused to go despite speech therapy and relaxation techniques. Surprisingly, this stutter was cured when Emily was asked to speak in an accent during the rehearsals of a school play. No surprises why Emily Blunt chose acting as a career!

Jackie the Singer

We all know Jackie Chan as an action star who has entertained us with his amazing action and comic moves through the years. But did you know that Jackie is also a talented singer? Over twenty albums of his have released in China, and he is a big singing star there!

Foxy Lady

It was rumoured that Megan Fox decided to audition for her role in *Transformers* (2007) by washing director Michael Bay's Ferrari in her bikini. Though she reportedly debunked the story, need we say that she nonetheless got the role?

Jim's Loss is Johnny's Gain

Jim Carrey and not Johnny Depp was director Gore Verbinski's first choice to play the celebrated on-screen pirate Captain Jack Sparrow. But the production schedule of *Pirates of the Caribbean: The Curse of the Black Pearl* (2003) clashed with the filming of *Bruce Almighty* (2003) and Jim had to say no. He must have kicked himself later!

Gone Fat

To play Amy in *Gone Girl* (2014), actress Rosamund Pike gained and lost 13 lb thrice to depict the character at various stages of her life. To gain weight, she ate hamburgers and drank malts. Then, to lose weight, she trained daily with a professional boxer for four hours and ran five miles in forty-two minutes flat.

Private Parts of an Autobiography

Mark Wahlberg wrote a dedication to his penis in his 1992 autobiography. Years later, he regretted the action, saying he thought it would be funny. Well, you certainly have the humour bone, Mark!

The Generous Keanu

Al Pacino hated the script of *The Devil's Advocate* (1997), which was initially action-oriented. The script was modified three times, but Al still had some doubts. He was finally persuaded when he received a salary hike. Keanu Reeves sacrificed $2 million from his own remuneration so that Pacino would act in the movie.

Jolie in Cambodia

Angelina Jolie surprised everyone when she decided to buy 60,000 hectares of land in Cambodia. The land was dangerous as it was infested with poachers. But surprise turned to admiration when Jolie transformed the land into a wildlife reserve and employed some of the poachers as rangers.

Brad Pitt

A Narrow Escape for Brad Pitt

Brad Pitt escaped being beaten by Mike Tyson when he was caught dating Tyson's estranged wife Robin Givens. Tyson thought he saw a blonde woman getting out of Robin's car who was actually Brad Pitt. The terrified actor explained to Tyson that they were rehearsing their lines in the car and got away with it.

Good Will Hunting

Robin Williams's last line in *Good Will Hunting* (1997), 'That son of a bitch stole my line', was ad-libbed. Williams would say a different line in each take, totally confusing director Gus Van Sant and Matt Damon. The moment Williams said this, Damon grabbed the director as it was the perfect shot.

Natalie Portman's Stand-In

Chris Hemsworth and Natalie Portman's kissing scene in *Thor: The Dark World* (2013) is so hot because Portman was absent. Chris's wife was her stand-in as the couple was vacationing in Hong Kong, where Portman couldn't reach on time. So, the makers filmed with Chris's actress wife Elsa Pataky in Portman's wig and costume.

Being Frank

The great Frank Sinatra has a unique achievement to his credit. He has three stars on the Hollywood Walk of Fame: one for film, one for music, and one for television. There is only one Frank Sinatra!

Insuring Jackie Chan

Jackie Chan does his own stunts and has had over seventy injuries while shooting, including a hole in his skull. Because of his dangerous stunts, no one is willing to insure Jackie Chan as he is certain to injure himself. So, Jackie pays for his entire stunt team himself.

Michael Corleone

Actors Jack Nicholson and Robert De Niro were both considered to play the part of Michael Corleone in *The Godfather* (1972). But director Francis Ford Coppola decided to go with Al Pacino, who delivered an iconic performance.

The Great Dictator

Charlie Chaplin decided to make his movie mocking Hitler with his own money (*The Great Dictator* [1940]) because Hollywood was afraid of losing money if they took a stand and invested money in the movie.

It's a Wonderful Life (1946)

The lead actor Jimmy Stewart returned from World War II after serving as a fighter pilot. He was not keen on doing the film and wanted to quit acting. Also, the movie was about suicide, which he felt was negative. He was somehow convinced, and the film not only relaunched his acting career but became one of the greatest life-affirming films ever.

Jackie's Silent Heroes

Apart from action, Jackie Chan loves comedy, and his movies offer a unique mix of both genres. But Jackie's commitment is commendable as his heroes are the silent film stars like

Charlie Chaplin and Buster Keaton. Jackie studied the silent era diligently to understand physical comedy better.

Proud Papa Pacino

Al Pacino has never been officially married, except in his movies of course. However, Al's first child was born just before he turned fifty. Eleven years later, he got lucky again in 2001 when he became the father of twins. At 83, he fathered a baby boy in 2023.

Cannonball

Even as a child, Jackie Chan was super energetic and always pretending to do his own stunts in a movie by rolling around on the ground. Years later, he was actually doing all that stuff without any pretensions. No wonder his nickname was 'Cannonball' as a child! He also acted in a movie called *The Cannonball Run* (1981).

Corleone

Coincidentally, Al Pacino, who played the role of Michael Corleone in *The Godfather* (1972) is actually connected to the Italian town of Corleone in Sicily. His grandparents migrated to the US from there.

Jane Russell's Contribution

Jane Russell could not bear children herself but placed 51,000 children with adoptive families in the US. Through her organization, World Adoption International Fund (WAIF), Russell pushed for the passage of the Federal Orphan Adoption Amendment of 1953, allowing children of servicemen born overseas to be adopted in the US.

The Great Escape

The Great Escape (1963) had a famous scene where Steve McQueen's character flees from German soldiers on a motorcycle during World War II. Ironically, McQueen was pulled over by the

German police during the production of the film and jailed for speeding!

Jackie Chan: Amazing Facts

- Jackie Chan speaks seven languages: Cantonese, Mandarin, English, Korean, German, Japanese, and Thai.
- He has a Pokémon named after him!
- Jackie loves football and supports Hong Kong, England, and Manchester United.
- His father was a spy.
- He has his own American cartoon called *Jackie Chan Adventures.*

Jackie Chan

Danny the 'Tunnel King'

Charles Bronson played Danny the 'Tunnel King' in *The Great Escape* (1963). Danny's an expert at digging tunnels but suffers from claustrophobia. The similarity Bronson shared with his character is uncanny. Bronson was a coal miner before his acting days and also suffered from claustrophobia. Did he write his own character?

Love on the Sets

Lauren Bacall and Humphrey Bogart fell in love on the sets of *To Have and Have Not* (1944). Bogart was married then, but the two were so much in love that they got married a year later. This marriage lasted till Bogart's death in 1957.

Chal Production

Al Pacino's studio is called Chal Production. 'Ch' in Chal stands for the first letters of his friend, mentor, and acting teacher, Charles Laughton, who is also a co-founder of the company. We all know what 'Al' stands for, don't we?

Al Pacino

Al Pacino: Fast Facts

- He is a big fan of Shakespeare.
- Al Pacino's favourite poet is Oscar Wilde.
- Nominated for an Oscar eight times, he only won once for *Scent of a Woman* in 1993.
- Al Pacino loves the opera.

What's in a Name?

Actress Whoopi Goldberg chose her on-screen name from a combination of Whoopee Cushion and her mother's suggestion of a Jewish surname. Her mom thought 'Goldberg' sounded Jewish enough for her daughter to make it big in Hollywood. Well, turns out she was right!

Playing the Grandmother

In 1992, Charlie Chaplin's daughter Geraldine Chaplin essayed the role of her grandmother/Chaplin's mother in his film biography named *Chaplin* (1992) of course.

Enter the Dragon

The great Bruce Lee was born in the Year of the Dragon, on the Day of the Dragon, and on the Hour of the Dragon. We are not surprised that his nickname was also 'Little Dragon' or that he was in a famous movie called *Enter the Dragon* (1973).

For the Sake of Tears

The eight-year-old actor Jackie Cooper was filming for *Skippy* (1931) when his director Norman Taurog did something cruel

Charlie Chaplin: Fast Facts

- Charlie Chaplin detested his first movie *Making a Living* (1914), in which he played a swindler. He felt he was too stiff.
- He had four very young wives and eleven children.
- The asteroid 3623 Chaplin has been named after Charlie Chaplin.

to make him cry in a scene. He told Jackie that his dog would be taken to the pond and had someone shoot a gun in the distance. Cooper thought his dog was dead and cried hysterically.

No Undershirts Please

Actor Clark Gable set off an unimaginable trend when he went without an undershirt while filming *It Happened One Night* (1934). All the wives in America stopped buying their husbands the undergarment. Remarkably, this caused a decline in undershirt sales in the 1930s.

Real-Life Heroine

Elizabeth Taylor saved Montgomery Clift's life when he was involved in a deadly car crash after a dinner party at her home in 1956. His car collided with a utility pole at a hairpin turn amidst fog, and due to its impact, a heavy transformer had narrowly missed hitting the car. The car doors were jammed, several of his teeth had broken, and some got stuck in the back of his throat. Taylor entered the wrecked car through the back door and crawled to the front seat. Then she quickly removed the two teeth from Clift's throat that threatened to choke him to death.

As you think, so shall you become.
If you spend too much time thinking about a thing, you' ll never get it done.

Water can flow, or it can crash. Be water, my friend.
I fear not the man who has practiced 10,000 kicks once, but I fear the man who has practiced one kick 10,000 times.

Standing Tall

Because Ingrid Bergman was 5'9" tall, her shorter co-stars like Claude Rains and Humphrey Bogart had to wear lifts in their shoes not to look small next to her. Humphrey Bogart was two inches shorter and had to stand on boxes and sit on cushions to look taller in *Casablanca* (1942).

Brando the Liftman

Before his elevated status in Hollywood, Marlon Brando was employed as a modest department store elevator operator. But he quit after just four days because he was too embarrassed to call out the lingerie floor.

The Real Hollywood Hero

Adolf Hitler liked Clark Gable above all other Hollywood actors and offered a reward during the war to anyone who could capture and bring Gable to him unharmed. In 1942, the brave Gable enlisted in the Army Air Forces (AAF) to honour his late wife, Carole Lombard (whose plane crashed while she was returning from Indianapolis after raising $2 million in war bonds in the national campaign during war), and flew combat missions over Germany.

Speed King

Film directors had to shoot Bruce Lee's fight scenes at thirty-two frames per second instead of the normal twenty-four frames per second. This was because Bruce Lee was lightning fast and the directors wanted his fight scenes, especially his kicks, to appear more realistic on-screen.

Rita Hayworth's Bombshell Status

After World War II, a fourth atomic bomb was detonated as part of the Operation Crossroads Mission by the US. This bomb was decorated with a photograph of Rita Hayworth. Her film *Gilda* had just released in 1946, and the American soldiers wrote the name 'Gilda' stencilled in black letters above the actress's image to showcase Hayworth's 'bombshell' status among her fans.

Hayworth's Anger

Hollywood actress Rita Hayworth was furious and took great offence when she learned how her image and name had been used by American soldiers in an atomic bomb that had caused so much destruction. That probably earned her more fans across the world.

The Strong Rita Hayworth

Rita Hayworth was certainly a strong woman in every sense of the word. Once she accidentally broke two of Glenn Ford's teeth when she slapped him during a scene in *Gilda* (1946).

The Tallest and Darkest Leading Man in Hollywood

When director Merian C. Cooper promised Fay Wray that she would be starring opposite "the tallest, darkest leading man in Hollywood", she accepted thinking she'd be working opposite Cary Grant. She realized she'd been tricked when the man turned out to be an ape. The movie was *King Kong* (1933).

James Dean's Overspeeding

In 1955, James Dean was issued a speeding ticket for going ten miles over the speed limit. This happened just two hours before his fatal car accident and he was scheduled to appear in court two weeks later. If only he had listened to the warning sign!

Richard Burton vs. Kennedy

Once, Richard Burton decided to have a contest with Robert F. Kennedy. The two men tried to outdo each other by reciting William Shakespeare's sonnets. Both men were equally strong in the subject, but Burton won the contest by quoting one of the sonnets backwards. Well done, King Richard!

Judy's Memory

Actress Judy Garland was blessed with a powerful gift of retention and could remember all her lines easily. But what was most wonderful was that she could view a piece of music only once and memorize the entire thing.

The Leading Man of Hollywood

Hollywood star John Wayne holds the record for the actor with the most leading roles. Wayne played the leading role in 142 movies. He did not do so in only thirty-three films in his career.

The Defiant Ones

In the 1950s, actor Tony Curtis broke an old Hollywood taboo. He vociferously insisted that African American actor Sidney Poitier be given star billing next to him in the movie *The Defiant Ones* (1958). That's certainly good defiance, Mr Curtis!

The Fear of Drowning

Natalie Wood had a deep phobia of drowning. This fear had been deeply instilled in her after she narrowly escaped an accident as a little girl while she was filming *The Green Promise* (1949). In a tragic turn of events, Natalie Wood actually died from drowning in 1981.

Saying No to *Dr. No*

Actor Cary Grant said no to the role of superspy James Bond in the film *Dr. No* (1962). This was because Cary Grant rightly thought that he was too old at fifty-eight to play the character of James Bond. It was then that the role went to Sean Connery, who played 007 till the age of forty-one. The oldest actor to play Bond was Roger Moore, who stepped into 007's shoes at forty-five, and played the role till he was fifty-seven.

Bruce Lee: Fast Facts

- During his young days, Bruce Lee was the leader of a street gang called 'Junction Street Eight Tigers'.
- He could do push-ups with two fingers and also with a man weighing 250 pounds on his back.
- He loved reading and had over 2,500 books in his personal library.

Challenging the Big Boss

At the height of his stardom, Bruce Lee was forced to carry a .357 Magnum because he was challenged to a fight by several people whenever he was recognized in public. Everyone wanted to prove their strength to the Big Boss.

Dumbledore

Professor Dumbledore's character was essayed by Richard Harris in *Harry Potter and the Philosopher's Stone* (2001) and *Harry Potter and the Chamber of Secrets* (2002). After Harris's unfortunate death in October 2002, Michael Gambon played Dumbledore's part in the six Harry Potter films that followed during the period from 2004 to 2011.

The John Wayne Punch

During the filming of *The Barbarian and the Geisha* (1958), actor John Wayne punched director John Huston. Wayne was frustrated with the script and Huston's directorial style and resorted to extreme action after expressing his displeasure several times. The film flopped after release, and we hope

Wayne didn't punch Huston again. The movie was actually disowned by Huston when it released.

Launching Marilyn Monroe

Marilyn Monroe, however, claimed that John Huston was a genius. That's understandable because the director launched her in *The Asphalt Jungle* (1950), considered one of his best films. Even though a young Monroe had a small role, the film launched her Hollywood career.

The Cursed Movie

In 1961, Huston cast Marilyn Monroe in *The Misfits*. Despite its commercial success, the movie was thought to be cursed. Monroe struggled with a serious drug addiction while working on this movie and her marriage to Arthur Miller also ended. This was Monroe's last film as she died in less than a year. This was also Clark Gable's last film.

Gentlemen Prefer Blondes

During the filming of *Gentlemen Prefer Blondes* (1953), Marilyn Monroe and Jane Russell became rather good friends. Russell nicknamed Monroe 'Blondie' and was the only one who could persuade Marilyn Monroe to come to the set when she was too nervous and upset to emerge from her trailer.

Friends with 'The Snake'

During the production of *The Godfather* (1972), actor James Caan became friends with dreaded mafioso Carmine Persico while he researched his role as a gangster. Persico was called 'The Snake' in mafia circles, and government investigators thought Caan was an upcoming gangster as he was relatively unknown as an actor then.

Rear Window Jealousy

Jimmy Stewart's wife Gloria was against him working in *Rear*

Window (1954) with Grace Kelly. There were rumours of Kelly having affairs with her co-stars, and Gloria was paranoid she would seduce Jimmy. But nothing happened between the actors. But Grace Kelly went on to become Princess Grace of Monaco later. Incidentally, this also happened during the shooting of another Hitchcock film – in Monaco.

Fred Astaire's First Screen Test

Fred Astaire was an actor, dancer, vaudevillian, and movie star with a career that spanned almost eight decades. He started dancing at age four and performed professionally at six. Strangely, the evaluation of his first screen test was: 'Can't act. Can't sing. Balding. Can dance a little.'

The Great Composer

Charlie Chaplin was also a great composer and musician even though he had received no formal music training. Chaplin composed the music of several of his own movies, and in 1972, won the Oscar for the music in *Limelight* (1952), which he helped compose.

Bruce Lee Travels to America

Bruce Lee's early life was strangely similar to a movie script. In 1958, his father shipped him to the US with $100 when he got into a fight with the son of a Hong Kong triad boss. Bruce gave cha-cha dance lessons to first-class passengers to earn some extra money.

Uma Thurman's Buddhist Dad

Hollywood actress Uma Thurman's dad is a Tibetan Buddhist monk. Robert A.F. Thurman was the first westerner to be inducted into the Buddhist religion. He is also a professor of Indo-Tibetan Buddhist Studies at Columbia University. Now we know where Uma gets her wisdom from.

Tom's Audition Gone Wrong Gone Right Again

When Tom Hiddleston auditioned for the role of *Thor*, he lost out to actor Chris Hemsworth. But the movie bosses were so impressed with Tom's audition that they gave him the role of the wicked Loki instead. Looks like Tom's blessed by the gods of Norse mythology.

Halle Berry

It does seem unbelievable, but Halle Berry was actually named after a department store. Her parents named her Maria Halle Berry, and the middle name 'Halle' was a tribute to Halle Brothers, a department store in Cleveland, Ohio. This became her stage name later. As they say, what's in a name?

Johnny Depp

Johnny Depp's Weird Suggestion

Johnny Depp as Captain Jack Sparrow in the *Pirates of the Caribbean* (2003) series entertained us all with his crazy antics and eccentric charm. But what the producers at Walt Disney Pictures didn't exactly approve of were Johnny's weird suggestions. For instance, Johnny proposed that his character shouldn't have a nose.

Techniques of Bruce Lee

In a technique called 'the one-inch punch', Bruce Lee could strike a lethal blow with his fist travelling only an inch. He also demonstrated a trick to display his superhuman speed. As a person held a coin in his palm and closed it, Lee could take away the coin, replacing it with another before the palm closed.

The Bodybuilder Bricklayer

Arnold Schwarzenegger built a successful business before he became a legendary bodybuilder and famous Hollywood star. He began a bricklaying business in California in 1968 after moving to the US as a penniless twenty-one-year-old. It's easy to understand why people would trust someone like Arnie to lay their bricks, right?

The Signature Stallone Smirk

Sylvester Stallone's signature smirk has become synonymous with the identity of the iconic star. But Stallone's frown actually resulted from the wrong handling of forceps by an intern when Stallone was born. The forceps grabbed his face by mistake, and his facial nerves in the lips and eyelids were severed.

Bruce Lee vs. Jackie Chan

Jackie Chan worked in minor roles with Bruce Lee early on in his career on two films: *Fist of Fury* (1972) and *Enter the Dragon* (1973). The two faced off in a couple of iconic fight scenes. Jackie has fond memories of the time when Bruce Lee accidentally hit him in the face with a stick.

Bruce Lee the Voracious Reader

Bruce Lee loved reading and had more than 2,500 books in his personal library. Among his favourite books were Sun Tzu's *Art of War,* Herman Hesse's *Beneath the Wheel,* Chang Chen Chi's *The Practice of Zen,* Rene Descartes' *Meditations,* and obviously, Tsai Lung-Yun's *Fundamental Training on Martial Arts.*

Most Expensive Cable Guy

Jim Carrey became the first Hollywood star to ask for and receive $20 million for a single movie. The movie was *The Cable Guy* (1996). Not bad for someone who relied on excessive energy, funny dialogue delivery, and facial contortions to display comedy on film.

Nominated for the Oscars Eleven Times

Hollywood actress Bette Davis was nominated for a whopping eleven Academy Awards for Best Actress in a Leading Role. Her first Oscar win was for *Dangerous* (1935), and she won her second Academy award for *Jezebel* (1938). She was nominated for *Of Human Bondage* (1934), *Dark Victory* (1939), *The Letter* (1940), *The Little Foxes* (1941), *Now, Voyager* (1942), *Mr. Skeffington* (1944), *All About Eve* (1950), *The Star* (1952), and *What Ever Happened to Baby Jane?* (1962).

The Pair Most Likely to Succeed

Dustin Hoffman and Gene Hackman met each other as students at California's Pasadena Playhouse. Their classmates voted them as 'the pair most likely to succeed'. (Boy, were they right!) The two moved to New York City, where they briefly shared an apartment before making it big.

American Actors in Harry Potter

American actor Verne Troyer played Griphook in the very first *Harry Potter* film in 2001. His voice was dubbed by English actor Warwick Davis. American director Chris Columbus also cast his daughter Eleanor Columbus as Hufflepuff student Susan Bones in the first two films. Rowling, the British author, would have probably disapproved.

The Self-Made Millionaire of Hollywood

Arnold Schwarzenegger is one of the most successful self-made millionaires. Arnie first made money with his successful bricklaying business and then added to it a thriving mail-order business selling exercise equipment and instructional videos. Then he became a champion bodybuilder and transformed this career into Hollywood action movies.

Sly Struggle

Sylvester Stallone fought hard to make ends meet before he

made it big as an actor. The odd jobs he did included cleaning out lion cages at the Central Park Zoo, working as a hairdresser, and being employed as an usher at the Walter Reade Theater.

Danny Boy's Destiny

Daniel Radcliffe was the only one among the three leads in the Harry Potter films who was selected by the director. Though his parents initially declined the offer, producer David Heyman eventually convinced them to allow him to audition for the role. Chris Columbus was impressed by Radcliffe's performance as the young *David Copperfield* in the 1999 BBC TV miniseries.

Freeze!

Arnold Schwarzenegger delivered a spine-chilling performance as Mr Freeze in *Batman & Robin* (1997), getting $25 million for his villainous efforts. But Arnie desperately wanted the Mr Freeze costume as a souvenir and only got it after he agreed to pay a rental of $1 per year. Peanuts, we say!

Fastest Draw in the Westerns

Glenn Ford, star of the Western *The Fastest Gun Alive* (1956) actually had a gun-from-holster speed of an astonishing 0.4 seconds. That made him the quickest on the draw among all Hollywood Western stars in the 1950s. Even Billy the Kid would have been impressed.

Expensive Martial Arts Lessons

In the 1960s, Bruce Lee charged $275 per hour for private martial arts lessons. Based on inflation, the amount was $2,500 in 2020. Bruce Lee was a busy man and preferred to teach only a few people. But many were willing to pay the amount to receive the best from the best.

Rocky Days in School

Sylvester Stallone was a terror in his teenage years and was reportedly expelled from fourteen schools, mostly for fighting and acts of vandalism. His teachers in junior high school voted him as 'the most likely to end up in the electric chair'. Instead, Stallone pursued higher education from a college in Switzerland.

A Tragic Death in Hollywood

It appeared that young actress Peg Entwistle had a promising Hollywood career after her Broadway success. But she just did one movie called *Thirteen Women* (1932) before she died tragically. Entwistle is famous today for how she died. She committed suicide by jumping from the 'H' on the 'Hollywood' sign.

Joan Crawford's Beauty Regime

Hollywood actresses of yesteryears were obssessed with their looks on-screen. As a part of her beauty ritual, actress Joan Crawford soaked her eyes in boric acid to make them sparkle. To accentuate her cheek bones, she had her back molars removed.

Japanese Honour for Tom Cruise

Tom Cruise has a special affinity with Japan. He has visited the Asian country more than any other Hollywood star. Japan reciprocated lovingly in 2014 when 10 October was declared as 'Tom Cruise Day' in Japan.

Five Consecutive 100-million Hits

The first Hollywood actor to star in five consecutive films that grossed $100 million at the box office was Tom Cruise. This feat was achieved with *A Few Good Men* (1992), *The Firm* (1993), *Interview with the Vampire: The Vampire Chronicles* (1994), *Mission: Impossible* (1996), and *Jerry Maguire* (1996).

The Untouchables

For *The Untouchables* (1987), Robert De Niro took method acting to a new level. He insisted on wearing the same underwear that Al Capone used to wear. Even though this wouldn't be seen on camera, the producers agreed. They tracked down Capone's former tailors to make the special underwear, the same silk-styled undies like that of Capone.

She's Got the Look!

Audrey Hepburn was famous for her eyelashes that led to her doe-eyed expressions on camera. But this look was achieved rather painstakingly. At first, she would apply a heavy layer of mascara. Then her makeup artist Alberto de Rossi would laboriously separate each individual eyelash with a safety pin.

Against All Odds

Arnold Schwarzenegger achieved success in Hollywood against all odds. He moved to America from Austria when he was just twenty-one years old. He barely spoke any English and had little money. It is like a fairy tale to have become not only hot Hollywood property but also the governor of California.

What's in a Name?

Hollywood producers thought that a name like Arnold Schwarzenegger would be confusing for audiences. Hence they initially christened him as 'Arnold Strong' in the movie credits. But Arnold demanded in later films that his real name be used, which is one of the most recognized names in the world today.

Bruce Lee's Superhuman Feat

Bruce Lee could do as many as fifty one-arm chin-ups. There were reports of him doing push-ups with 250 pounds of weight placed on his back. This is particularly unbelievable because Bruce Lee weighed just 130 pounds.

Packing a Speedy Punch!

Bruce Lee's punching speed and reaction time was impressive and unrivalled. When he was at a distance of three feet from his opponent, Lee could punch in almost one-twentieth of a second. That is equivalent to 0.05 second.

Mission accomplished!

I want the truth!

I feel the need... the need for speed.

Show me the money!

Brando's Oscar Refusal

Marlon Brando refused to accept his Best Actor Oscar for his superlative performance in *The Godfather* (1972). Instead, he sent an Apache activist named Sacheen Littlefeather to accept the award on his behalf and deliver a speech about Native American rights.

Cleopatra

To star in the movie *Cleopatra* (1963), actress Elizabeth Taylor was paid the record-breaking sum of $1 million and 10 per cent of the film's gross profit. Considering the fact that the movie was made in 1963, it is an astronomical amount, which made Elizabeth Taylor the highest-paid actress of her time.

Marilyn Monroe's IQ

Whoever coined the notion that blondes were blessed with average intelligence must be dumb. Marilyn Monroe is believed to have had an IQ of 168, much higher than the average IQ of 100.

Marilyn Monroe's Expensive Movie Costume

In 2011, the dress that Marilyn Monroe wore in the film *The Seven Year Itch* (1955) sold at an auction for $4.6 million, making it one of the most expensive movie costumes ever sold in Hollywood history.

Related to Abraham Lincoln

Tom Hanks is a distant relative of the sixteenth president of the United States, Abraham Lincoln. George Clooney is also related to the former president. Wonder if we'll see a biography of Lincoln soon with Hanks or Clooney playing the leading role.

Highest Grossers in the US

The highest-grossing movie of all time in the US is *Star Wars: The Force Awakens* (2015), which grossed over $936 million domestically. The highest-grossing film franchise of all time in

Tom Cruise

Tom Cruise: Fast Facts

- Cruise purchased his first motorcycle when he was ten years old but soon ended up crashing it.
- He received his pilot licence in 1994. He owns a private jet, Gulfstream G450.
- Cruise also sky-dives and scuba-dives.
- In 1998, he helped chase down robbers who stole jewellery worth nearly $160,000 in London.

the US is the Marvel Cinematic Universe, grossing over $11.8 billion domestically as of 2024.

The Talented Teenager

When Woody Allen was fifteen years old, he started writing jokes or gags for a newspaper column as a fund-raising exercise. He received great appreciation and was invited to join the National Broadcasting Company (NBC) Writer's Development Program in 1955 receiving $25 weekly.

Woody's Greatest Hit

In 1979, Woody Allen delivered his biggest hit with the romantic comedy-drama *Manhattan*. He directed as well as starred in this movie that collected $39.9 million at the box office.

Woody Allen: Fast Facts

- Woody Allen has written all his film scripts on a typewriter bought when he was sixteen.
- A young Woody worked almost fifteen hours a day, writing. In 1962 alone, he wrote more than 20,000 comic book jokes.
- He's a fan of Alfredo Zitarrosa, one of the best Uruguayan musicians.

Elizabeth: The Golden Age (2007)

This period film has a scene that shows ongoing construction work in St Paul's Cathedral. The cathedral actually needed repair work and director Shekhar Kapoor decided to improvise. He hired stonemasons and construction workers and gave them costumes and period tools. As the scene was filmed, the construction work happened simultaneously.

Interstellar (2014)

Director Christopher Nolan decided to grow corn over a 500-acre piece of land for a cornfield scene in this movie. After the movie was completed, the corn was sold and actually made a profit.

The Godfather (1972)

The cat in Marlon Brando's arms in a famous scene was a stray. Director Francis Ford Coppola found the cat running about on set and put it in Brando's arms, thinking it was a good addition. It is remembered as one of the best shots of the movie.

Psycho Loo

Strangely, the first toilet flushed on the big screen in Hollywood was in 1960. It was probably considered indelicate to do so before that. In a first, Alfred Hitchcock took the first shot of a flushing toilet to set up his infamous shower scene in his horror classic *Psycho* (1960).

Squirrel Stars

Director Tim Burton decided to employ forty squirrels in his 2005 remake of the classic *Charlie and the Chocolate Factory*. The little creatures were trained by a professional animal trainer till they were ready after nineteen weeks to sit on stools and a conveyor belt and open nutshells.

The Finch

Director David Fincher is not popular among stuntmen for sure. When he was filming *Fight Club* (1999), Fincher asked a stuntman to fall down the stairs as many as twelve times during a fight scene. Then, he used the first take. Evil!

Get Welles Soon

Orson Welles directed most of his cult film *Citizen Kane* (1941) sitting on a wheelchair as he had injured himself on set in the initial stages of filming.

Orange Stones

Before Stanley Kubrick was roped in as director for *A Clockwork Orange* (1971), author Anthony Burgess had sold the film rights to Mick Jagger, who desperately wanted to play Alex with the other Rolling Stones members playing the other Droogs. But eventually he sold the rights to film producer Si Litvinoff, who would go on to produce the film with Kubrick. And Kubrick for sure didn't roll with the Stones.

Titanic Ending

James Cameron also had an alternative second ending for *Titanic* (1997) in mind in which Bill Paxton and the old lady would fight with each other over the million-dollar necklace. If you thought the original ending was lame, we wonder what you think about this one.

Slumdog Millionaire (2008)

It is often alleged that Danny Boyle did not pay his three lead child actors in *Slumdog Millionaire*. However, he and the producers of the film placed an undisclosed amount in a trust that would give them the money when they finished grade school at sixteen years of age. He also arranged for an autorickshaw driver to ferry the kids to school every day.

Avatar (2009)

James Cameron has a reputation of being a tough director on the sets. No cell phones were allowed on the sets of *Avatar* and Cameron had a nailgun with him to nail the cell phones that rang to a wall above the exit sign.

2001: A Space Odyssey (1968)

Director Stanley Kubrick was paranoid that someone else would use his props and sets to create another science fiction film. He destroyed most of his props and sets from *2001: A Space Odyssey* after production was over.

Hostel Blues

When the film *Hostel* (2005) released, it damaged Slovakia's tourism economy so badly that director Eli Roth was invited to the country on an all-expenses-paid trip. This was to clear false allegations made in the film that projected Slovakia as a crime-infested, corrupt, poor, lawless, and dangerous country.

Action by the Bay

Director Michael Bay got hooked to action films as a boy. He attached firecrackers to a toy train and filmed the fiery stuff that ensued with his mother's 8mm camera. The fire department had to be summoned, and the boy was grounded but a great director was born.

Spielberg's First Commercial Success

Seventeen-year-old Steven Spielberg directed a sci-fi film called *Firelight* with a budget of $500. A local cinema showed the film with tickets priced at a dollar each. Five hundred people came to watch, but one person paid $2. That meant a profit of $1 as Spielberg tasted his first commercial success.

Scorsese's Loyal Editor

Hollywood director Martin Scorsese is famous for his violent gangster films. But this legendary director has worked with the same female editor since he made *Raging Bull* in 1980. Thelma Schoonmaker has edited every single movie of his after that.

The Terminator Nightmare

On a film set in Rome, director James Cameron was down with food poisoning. As he slept, he had a nightmare about a powerful robot assassin sent from the future to kill him. That nightmare gave birth to the idea for *The Terminator* (1984) and catapulted him into stardom.

The Spider Collector

The director of *Spider-Man: Homecoming* (2017), Jon Watts, has an impressive collection of pet spiders, which includes rare South American spiders. We bet he was thrilled to be chosen to direct a Spidey movie.

Hating Matt Damon

Steven Spielberg intentionally did not allow Matt Damon to

attend the pre-production boot camp for all actors for the movie *Saving Private Ryan* (1998). Spielberg wanted the rest of the cast to hate Matt Damon genuinely so that their feelings would be reflected on-screen as the film demanded.

Spaced Out

Director Christopher Nolan is of the opinion that his audiences are mature enough to realize the difference between real sets and computer-generated ones. So, he built large-scale practical sets for the spacecraft in the movie *Interstellar* (2014) for both the interiors and exteriors.

The Film Buff

Director Quentin Tarantino never went to any film school. He is quoted as saying, 'When people ask me if I went to film school, I tell them, "No, I went to films".'

Goodfellas (1990)

After Martin Scorsese read the book *Wiseguy*, he called up author Nicholas Pileggi to adapt the book into a movie.

'I've been waiting for this book my entire life,' Scorsese said. 'I've been waiting for this phone call my entire life,' Pileggi replied.

The movie that rolled out was *Goodfellas*.

Peter's Social Experiment

Peter Weir, director of *The Truman Show* (1998), wanted to have cameras installed behind all the theatres showing the movie. He ordered the projectionist to cut the power during the film at some point, cut to the viewers who would watch each other, and then cut back to the movie again. Weird!

Legal Eagle

The 1992 film *My Cousin Vinny* is iconic, especially for its accurate depiction of the legal community. The director, Jonathan Lynn, is armed with a law degree from Cambridge. The film is highly regarded in the legal community for the realistic depiction of courtroom procedure and trial strategy.

Mad Max

Director George Miller was inspired to make *Mad Max* (1979) when he was an MD. The car accident victims he saw as a doctor in emergency disturbed him greatly. And it is also then he was led to the idea of making Mad Max.

No Technology for Nolan

Director Christopher Nolan, maker of *The Dark Knight* (2008) and *Inception* (2010) among others, absolutely hates using email or a cell phone. He says doing so does not give him time to think, and he has banned the use of cell phones on his movie sets.

The Rise of Cameron

James Cameron was homeless when he was writing the screenplay of *The Terminator* (1984). He sold the rights for the screenplay for just $1 on the condition that he would direct the movie.

The Lord of Cricket

Peter Jackson, director of *The Lord of the Rings* film series, orchestrated as many as 25,000 cricket fans during a cricket match to create the sound of the Uruk-hai army in *The Two Towers* (2002). Well played, sir!

Home Alone

Director Chris Columbus abandoned *National Lampoon's Christmas Vacation* (1989), which he was supposed to direct, after things didn't work out with star Chevy Chase. He went on to direct *Home Alone* (1990) instead, which became the highest-grossing Christmas film of all time.

Dedicated Director

A young John Ford was sent to the island of Midway to film a documentary on life at a small, isolated military base on the island. But he was wounded by shrapnel while filming the Japanese attack in the *Battle of Midway* (1942). However, Ford managed to film the entire battle.

Intimidated Burton

Director Tim Burton was initially uncomfortable about casting actor Christopher Walken as Max Shreck in *Batman Returns* (1992). He told the casting director that the man scared the hell out of him.

Realistic Fury

David Ayer, the director of the film *Fury* (2014), insisted that the cast of the film live in the tank together for a long time where they ate, slept, and did everything else. He also urged them to fight each other, causing bruises, black eyes, and bloody noses.

Deadly Website

Writer-director Eli Roth of *Hostel* (2005) came up with the idea of the movie after he stumbled upon a Thai website on the internet that offered services to kill human beings.

Blood Money

Steven Spielberg refused to take his remuneration for directing *Schindler's List* (1993). He said it would have been 'blood money' and insisted that all profits made from the movie should be returned to the Jewish community.

The Birds

In *The Birds* (1963), Hitchcock tied live birds to Tippi Hedren and also threw them at her in the attic scene. Initially, fake birds were supposed to be used. But after mechanical hiccups, live birds were used. Cary Grant visited the set and complimented Hedren: 'You're the bravest woman I've ever seen.'

No Fake Blood!

In the film *Snow White and the Huntsman* (2012), director Rupert Sanders felt that fake blood didn't look realistic enough in a scene at the start of the film. So, he decided to prick his own finger and use real blood.

A Director's Artistic Side

The person who was the stand-in for Leonardo DiCaprio and drew the famous picture of Kate Winslet in *Titanic* (1997) was none other than director James Cameron himself. But as Leo and Cameron use different hands (Leo is a righty and Cameron is a lefty) a mirror image of the actual shot was used in the movie to maintain continuity.

The Shawshank Redemption

Directed by Frank Darabont, *The Shawshank Redemption* released in 1994. Made at an estimated budget of $25 million, it only collected $16 million in its initial theatrical run. But like all good things that take time, the movie collected $80 million after its Home Media release. That's redemption of sorts!

Cutting it Fine

David Lynch finished editing *Wild at Heart* (1990) only a day before its Cannes premiere. But the film almost didn't make it to Cannes. Lynch tried to board his flight with the film in his carry-on. After arguing with Swiss Air employees, he succeeded. All that effort paid off as *Wild at Heart* won Cannes.

Full Metal Jacket

When Stanley Kubrick asked actor Dorian Harewood for more time while *Full Metal Jacket* (1987) was being filmed, the actor demanded more money. A furious Kubrick decided to terminate Harewood, or rather, his role in the film. Kubrick had Harewood lie on the cold ground for hours and had him riddled with false bullets.

Two Spaced Out Ideas

Steven Spielberg wanted to produce film-maker John Sayles's *Night Skies* script involving a rural family invaded by murderous aliens. But Spielberg wanted a family film and thought of *E.T. The Extra Terrestrial* (1982). Sayles refused to rewrite the script, and Spielberg decided to keep his idea for *Poltergeist* (2015) which was later directed by Gil Kenan.

Underground for Ninety-Four Years

The director of *The Ten Commandments* (1923), Cecil B. DeMille, thought his film set with twenty-one Sphinx replicas was too valuable for other film-makers to exploit. So, he buried the set as that was cheaper than destroying it. The set remained buried for ninety-four years near the California coast before archaeologists found it in 2017.

Diving for the Titanic

Director James Cameron wanted Hollywood funding to make *Titanic* (1997) not because he lacked funds. It is just that Cameron wanted to dive to the scene of the actual shipwreck underwater to make filming even more realistic. Unfortunately, that came at an astronomical cost.

Bergman's Love for the Cinema

Swedish director Ingmar Bergman was spellbound when he saw his first film as a six-year- old. Even when he was eighty-three, the enthusiasm did not diminish when he went to watch *Ocean's Eleven* (2001) with his family. Bergman loved the film and told his son-in-law, 'Jesus! We need to see this again next week.'

The Ambulance Man

Orson Welles had a busy schedule with several radio shows in different parts of New York City. It was tough to navigate through the busy NYC traffic. As no law stated that only the sick could travel in an ambulance, Welles hired ambulances to reach the radio stations, sirens blazing.

12 Angry Men (1957)

While making the classic *12 Angry Men,* director Sidney Lumet ordered the actors to go over the script for several hours huddled in an actual jury room. The idea was to make the actors feel how it was to be stuck in the same room with the same people for hours.

Twice the Heat

Michael Mann directed *Heat* twice. The first on the same plot was a low-budget television movie called *L.A. Takedown* (1989), and the second a big-budget box-office hit *Heat* (1995). Both films had the same script, but the latter is a classic in the crime film genre with an impressive star cast of Al Pacino, Robert De Niro, and Val Kilmer.

The Matrix (1999)

When the Wachowski brothers approached kung fu choreographer Yuen Woo-ping, he charged an exorbitant fee for the film, not wanting to work on it. When the Wachowskis agreed, he demanded complete control of the fights and to train the actors for four months. The Wachowskis agreed, and Yuen was forced to work.

The Angry Heston

Controversial film-maker Sam Peckinpah's chronic alcoholism almost killed his directing career. During the filming of *Major Dundee* (1965), actor Charlton Heston was so angry with Peckinpah's drunken behaviour and verbal abuses that he threatened to attack Peckinpah with his sabre. Once, he angrily charged at Peckinpah on horseback during a scene.

Loyalty Towards the Director

While Sam Peckinpah's erratic behaviour on set antagonized the cast and crew, they were also fiercely loyal to him. Once, when Peckinpah was starved of funds by the studio, Charlton Heston offered to give up a part of his salary so that he could continue shooting the film.

The Movie Brats

In 1970, Martin Scorsese was introduced to the 'movie brats' and became friends with these influential people in Hollywood. They were Brian De Palma, Francis Ford Coppola, George Lucas, and Steven Spielberg. It was Brian De Palma who introduced Scorsese to his future long-time collaborator–actor Robert De Niro.

Scorsese Advises Spielberg

Steven Spielberg was developing *Schindler's List* (1993) in the early 1990s and did not want to direct the movie. So he asked good friend Martin Scorsese if he'd be willing to. Scorsese advised Spielberg that a Jewish director would do a better job because of the Holocaust theme and asked Spielberg to direct it himself.

Swapping Movie Projects

Steven Spielberg was about to direct a remake of the classic thriller *Cape Fear* when Martin Scorsese advised him to direct *Schindler's List* (1993) instead. So the two legendary directors decided to swap movies, and Scorsese ended up directing *Cape Fear* (1991).

The Reservoir Film

Quentin Tarantino's cult film *Reservoir Dogs* (1992) made him a household name. It is often believed that the title was inspired from Tarantino's working days in a video shop. His incapability to pronounce the title of the inspiring Louis Malle film *Au Revoir Les Enfants* (1987) prompted Tarantino to name it 'the reservoir film'.

Sunset Boulevard

For *Sunset Boulevard* (1950), director Billy Wilder wanted the corpse of Joe Gillis to be seen from the bottom of the pool. But he was dissatisfied with the shots taken from the underwater camera and filmed the corpse's reflection instead in a mirror on the bottom of the pool.

Chewbacca

Director George Lucas's inspiration to create the Wookiee character Chewbacca for *Star Wars* was his Alaskan Malamute called Indiana.. The word 'Chewbacca' sounds similar to 'sobaka', the Russian word for dog. The character brief was a gentle, hairy, non-English-speaking co-pilot after all!

Scorsese's Cameo

Martin Scorsese is known to make cameo performances in his movies, but his most famous cameo wasn't planned. In *Taxi Driver* (1976), Scorsese played one of Robert De Niro's passengers planning murder because of his cheating wife. The actor supposed to play the role suffered a serious head injury, and Scorsese stepped into his shoes magnificently.

Steven Spielberg and Martin Scorsese

Banned from China

Martin Scorsese directed the biographical film *Kundun* (1997) based on the life of Tenzin Gyatso, the exiled Tibetan political leader. The film was not only criticized and banned by Chinese leaders after its release but Scorsese was added to a list of fifty people who are banned from entering China. However, it was a temporary ban, which was lifted later.

The Idea for *ET: The Extra-Terrestrial*

Director Steven Spielberg conceived *ET: The Extra-Terrestrial* (1982) to sum up his feelings as a child after his parents got divorced. It was a film that was inside him for many years as he escaped from his loneliness by seeking an imaginary friend in his childhood.

Death Threats against Scorsese

Martin Scorsese's 1988 adaptation of Nikos Kazantzakis's 1952 novel *The Last Temptation of Christ* led to death threats and Catholic protests outside theatres. As Jesus Christ had been depicted with human flaws and sexual desires, the movie was deemed blasphemous. Scorsese lived in the shadow of bodyguards for a while.

A Psycho for Perfection

Alfred Hitchcock was certainly not a director to shy away from perfection. The famous shower scene in his legendary film *Psycho* (1960) took an entire week to film and involved as many as seventy-eight set-ups and fifty-two cuts.

Hollywood Plagiarism

The spaghetti western *A Fistful of Dollars* (1964) by Sergio Leone was a rip-off from Kurosawa's film *Yojimbo* (1961). Toho, the production company of *Yojimbo,* sued for plagiarism. Fifteen per cent of the international sales of *A Fistful of Dollars* had to be given to compensate Toho. That's more than a fistful of dollars!

Cate Plays the Monkey

Cate Blanchett wanted a part in *Pinocchio* (2022). But all the characters were cast except Spazzatura, the monkey. Blanchett wanted to voice the character even though it had few actual lines and mostly sounds. She told Guillermo del Toro, 'I would do anything. I would play a pencil in a movie for you.' She did a fantastic job.

***Pinocchio*'s Amazing Facts**

- The longest stop-motion animated film.
- Geppetto's deceased son is named Carlo – a tribute to Carlo 'Collodi' Lorenzini, the writer of the original Pinocchio story.
- Unlike most Pinocchio versions set in nineteenth-century Italy, this is set in 1930s Italy under the rule of Benito Mussolini and the National Socialist Fascist Party.

Kubrick's Reading Habit

Stanley Kubrick would read novels, looking to adapt one into a movie. His secretary often heard the noise of a book hitting the wall as it was thrown into a reject pile. Once, it was eerily silent, and she entered the room to find Kubrick deeply immersed in *The Shining*.

Eraserhead Days

David Lynch took five years to make his first feature film *Eraserhead* (1977). To support himself financially during this tough period, Lynch took up several odd jobs, including that of a paperboy delivering copies of *Wall Street Journal* around the neighbourhood.

The Angriest Dog in the World

David Lynch had major anger issues in his younger days. Meditation solved the problem, but the memory of his rage inspired Lynch to write and draw a comic strip called *The Angriest Dog in the World.* This ran in the *Los Angeles Reader* and other publications from 1983 to 1992.

Orson Welles in Ireland

Orson Welles had excellent grades when he was supposed to attend college. He was offered a full scholarship to Harvard University. But he declined and travelled to Ireland, where he conned a theatre group to believe he was a New York star. Thus began his love affair with the performing arts.

Dictator Director

Director John Ford was quite the tyrant on his sets. If an actor asked him too many questions, Ford would do one of the two things. Either he would take the particular pages and tear them from the script or he would insult the actor in the worst way possible.

The Jazzy Director

Director Woody Allen's real name was Allen Stewart Konigsberg. He was a big fan of the jazz clarinettist Woody Herman and chose his artist name from his idol. Woody Allen played the jazz clarinet and is a regular musician at the Carlyle Hotel on Monday evenings with his band.

The Magical Director

Orson Welles developed a strong interest in magic when he was a boy being taught his first magic tricks by famous magician Harry Houdini. He performed magic tricks in several films and television programmes and was a member of the Society of American Magicians and the International Brotherhood of Magicians.

The Trial

Orson Welles achieved enormous fame for his masterpiece *Citizen Kane* (1941), which is hailed as one of the best films ever. But Welles considered *The Trial* (1962) as the best film that he had ever made, which was adapted from a novel by Franz Kafka about a prosecuted man awaiting trial.

Spielberg's First Film

The first film that Steven Spielberg made was nine minutes long and recorded on 8mm film. Titled *The Last Gun* (1959), this film was made by Spielberg to earn his photography merit badge for the Boy Scouts. We forgot to mention that he was only thirteen years old then.

The Birth of Camera Techniques

D.W. Griffith was the first director to use the close-up shot, the fade-out, the long shot, and many other camera movements that we can see in the movies today. He introduced these techniques in his classic *The Birth of a Nation* (1915), which unfortunately also highlighted the Ku Klux Klan.

The Perfect Take

Stanley Kubrick would get the perfect shot no matter what. While filming *Paths of Glory* (1957), Kubrick wanted another take from actor Adolphe Menjou after seventeen takes. Menjou lost his cool and shouted insults at Kubrick, who sat silently. After Menjou stopped, Kubrick requested for a retake again and Menjou agreed.

Orson's Blues

Orson Welles could not keep his Oscar for long. When he was filming in 1971, Welles realized he could not afford to pay his cinematographer Gary Graver. He decided to continue the film by offering his only Oscar as remuneration to Gary. Sadly, even then, the film was never finished.

Hitchcock's Cameo Appearances

One of director Alfred Hitchcock's signature moves was the small cameo appearance he made in his movies. This trend was observed from the 1927 film *The Lodger: A Story of the London Fog*. Hitchcock's last film was *Family Plot* (1976) and also his last cameo appearance, but as a silhouette. Sometimes,

Alfred Hitchcock

Hitchcock would appear as a passenger who missed his bus, or he could be seen winding a clock in a scene. He made more than thirty-five cameo appearances in more than fifty movies throughout his career.

Little Marty Goes to the Movies

As a boy, Martin Scorsese couldn't participate in sports or engage in physical activities with other kids because of his asthma problem. So his parents and elder brother Frank would often take little Marty to the movie theatre. This developed Scorsese's love and passion for cinema at an impressionable age.

Dog Tattoo Artist to Film Director

Before he became a director, Robert Altman had a brief offbeat career after World War II – dog tattooing! Altman and a friend began a business tattooing identification numbers onto pet dogs. They were also invited to Washington D.C. to tattoo President Harry Truman's dog, but the business didn't take off.

Gracious Gregory

Gregory Peck's breakout role as Atticus Finch in *To Kill a Mockingbird* (1962) earned him an Academy Award for Best Actor. It is often believed that he had initially turned down the iconic role. It was only after persistent persuasion from the director that he accepted the part.

J. Lo's Milestone

Jennifer Lopez made history with her role in *Selena* (1997), becoming the first actress of Latin origin to earn a million-dollar pay cheque for a single film. Her portrayal of the legendary singer not only showcased her talent but also broke barriers in Hollywood pay standards.

Cannot Do the Dirty

Patrick Swayze, famous for his moves in *Dirty Dancing* (1987), did not know how to do the 'dirty' dancing, having been trained by his mother for years in ballet. He had to unlearn years of technique to get the role right.

Hudson's Leading Secret

Rock Hudson, a leading man in the 1950s and '60s, kept his homosexuality a secret during his Hollywood career due to societal norms. It was only after his death that his struggle with AIDS brought attention to LGBTQ+ issues in the industry.

Sir Roger Moore

Best known for taking over the reins from Sean Connery to play the second James Bond, Roger Moore was not just an actor; he was an animator before joining the movies. He was also one of the longest-serving UNICEF Goodwill Ambassadors since 1991 up till his death in 2017. He was knighted by Queen Elizabeth II in 2003 for his charity services.

Bond, the Painter

Pierce Brosnan, the James Bond of the 1990s and early 2000s, has a hidden talent – he is an accomplished painter. Before entering the world of acting, he trained as a commercial artist. His wide range of artworks, from abstract to representational pieces, show his artistic prowess.

McConaughey's Oscar Journey

Matthew McConaughey underwent a transformative career shift, known as the 'McConaissance', leading to his Oscar win for *Dallas Buyers Club* (2013). His dedication to unconventional roles marked a significant turning point in his acting trajectory.

Moore's Pottery Prowess

Demi Moore took pottery lessons to prepare for her iconic

scene in *Ghost* (1990). The sensual pottery wheel scene with Patrick Swayze became one of the most memorable moments in cinematic history.

Caine's Perseverance

For almost a decade, Michael Caine's career was dotted with small, unnoticed, uncredited roles in movies like *Sailor Beware* (1956) and *A Hill in Korea* (1956). Little did he know that this humble start would lead to a legendary career, earning him two Academy Awards and countless accolades.

Bluegrass, Banjo, and Grammy

Steve Martin, known for his comedic genius, is also an accomplished banjo player. In addition to his acting career, Martin's love for bluegrass music has led to multiple Grammy Awards for his banjo albums.

Avid Humanitarian

Beyond his on-screen success, Richard Gere is an avid humanitarian. He founded the Gere Foundation in 1991, focusing on global humanitarian causes. Gere's commitment to social issues, including his support for a free Tibet, mirrors his passion for making a positive impact beyond the silver screen.

Superhero Sacrifice

Before becoming Captain America, Chris Evans initially turned down the role three times due to anxiety about the massive commitment and its potential impact on his personal life. Eventually, he overcame his concerns, donned the iconic shield, and became one of the defining actors in the Marvel Cinematic Universe.

Dead Men Earn Millions

Two of the greatest music personalities who are still making the world groove years after their death, Michael Jackson, followed by Elvis Presley, have topped the *Forbes List of The Highest-Paid Dead Celebrities Of 2023,* still earning millions out of their estates, museums, merchandise, royalties, etc.

Million-Dollar Smile

Julia Roberts's infectious smile is not only her trademark, but a million-dollar asset. In *Erin Brockovich* (2000), her performance was so captivating that not only did it earn her an Oscar for Best Actress but also a record-breaking $20 million pay cheque, making her the first actress to reach this milestone in Hollywood.

Prosthetic Make-Up

Film, theatre, and television regularly employ prosthetic make-up, which is a form of effects make-up. Make-up artists may create augmented body parts that look very natural and convincing by modelling them after the wearer's actual body. Gypsum cement, foam latex, gelatin, and silicone rubber are some of the popular and most-used substances used in prosthetics.

These days, prosthetics are mostly used in combination with computer-generated special effects, but the first use of prosthetics goes back to as early as the twentieth century. As the horror genre began to take off in the 1920s, make-up for movies began to grow increasingly complex, notably in *The Phantom of the Opera* (1925). However, the first extensive usage of prosthetics was in the 1930s, during the production of *The Wizard of Oz* (1939). To accurately recreate the characters, foam latex pieces were utilized on the bulk of them to construct fake face characteristics.

Attraversiamo...

I'm also just a girl, standing in front of a boy, asking him to love her.

Because I know in my heart, you're the only one for me.

I'd rather have thirty minutes of wonderful than a lifetime of nothing special.

Notable Hollywood Movies with Amazing Prosthetic Make-Up

- ***Frankenstein* (1931)**
  Boris Karloff as Frankenstein
  Today, nobody can imagine Frankenstein without his signature scar on the forehead, bolts on either sides of the neck, and his green-coloured skin. This all became intrinsic to the character because of Jack Pierce, the make-up artist for the 1931 film. It was his research, vision, and skills with prosthetic make-up that made this version of Frankenstein iconic across all generations.

- ***Planet of the Apes* (1968)**
  One movie that made way for fantasy movies in Hollywood was *Planet of the Apes*, establishing the fact that non-human characters may be portrayed by performers with all the emotion and nuance that they would typically bring to a human character. It was made possible by the amazingly believable prosthetic make-up by John Chambers and Thomas Burman, the major factor behind the success of the film.

- ***The Godfather* (1972)**
  Marlon Brando as Don Vito Corleone
  Dick Smith, one of the pioneers of the make-up industry in Hollywood, thinned and coloured the actor's hair, used old-age stipple (a latex preparation that tightens the skin, creating realistic wrinkles), teeth discolouration, and dental plumpers that fit between Brando's lower teeth and cheeks.

- ***The Elephant Man*** **(1980)**
  John Hurt as Joseph Merrick
  Christopher Tucker, celebrated prosthetic artist, created latex prosthetic moulds to transform Hurt into Merrick, evoking both terror and sympathy.

- ***An American Werewolf in London*** **(1981)**
  David Naughton as David Kessler (who becomes a werewolf)
  The success of the prosthetics and effects make-up of this movie can be adjudged from the fact that Rick Baker was honoured with the first-ever Academy Award for Best Make-Up. The movie also went on to inspire Michael Jackson's *Thriller* look.

- ***Mrs. Doubtfire*** **(1993)**
  Robin Williams as Mrs Euphegenia Doubtfire
  Renowned make-up artist Ve Neill used the multi-piece mask created by Dick Smith and Greg Cannom and blended it into one with his skills, spending over four hours in make-up before every shoot.

- ***The Chronicles of Narnia: The Lion, the Witch and the Wardrobe*** **(2005)**
  There were cyclops, ogres, fauns, boggles, goblins, dwarves, etc., in this movie, and the entire cast required a lot of make-up, power of prosthetics, and CGI to bring them all to life. The success of the team can be adjudged from the fact that Tami Lane, the prosthetic make-up artist for the movie, won an Academy Award for her work in the film.

- ***Tropic Thunder* (2008)**
  Tom Cruise as Les Grossman
  Tom Cruise was unrecognizable in this movie, with his bald cap, bodysuit, fat hands, body hair, and what not. He took the support of multiple prosthetic pieces to play the part.

- ***Darkest Hour* (2017)**
  Gary Oldman as Winston Churchill
  Bringing a famous personality to real life on screen is a huge challenge that prosthetic designer Kazu Hiro responded to by receiving an Oscar for his work in this movie, transforming Oldman into the UK's then PM, Winston Churchill, during WWII.

- ***The Whale* (2022)**
  Brendan Fraser as Charlie
  This movie included some next-level prosthetic designing, with the use of digital scanning and 3D printing to transform Fraser into 600 lb Charlie. The efforts paid off as Fraser brought home an Oscar for his performance.

INDIAN CINEMA

INDIAN CINEMA'S GOLDEN ERA BEGAN IN 1947 WHEN INDIA GAINED INDEPENDENCE FROM BRITAIN. DIRECTORS, WRITERS, AND ARTISTS WERE INSPIRED TO MAKE THE FILM INDUSTRY REACH ITS ZENITH. THE FILMS IN THE GOLDEN AGE WERE INFLUENCED BY THE ANTI-COLONIAL AND INDEPENDENCE MOVEMENTS THAT LED TO THE BIRTH OF A GREAT NATION. THE GOLDEN ERA OF HINDI CINEMA SAW THE RISE OF SUCCESSFUL AND POWERFUL FEMALE ACTORS LIKE NARGIS, VYJAYANTHIMALA, MEENA KUMARI, MADHUBALA, NUTAN, WAHEEDA REHMAN, AND SADHANA. THE LEGENDARY AND MERCURIAL MALE ACTORS INCLUDE RAJ KAPOOR, DILIP KUMAR, GURU DUTT, AND DEV ANAND.

BOLLYWOOD

The First Movie in India

The first moving picture in India was *The Wrestlers* that was released in 1899. The first indigenously produced, full-length feature film (silent) in India was *Raja Harishchandra* that released in 1913. The first Indian movie shot in colour was *Kisan Kanya* that released in 1937.

First Female Director

Fatma Begum is acknowledged as India's first-ever female director when she directed the silent film *Bulbul-e-Paristan,* which released in 1926.

Light of the Universe

It was 14 March 1931 that saw the debut full-length Indian talkie *Alam Ara* (Light of the Universe) premiere at the Majestic Cinema in Bombay. Directed and produced by Ardeshir Marwan Irani of Imperial Film Company, the film was based on Joseph David's successful Parsi drama of the same name.

Multilinguals

In the 1930s, Indian films were made in different Indian languages and were known as multilinguals, like V. Shantaram and Prabhat Studios' Ayodhyache Raja/Ayodhya ka Raja (Marathi/Hindi 1932).

The Longest Kiss

The longest kiss in an Indian movie is from the 1933 film *Karma*. The actress Devika Rani and her real-life husband Himanshu Rai starred in this movie, where their kiss is four minutes long. This film also has the distinction of having the first English song in an Indian movie.

The First Lady of Indian Cinema

Devika Rani is considered the first lady of Indian cinema. Unlike other women of her time, she was educated, unconventional, and involved in most aspects of film-making. Through her production studio Bombay Talkies that she ran with her husband Himanshu Rai, Devika Rani launched stars like Dilip Kumar, Raj Kapoor, and Madhubala.

Neecha Nagar (1946)

The first Hindi-language film to receive global recognition was *Neecha Nagar.* It was honoured with the Palme d'Or (then known as Grand Prix du Festival International du Film) at the first Cannes film festival in 1946 and remains the only Indian film to have received it till date.

The First Indian Theatre

The distinction of the first cinema theatre in India goes to Elphinstone Picture Palace in Calcutta, which was set up in 1907. It was renamed Minerva Cinema in the '60s and then Chaplin in the 1980s and finally demolished in 2013.

The Father of Indian Cinema

Dadasaheb Phalke (Dhundiraj Govind Phalke) was a writer, director, and producer. He is regarded as the father of Indian cinema. His debut film, *Raja Harishchandra* (1913) was India's first full-length feature film.

Dadasaheb Phalke Commemorative Stamp (issued by Government of India, 1971)

The Golden Era of Bollywood Music

The 1970s is often considered to be golden era of Bollywood music. But it began in the 1950s when a powerhouse of musical talent like Mohammed Rafi, Kishore Kumar, Lata Mangeshkar, and Naushad, to name a few, tasted success. Composers like Salil Chowdhury, S.D. Burman, and Shankar–Jaikishan laid the foundation stones.

Kismet

In 1943, *Kismet* became a huge blockbuster. One of the highlights was the celebrated song 'Door Hato Aye Duniya Walon Hindustan Hamara Hai' (Go away, O people of the world, India is ours). The film is significant as it released at the height of the Quit India Movement against the British.

Teen Batti Char Rasta

Film-maker V. Shantaram's career lasted sixty-five years (1921 to 1986). In 1953, he made *Teen Batti Char Rasta*, a unique film themed on how important it was for Indians to live together despite linguistic and cultural differences. It was the story of a family where five of the six sons were married to five women from different states in India.

New Delhi

Director Mohan Sehgal focused on the antagonism between north Indians and south Indians in *New Delhi* (1956). A famous line has the Punjabi hero say to his Tamil lover that his father believed if one encountered a cobra and a madrasi, the latter, being more poisonous, should be killed first.

First Indian Film to Receive an A-Certificate

The first Indian film to receive the 'only for adults' certification was the Madhubala and Motilal starrer *Hanste Aansu* (1950). The A-certificate came about following the amendment of the original Indian Cinematograph Act (1918) in December 1949.

Snakes in Bollywood

Nagin (1954) was a tribal tale, featuring immortal melodies by composer Hemanta Mukherjee and starring Vyjayanthimala in the lead role. This movie probably started the Indian obsession with snakes in popular culture.

Indo-German Collaboration

The early years of Indian cinema saw collaborations with Germany. The West, especially Germany, provided both equipment and technicians for Indian films. In the 1920s, a co-production deal was signed between film-maker and actor Himanshu Rai and German firm Emelka to make successful movies together.

German director Franz Osten directed sixteen films for Himanshu Rai. But after the beginning of the World War II, all the German technicians were deported by the British government. This brought an end to the fruitful Indo-German collaboration.

The First Hub of Indian Cinema

It was Calcutta (now Kolkata) and not Bombay (now Mumbai) that was the hub of India's film-making until the 1930s. During the war, when there was a threat of Japanese invasion to India's eastern borders, many film-makers moved to Bombay from Calcutta.

Some Other Firsts of Indian Cinema

- Devika Rani was the first Indian woman to receive the Dadasaheb Phalke Award.
- *1942: A Love Story* (1994), the swan song of music maestro R.D. Burman, was the first Indian film to use Dolby sound.
- *The Court Dancer: Raj Nartaki* from 1941 is the first all-English talkie made in India by an all-Indian cast and crew.

The Largest Movie Industry

Today, the largest movie industry in terms of content production is based in India with more than a thousand movies produced annually in various languages. That's more than double of what Hollywood manages to produce!

Yaadein

In 1964, a unique film named *Yaadein* was released in India. Sunil Dutt was the director, producer, and sole actor in this film. It found a place in the *Guinness Book of World Records* for the 'Fewest Actors in a Narrative Film'.

'B' for Bombay, 'B' for Bollywood

In the 1970s, Indian cinema surpassed the American film industry (Hollywood) as the world's largest film producer. The name Bollywood came into existence, referring to the Hindi movie industry in Bombay (presently Mumbai).

Tragedy King

Dilip Kumar was also known as the 'Tragedy King' of Bollywood because of the roles he essayed on celluloid. He was offered the part of Sherif Ali in the legendary film *Lawrence of Arabia* (1962), which he turned down. The part then went to Egyptian actor Omar Sharif.

Dilip Kumar

Movie with the Most Songs

The Indian movie that features the most songs is *Indrasabha* (1932), which has a mind-boggling seventy-one songs. The makers were certainly musically inclined just like the Indian Gods.

Maximum Run

The Shah Rukh Khan and Kajol starrer *Dilwale Dulhania Le Jayenge* or *DDLJ* (1995) ran for over a thousand weeks at a Mumbai theatre, breaking the earlier record held by *Sholay* (1975), and setting a new record that no movie has broken yet.

The First Oscar Winner

In 1983, Bhanu Athaiya became the first Indian to win an Oscar. She received the Academy Award for Outstanding Costume Designer for Richard Attenborough's 1982 film *Gandhi*. Bhanu Athaiya has been a part of Bollywood for over fifty years.

A Perfect Love Story

A young Sunil Dutt was a radio jockey for Radio Ceylon (now Sri Lanka Broadcasting Corporation). When he interviewed his favourite actress Nargis, he was so tongue-tied that the interview was cancelled. Years later, he got the opportunity to work with her in *Mother India* (1957). Soon they fell in love and were married.

The Koechlins

Bollywood actress Kalki Koechlin's great-grandfather Maurice Koechlin was the chief engineer who supervised the construction of two iconic monuments – the Eiffel Tower in Paris and the Statue of Liberty in the US.

Mughal-E-Azam (1960)

The Hindi film *Mughal-E-Azam* was initially planned as a trilingual movie. All the scenes were shot thrice in three languages – Hindi, Tamil, and English. But when the Tamil version flopped miserably, the English version was abandoned instantly.

Gabbar Singh

Actor Amjad Khan, who became a household name in India after playing the character of Gabbar Singh in *Sholay* (1975), was almost rejected for the film initially. Screenwriter Javed Akhtar thought his voice was weak for the role. But Amjad Khan was retained, and the rest is history.

Designer Heroine

Actress Kareena Kapoor was clad in 130 different dresses created by the best designers from all over the world for the film *Heroine* (2012). This expensive wardrobe could not stop the movie from sinking at the box office. Clearly, content and not costume is king!

SRK Replaces Tom Cruise

Saif Ali Khan was the first choice for the role of Raj Malhotra in *Dilwale Dulhania Le Jayenge* (1995). In fact, SRK was not even the second choice as none other than Tom Cruise was considered after Saif could not do the film.

Rehman's 'K' Nemesis

Bollywood actor of the 1950s and '60s, Rehman had trouble speaking dialogues that began with the 'K' sound. If the dialogue went, '*Kaash tum yahaan aa jaate, toh main kitna khush hota*' (If only you had come here, I would have been so happy), Rehman would fumble with the dialogue and would be unable to deliver it. The solution to Rehman's problem was finally found, and the director heaved a sigh of relief. The dialogue writer cleverly switched the sentence to '*Main kitna khush hota, kaash tum yahaan aa jaate*', which basically meant the same thing. Now, Rehman delivered the dialogue easily.

Baby Mumtaz

Madhubala was born as Mumtaz Jehan Begum Dehlavi and began her journey in the film industry as the child artiste Baby Mumtaz in the film *Basant* (1942). She went on to become one of the most beautiful and talented actresses of the Hindi film industry.

Neel Kamal

In 1947, fourteen-year-old Madhubala made her debut as a lead heroine in *Neel Kamal* opposite Raj Kapoor, who also made his debut as a lead hero in this film. Madhubala's name was in the credits as Mumtaz.

Mumtaz becomes Madhubala

The producer of *Basant* (1942) and *Neel Kamal* (1947) was Bombay Talkies. Devika Rani, the owner of Bombay Talkies, was very impressed with Mumtaz's beauty and acting skills. To make her more acceptable to the audience, Devika Rani gave her the screen name of Madhubala, meaning 'sweet girl'.

Versatile Actress

Actress Waheeda Rehman has played both on-screen mother and lover to Amitabh Bachchan. She played his love interest in *Adalat* (1976) and mother in *Trishul* (1978).

Rockstar Hair

The Bollywood film *Rockstar* (2011) was shot in reverse as the climax of the movie was filmed first. This is because the makers did not want to mess Ranbir Kapoor's hairstyle.

Struggle Days

Stories of Bollywood struggle are pretty common. But Anil Kapoor's family initially lived in Raj Kapoor's garage when they first moved to the city of Bombay.

Two Movies, Two Intervals

Two of Raj Kapoor's movies, *Sangam* (1964) and *Mera Naam Joker* (1970), are the only two Bollywood movies to have two intervals, with both having a runtime of almost four hours. The former was the first Hindi movie to have not one but two intervals during its screening.

Most Awards

Hrithik Roshan's debut movie *Kaho Naa Pyaar Hai* (2000) found a place in the *Guinness Book of World Records*, 2002 edition, for winning the most number of awards for a movie. The Bollywood movie won a total of ninety-two awards!

Longest Song

The song *'Ab Tumhare Hawale Watan Saathiyo'* in the 2004 Bollywood movie of the same name is the longest Hindi film song. The song is twenty minutes long, and it is featured in three instalments in the movie.

From Lab Assistant to Star

Before Ashok Kumar became an actor in Hindi films in 1936 with *Jeevan Naiya*, he worked as a lab assistant in Bombay Talkies.

Longest Bollywood Films

The longest Bollywood films to run in theatres with run times of 255 minutes each are Raj Kapoor's *Mera Naam Joker* (1970) (original cut) and the war movie *LOC: Kargil* (2003).

On-Screen Brothers

The only Bollywood movie in which Shashi Kapoor has played Amitabh Bachchan's elder brother is *Silsila* (1981). In all other movies, Shashi Kapoor has played Big B's younger brother.

International Stars in Bollywood Movies

Sylvester Stallone, Denise Richards, Brandon Routh, and Holly Valance can be seen in cameo roles in Bollywood movie *Kambakkht Ishq* that released in 2009. The Hollywood stars play themselves in the movie. Some other examples of movies with a foreign star cast include *Lagaan* (2001), *Mangal Pandey* (2005), *English Vinglish* (2012), *RRR* (2022), etc.

Karz

The 1980 film *Karz* had some memorable songs. Apart from the theme song and 'Kamaal Hai', all the songs of *Karz* have been used as Bollywood film titles like *Dard-E-Dil* (1983), *Paisa Yeh Paisa* (1985), *Main Solah Baras Ki* (1998), *Ek Hasina Thi* (2004), and *Om Shanti Om* (2007).

The Pakeezah Delay

The Hindi film *Pakeezah* (1972) took almost fourteen years to shoot. The main reason for this was the separation of the lead actress Meena Kumari and director Kamal Amrohi who were married to each other before.

The Shower of Soap Flakes

Hariyali Aur Raasta (1962) was Manoj Kumar's first jubilee hit. The snow for a scene had been created artificially using soap flakes. The experienced Mala Sinha delivered her lines despite the heavy shower of soap flakes. But Manoj Kumar couldn't say a word as his mouth was full of soap flakes.

War of Words

Instead of being sympathetic because of the soap flakes fiasco, Mala Sinha snapped at Manoj Kumar for failing to speak his lines, 'Who invited you to join the industry?' Manoj Kumar retorted that while she might be in the industry for money, he was there for the love of acting.

No Smoking, John!

For the 2007 film *No Smoking*, actor John Abraham had to smoke 80–120 cigarettes a day to get into character. Sadly, John's lungs were affected, and the title of the film is always on his mind now.

Star on Moon

Shah Rukh Khan owns property on the moon. Every year, on SRK's birthday, one of his die-hard fans from Australia buys him a piece of land on the moon. She has gifted him several acres on 'The Sea of Tranquillity', one of the most sought-after addresses on the moon.

Naushad's Wedding Song

The Hindi film industry was considered such a low profession to be in, back in the 1940s, that music director Naushad's parents introduced him to his would-be-bride's family as a tailor. Ironically, the music that played at Naushad's wedding was from the 1944 film *Rattan*. The music was composed by Naushad.

French Awards for SRK

The Government of France has awarded Indian superstar Shah Rukh Khan both the Ordre des Arts et des Lettres and the Légion d'honneur, the greatest French honour, equivalent to the Bharat Ratna in India.

Shah Rukh Khan

World Honours for SRK

Shah Rukh Khan was the first Indian to have a statue in Grevin Museum in Paris, France, after Mahatma Gandhi. He was the first Bollywood actor to be featured on the cover page of the *Los Angeles Times* Calendar section and the first Bollywood personality to be honoured with the prestigious Chubb Fellowship at Yale University's Timothy Dwight College.

Mother India (1957)

Mother India with Nargis Dutt in the lead role supported by Sunil Dutt and Rajendra Kumar was India's first Oscar nomination. It was nominated in the category of Best Foreign Language Film.

Naya Daur (1957)

B.R. Chopra's classic *Naya Daur* originally had Madhubala as the female lead opposite Dilip Kumar. But Madhubala's father objected when they had out-of-town shooting schedule, because of her budding romantic relationship with Dilip Kumar. So, Vyjayanthimala was roped in as the female lead.

The First Indian Movie That Ran for a Year

The Kannada movie *Mungaru Male* (2006) is the first Indian movie to be screened in multiplexes continuously for a year. The movie was a game changer for the Kannada film industry.

Dharmendra's First Salary

Bollywood stars are paid an obnoxious sum of money as remuneration today. But when Dharmendra first joined the Hindi film industry, he received a salary of ₹51 only! He received the same as signing amount for his debut movie *Dil Bhi Tera Hum Bhi Tere* (1960) by the movie's three co-producers, who gave him ₹17 each.

Salman Khan's Horses

Bollywood superstar Salman Khan was so thrilled at the success of his film *Bajrangi Bhaijaan* (2015) that he promptly bought two new horses for his farmhouse. No prizes for guessing what he named them. Bajrangi and Bhaijaan of course!

Jumping Jack

Jeetendra's unique dancing skills had earned him the nickname of Jumping Jack. The secret behind his nimbleness and flexibility was probably that he began his career as a body double, and that too for actress Sandhya in her film *Navrang* (1959).

A Light Love Affair

During the filming of *Sholay* (1975), Dharmendra bribed the light boys to deliberately make mistakes during a scene where he had to hug Hema Malini, whom he was head over heels in love with in real life as well. He did this so he could hug Hema Malini again and again!

Zindagi Na Milegi Dobara (2011)

Thanks to the Bollywood film *Zindagi Na Milegi Dobara*, Spain's tourism business witnessed a spectacular hike of 65 per cent. Part of the film was shot in Spain, which has naturally thrown its doors wide open for Bollywood since then.

Tomatoes Na Milega Dobara!

Zindagi Na Milegi Dobara (2011) had a scene from the famous Tomatina Festival. But unfortunately, it was off-season when the movie was being shot in Spain. So, 16 tonnes of tomatoes were flown in from Portugal to Spain and the festival was recreated for the movie. Tomatoes Na Milega Dobara!

The Most Expensive Song

The song 'Pyar Kiya Toh Darna Kya' was an integral part of the film *Mughal-E-Azam* (1960). It was rewritten 105 times before being approved and cost ten million rupees to shoot. This amount was astronomical in those days and far too expensive for one song.

Hunterwali

Sequels are pretty common in Bollywood now, but the first Hindi film to have a sequel was *Hunterwali*. The first film was released in 1935 and its sequel, *Hunterwali Ki Beti,* in 1943. *Hunterwali* is an action movie starring Fearless Nadia and is also one of the earliest female-lead Hindi movies.

Fearless Nadia

The first foreigner to act in Bollywood and achieve cult status was Australian-born actress Mary Ann Evans, better known by her screen name Nadia. She was also known as 'Fearless Nadia' or 'The Hunterwali' (the woman with the whip). She did this as early as 1935.

Gangs of Wasseypur

Gangs of Wasseypur (2012) is a classic in the crime genre. The film's associate director Vicky Kaushal also became a leading man in Bollywood later. But the film was in troubled waters when director Anurag Kashyap almost lost the original script. on a flight Thankfully, the airline managed to retrieve his bag in time.

Piku (2015)

The name of the Bollywood film *Piku,* starring Amitabh Bachchan, Deepika Padukone, and Irrfan Khan, was inspired by Satyajit Ray's short film *Pikoo* (1981), which was further adapted from his own short story *Pikoor Diary* (Pikoo's Diary). Irrfan Khan said no to a Hollywood project so that he could work in *Piku* instead.

The Punctual Superstar

Amitabh Bachchan is renowned for his punctuality on the sets apart from his other qualities. But this punctuality embarrassed everybody in his younger days as he reached Filmistan Studios before the watchman or gatekeeper to open the gates himself. No wonder he is called Big B.

Lata Mangeshkar

The Guinness World Record for 'Most Recorded Artist in History' was discontinued in 1991. But Bollywood playback singer Lata Mangeshkar held the record till then. From the beginning of her glittering career in 1942, the Indian nightingale has recorded more than 25,000 songs in thirty-six regional languages. Stupendous!

Alternative Use of Bollywood Songs

Bollywood songs are not only about entertainment. Some are being used in rural Indian villages to increase literacy rates. Roughly one-third of Indians don't speak English. Hindi subtitles in movies play an important role in India.

Bollywood Rap

In an attempt to woo both younger and international audiences, Bollywood used artists like Snoop Dogg and Pitbull to record songs in the late-2000s. However, the 'Rail Gaadi' song from the film *Aashirwad* (1968), sung by Ashok Kumar, was the first Indian rap song. Then it was in the Indie Pop Era of the 1990s that Harjeet Singh 'Baba' Sehgal made rapping popular in India and he is widely regarded as the country's first rapper.

Paanch Rupaiyya Barah Ana

The idea behind singer/actor Kishore Kumar's famous song 'Paanch Rupaiyya Barah Ana' is unique and interesting. Kishore Kumar had a debt of 5.75 rupees during his student days in the canteen of his college hostel. That's how the concept of the song originated.

The Versatile Singer

Kishore Kumar was also versatile apart from being supremely gifted and talented. He could sing in both male and female voices. The first Hindi film song that he sung in a female voice was 'Aake Seedhi Lagi Dil Pe'.

Guide

Dev Anand's first movie in colour, *Guide,* released in 1965. Two versions of *Guide* were made separately. The first was in Hindi and the second, in English.

Guru Dutt Replaces Dilip Kumar

For Guru Dutt's classic film *Pyaasa* (1957), Dilip Kumar was the first choice for the lead. But after his unprecedented absence, Guru Dutt decided to play the part himself. The rest is cinematic history.

Gol Maal

Director Hrishikesh Mukherjee filmed his iconic comedy *Gol Maal* (1979) mostly in and around his own bungalow in Bandra. Surprisingly, it took him just forty days to finish shooting the film.

School Anthem

The song 'Aye Malik Tere Bande Hum', was sung by Lata Mangeshkar in the Hindi movie *Do Ankhen Barah Haath* (1957). The song was adopted as an anthem by a school in Pakistan.

Madhumati

Director Bimal Roy was broke and needed money during the shooting of *Madhumati* (1958). Actor Dilip Kumar was the one who decided to help him out. He arranged a special screening of the film exclusively for distributors, who were impressed and put their money on the film.

The Legends of *Madhumati*

No wonder the distributors who watched *Madhumati* were impressed. Director Bimal Roy had an impressive ensemble of legends for the film. Ritwik Ghatak was the writer, Hrishikesh Mukherjee was the editor, Salil Chowdhury was the music composer, and Dilip Kumar was the actor. Naturally, *Madhumati* was the highest grossing film of 1958.

Inspired by French Literature

The Hindi film *Ram Aur Shyam* (1967) was a remake of the hit Telugu film *Ramudu Bheemudu*. This was again inspired from *The Corsican Brothers* by classic French author Alexandre Dumas, père.

Guru Dutt's Promise to Dev Anand

When Dev Anand helped Guru Dutt with a directorial break, he also extracted a promise out of him. Guru Dutt promised to cast Dev Anand in his next film. Fulfilment of that promise happened in 1956 as Dev Anand starred in Guru Dutt's film *CID*.

Jaane Bhi Do Naseer Saab!

Jaane Bhi Do Yaaro (1983) was made on such a shoestring budget that Naseeruddin Shah was paid just ₹15,000 as remuneration and was the highest-paid actor in the film. Naseeruddin Shah was instructed to bring his own camera as a prop, which was later stolen on the set.

Nana Stabbed

In the film *Salaam Bombay!* (1988), Nana Patekar actually got stabbed with a knife by one of the child actors. It appears that the child actor did not understand the director's instructions properly.

Big B's Double Punch

Two of the finest films in Amitabh Bachchan's impressive filmography are *Deewar* and *Sholay,* which both released in 1975. Interestingly, both movies were shot simultaneously. After shooting for *Sholay* in the morning, Amitabh Bachchan would rush to the sets of *Deewar* to shoot at night.

Kishore Kumar the Choreographer

The famous song 'Meri Pyari Bindoo' in the equally famous film *Padosan* (1968) did not have a choreographer. That is when the great Kishore Kumar stepped in, and the shoot was conducted under his impromptu instructions. K for Kishore Kumar and G for Genius!

Autograph Please!

The cast and crew of the film *Nau Do Gyarah* (1957) were

resting at night in a region in the dreaded Chambal Valley, where they were shooting. A fully armed dacoit arrived at Dev Anand's doorstep to ask for his autograph. These are the never-say-never moments in life!

QSQT

A strange business strategy was used by the makers of the film *Qayamat Se Qayamat Tak* (1988). They promised to give away a free poster of Aamir Khan and Juhi Chawla to anyone who bought eight tickets for the movie. Strangely, this marketing strategy worked even though the leads were debutants.

Enter the Angry Young Man!

Raaj Kumar was first offered the lead role in *Zanjeer* (1973) and Jaani apparently refused simply because he could not stand the smell of director Prakash Mehra's hair oil. Enter the angry young man of Bollywood who had no such qualms. Raaj Kumar must have torn his hair after the film's release.

The Rise of Sanjay Mishra

Sanjay Mishra's father's dream was that his son became an actor. Sanjay went to the National School of Drama (NSD), New Delhi, but achieved little success after that. When his father died, a devastated Sanjay decided to abandon his acting career went to Rishikesh and began working at a dhaba. Thankfully, director Rohit Shetty persuaded him to return.

The Curious Case of Film-Making

In a curious case of film-making, Kishore Kumar made *Chalti Ka Naam Gaadi* (1958) and the Bengali film *Lukochuri* (1958) hoping that they would both flop as he wanted to show losses to the Income Tax Department. Unfortunately for Kishore Kumar, both the movies were huge blockbusters.

The Superfast Music Director

Music director Naushad declined when approached to compose the music of *Azaad* (1955) as he was given only two weeks. He said he was a composer, not a factory. C. Ramachandra was hired, and he composed five songs within a fortnight, most of which topped the charts. Need for speed!

The Hit Pair of Hindi Films

The famous Raj Kapoor–Nargis pair first tasted on-screen success with the film *Andaz* (1949). They followed this up with seventeen films in Hindi cinema together. *Andaz* was also the only movie where Raj Kapoor and Dilip Kumar worked together.

North by North-East

Aradhana (1969) set a unique record for being the first Hindi movie to run successfully for more than a hundred days with four shows in a day in the non-Hindi-speaking belt of the north-eastern states of India.

I Can Talk English

The famous comedy scene with Amitabh Bachchan saying 'I can talk English' in the film *Namak Halal* (1982) was mostly improvised by the actor himself. Director Prakash Mehra was asked to stay outside the set as Bachchan kept bursting out in laughter whenever he tried to enact the scene to him.

Karz Remakes

There were several remakes of the popular Hindi film *Karz* (1980) in several languages, like *Yuga Purusha* (1989) in Kannada, *Enakkul Oruvan* (1984) in Tamil, and *Aatma Balam* (1985) in Telugu. The most recent adaptation was a Hindi film named *KARZZZZ* (2008). *Karz* itself is a remake of a Hollywood film, *The Reincarnation of Peter Proud* (1975).

Shalimar

Many international songs sampled the title song of the Hindi film *Shalimar* (1978). Among them were 'Mef Vs Chef 2' by Method Man, Raekwon, and Ghostface Killah, and 'The Hours' by Handsome Boy Modeling School featuring Chino Moreno, El-P and Cage. Mera Pyar Shalimar!

Anari

Director Hrishikesh Mukherjee had no takers after his debut film *Musafir* (1957) flopped at the box office. Raj Kapoor was the only one who realized Mukherjee's potential and recommended him as the director of his next film. The film was *Anari* (1959), which catapulted the careers of both Raj Kapoor and Hrishikesh Mukherjee.

Kaagaz Ke Phool

The iconic *Kaagaz Ke Phool* (1959) was the last Hindi film directed by Guru Dutt in his illustrious cinematic career. But it was India's first CinemaScope film.

Shakti

Shakti (1982) saw the cinematic face-off between the two great stars: Dilip Kumar and Amitabh Bachchan. But the Big-B fan club was a tad disappointed as he was overshadowed by Dilip Kumar in the movie.

When Mohammed met Muhammad

When Mohammed Rafi visited Chicago on a musical tour, he requested the organizers to arrange an appointment with Muhammad Ali. Rafi was a big fan of the legendary boxer, who normally didn't meet people. But when he heard how legendary Rafi was in India, Ali agreed and came all the way to Rafi's hotel.

Farhan Akhtar's Hollywood Project

Farhan Akhtar worked on a Hollywood project in 2004. He wrote the lyrics of the blockbuster *Bride and Prejudice,* which also had Aishwarya Rai as the lead. Farhan collaborated with sister Zoya for the lyrics of the songs after Javed Akhtar's recommendation. Listen without prejudice!

Practical Lessons in Method Acting

Actor Balraj Sahni wrapped a gamchha around his head and plied a rickshaw on the streets of Calcutta every day for two weeks. His son Parikshit and daughter Shabnam sat as passengers as Balraj Sahni practised hard to get into the skin of the character of a rickshaw puller for the classic *Do Bigha Zamin* (1953).

Pride of Hindi Cinema

Do Bigha Zamin is regarded as one of the ten best Indian films of all time. Also, it is one of the first Indian films to win awards and accolades in cities like Venice and Melbourne and many others in China, the UK, and the USSR, besides in film festivals held in Karlovy Vary, Cannes, etc.

Sahib Biwi Aur Ghulam (1962)

Guru Dutt's film *Sahib Biwi Aur Ghulam* was based on a Bengali movie *Saheb Bibi Golam* (1956), which in turn was based on the 1953 novel of same name by Bimal Mitra. Starring Meena Kumari, Guru Dutt, Rehman, and Waheeda Rehman in lead roles, the movie narrates the story of a disintegrating Bengali household, wherein the hopeless faithful wife adopts drastic measures in an attempt to keep her husband home, who only loves drinking and being with women. She starts drinking with him at home but ends up becoming an addict herself.

It was submitted to the Oscars as an official Indian entry. But the film where the female protagonist was shown drinking was rejected by the Academy of Motion Pictures on the grounds that in Western culture 'a woman drinking is not a taboo'.

Anand

Hrishikesh Mukherjee's *Anand* (1971) was a low-budget film by Hindi movie standards those days. Rajesh Khanna wanted to work with Hrishikesh Mukherjee so badly that he waived off his remuneration and accepted just ₹7 lakh for the film.

Dharmendra's Blues

Dharmendra was so hurt that Rajesh Khanna was preferred over him by Hrishikesh Mukherjee in *Anand* (1971) that he got drunk and called the director in the middle of the night to voice his grievance. Hrishikesh Mukherjee got no sleep that night as Dharmendra kept calling him.

Bribed with a Meal

To make famous singer Manna Dey sing the song 'Kaun Aaya Mere Man Ke Dware' in his film *Dekh Kabira Roya* (1957), music director Madan Mohan first bribed the singer with a meal of his favourite bhindi meat curry.

Don

Amitabh Bachchan played the leading role in the film *Don* (1978). But his remuneration was still less than Pran's, who had a supporting role in the movie.

Parinda Lingo

Bollywood has influenced people from all walks of life over the years and continues to do so. Most of the underworld slang that is used in Mumbai today has been heavily borrowed from the dialogues of the 1989 film *Parinda*.

Mogambo's Costume

For the costume of Mogambo, played by Amrish Puri in *Mr India* (1987), a sum of ₹25,000 was spent. This was a huge amount in the 1980s in Bollywood to invest in the costume of a villain. Mogambo khush hua!

Elephantine Memory

The elephant that acted in the Hindi film *Haathi Mere Saathi* (1971), recognized lead actress Tanuja many years later. It grabbed her sari with its trunk joyfully when she visited a circus with her young daughter Kajol. Elephantine memories during shooting!

Lady Luck

Actor Anil Kapoor was dying to play the leading man in a Hindi film but could only land the role of the villain in *Meri Jung* (1985). But when Amitabh Bachchan couldn't do the film, Anil Kapoor got the lead role. It was also after signing this movie that Kapoor decided to marry Sunita, his wife. This movie became a turning point in his life and he has been exclaiming 'Jhakkas' ever since!

The Simpsons Hum a Hindi Tune

The song 'Pal Bhar Ke Liye' from the Hindi film *Johny Mera Naam* (1970) starring Dev Anand was used in the popular American TV show, *The Simpsons*.

Joy in Hong Kong

The moves of the famous electric dance of Joy Mukherjee in the song 'Duniya Pagal Hai' in the movie *Shagird* (1967) was picked up by the actor from a dancer at a Hong Kong nightclub. This was when Joy Mukherjee was filming the movie *Love in Tokyo* (1966), strangely in Hong Kong.

Four Weddings and a Kishore Kumar

Kishore Kumar's first marriage to Ruma Guha Thakurta lasted from 1950 to 1958. He married Madhubala after that, and was rumoured to have converted to Islam back then. This second marriage lasted for nine years. He married Yogeeta Bali in 1976 and she left him in 1978. He finally married Leena Chandravarkar in 1980.

Why Kishore Kumar Stopped Singing for Mithun Chakraborty

After Yogeeta Bali left Kishore Kumar and married actor Mithun Chakraborty, it is reported that Kishore Kumar temporarily stopped singing for Mithun Chakraborty in his films. Love hurts!

The 80 Per Cent Blind Pianist

In *Andhadhun* (2018), Ayushmann Khurrana played a blind pianist to perfection. He trained under a professional pianist for two months to prepare for his role. A special pair of lens was fetched by the team from London that hindered his vision by 80 per cent.

Shah Rukh Khan's Hindi Grades

Shah Rukh Khan's least favourite school subject was Hindi, but he loved Hindi films. In an effort to increase his interest in the subject, SRK's mother offered to take him to watch a Hindi film if he improved his grades in Hindi. Mothers know best!

RRR's Remuneration

RRR star Jr NTR was eighteen years old when he made his debut in 2001 with *Ninnu Choodalani*. He received ₹4 lakh as remuneration. Cut to 2022 when Jr NTR received ₹45 crore as remuneration for *RRR*. That's an increase of 1,12,400 per cent!

Sholay Star

The remuneration that is paid to movie stars seems astronomical compared to what some actors were paid earlier. For *Sholay* (1975), Amjad Khan received only ₹15,000 for a fantastic debut. *Sholay* went on to make ₹15.50 crore way back in 1975. Wonder if Amjad Khan received a bonus later.

Jab Jab Phool Khile

The climax of *Jab Jab Phool Khile* (1965) involved a scene where Shashi Kapoor had to lift Nanda while she was running beside a moving train. To time the scene perfectly, Shashi Kapoor pulled her up at the last second. The director closed his eyes as he was sure Nanda would die.

Yaadon Ki Baraat (1974)

The title song, *'Yaadon Ki Baarat'* in the movie of the same name that was sung by the three brothers on-screen was in reality sung by three women playback singers.

Cool Chopra

Producer–director Yash Chopra kept a cool head when confronted with a crisis during the music recording for *Kabhi Kabhie* (1976). Faced with a musicians' strike, Yash Chopra got artists from the navy to record the music. The music was composed by Khayyam, and the lyrics were penned by Sahir Ludhianvi.

Big-B Style

When Amitabh Bachchan was shooting for *Sharaabi* (1984), he received an injury on his left hand during Diwali celebrations. While filming the movie, he kept his left hand in his pocket because of the injury. This became a cool mannerism among the youth when the film released.

Amitabh Bachchan

Aandhi Raises a Storm

Aandhi (1975) was banned by the government after its release because of the similarities between the lead character Aarti Devi, played by Suchitra Sen, and the then prime minister of India, Indira Gandhi. A scene was added later where the protagonist declares that she wants to serve India like her idol Indira Gandhi. Only then was the film approved and premiered on national television. Quite a storm this!

Ban on Kishore Kumar

Kishore Kumar faced a lengthy ban on national broadcasters like All India Radio and Doordarshan. This was because he had refused to sing for a rally of the Indian National Congress in Bombay.

The RK Logo

The iconic scene between Raj Kapoor and Nargis in *Barsaat* (1949) became the famous logo for Raj Kapoor's production house RK Studios. Raj Kapoor bought the rights from his remuneration from the same movie.

Desperate Measures

Anil Kapoor was desperate to work with Yash Chopra and pleaded to be cast in *Parampara* (1993). He signed the film blindly. But Anil Kapoor decided to run away when he realized he would be playing the on-screen father of Aamir Khan and Saif Ali Khan. Vinod Khanna replaced Anil Kapoor.

Kaala Patthar

The Hindi film *Kaala Patthar* (1979) was inspired by a coal mine disaster called the Chasnala Mining Disaster that took place on 27 December 1975 near Dhanbad, Jharkhand (then Bihar). This unfortunate disaster claimed the life of 372 miners.

Raj Refuses to Play *Anand*

Hrishikesh Mukherjee had written *Anand* (1971) keeping in mind his dearest friend Raj Kapoor. But Raj Kapoor, although liked the story and the script, had to decline due to health issues, and the director was understanding of his situation.

Big Star with a Big Heart

Shah Rukh Khan became the sole Indian to win UNESCO's Pyramide con Marni Award for supporting children's education. In 2014, SRK donated all the prize money of Kolkata Knight Riders' (KKR) Indian Premier League (IPL) win to the children's hospitals in Kolkata and Mumbai.

Kishore Kumar the Fan

Most Indians are huge fans of Kishore Kumar. But Kishore Kumar was such a big fan of the Hollywood actor and singer Danny Kaye that he used to hang his posters in his house.

Bimal Roy's Creative Strategy

Director Bimal Roy was aware that the songs of a Hindi film were instrumental in their success at the box office. For his films, he cleverly alternated between the two great music directors then – Salil Chowdhury and S.D. Burman – to make them compete with each other and produce world-class music.

Bawarchi Credits

The 1972 movie *Bawarchi* used an innovative and unconventional method instead of the usual title cards in the credits. Through a voice-over, the baritone voice of Amitabh Bachchan was used to narrate the titles and the credits.

Sunil Dutt's Japanese Walk

Bollywood star Sunil Dutt once walked from Nagasaki to Hiroshima when he was in Japan to appeal for global disarmament.

Bollywood Fans in Germany

Bollywood is extremely popular in Germany. In fact, it is the second biggest Bollywood market in Europe after the UK. Bollywood also has an impressive presence in Berlinale and other German film festivals.

Ardh Satya

Actor Om Puri has thanked Amitabh Bachchan in his biography. That is because Big B was first offered the lead role in *Ardh Satya* (1983). But after he turned it down, it went to Om Puri instead. Om Puri's performance in *Ardh Satya* cemented his position in Bollywood.

After Twenty Years

Director K. Asif liked to take things slow. His legendary film *Mughal-E-Azam* (1960) took fourteen years to complete. *Qais Aur Laila* (1986) took even longer, twenty years, to finish after hiccups like the deaths of actor Guru Dutt in 1964 and K. Asif himself in 1971. The incomplete movie was eventually released in 1986.

The Most Typecast Actor

Jagdish Raj Khurana is an actor with a difference in Bollywood. He is the most typecast actor in the world having played the role of a police inspector in 144 films. He holds a Guinness World Record for this repetitive yet unique achievement.

Most Expensive Bollywood Film

Shah Rukh Khan's science fiction Hindi movie *Ra.One* (2011) is one of the most expensive films to be produced by Bollywood standards. The huge budget was ₹130 crore (approximately US $24 million). Unfortunately, the film bombed at the box office.

Most Songs Recorded in a Single Day

Singer Kumar Sanu made a huge impact in Bollywood. But he also got carried away by recording as many as twenty-eight songs in a single day setting a Guinness World Record for the same.

Adaptations of *The Comedy of Errors*

There have been multiple Bollywood adaptations of Shakespeare's *The Comedy of Errors.* Rohit Shetty's *Cirkus* (2022) is inspired from *Angoor* (1982). Gulzar got the idea of *Angoor* (1982) working with Bimal Roy in *Do Dooni Chaar* (1968), which was based on Bengali author Ishwar Chandra Vidyasagar's novel *Bhranti Bilas,* which was again based on Shakespeare's play *The Comedy of Errors.*

Phantom Fixation

The famous comic character Phantom or 'the Ghost who walks' was the favourite of Bollywood superstar Rajesh Khanna. He was so taken up with the character that he designed an entire sequence on the Phantom for his movie *Bundal Baaz* (1976), which was directed by another famous actor named Shammi Kapoor.

Amazing Facts about Bollywood

- 'Bollywood' has been added to the Oxford Dictionary.
- Shah Rukh Khan runs a cancer ward in Mumbai's Lilavati Hospital.
- Danny Denzongpa was the first choice for the role of Gabbar Singh in *Sholay* (1975).

First Indian 3D Movie

The first 3D film released in India in 1984 was *My Dear Kuttichathan*. It was dubbed in Hindi later as *Chota Chetan* (1998).

Record Production

In the year 2013, the Indian film industry released as many as 1,724 films. That's a mind-boggling average of over 143 movies per month.

Raj Kapoor's Fees

When writer Shailendra produced the film *Teesri Kasam* (1966) and requested Raj Kapoor to star in it, the great actor charged a fee of ₹1 only to act in the film.

The Talented Salil Chowdhury

One of director Bimal Roy's many contributions to Hindi cinema was the introduction of the genius composer Salil Chowdhury, who was a songwriter, music director, lyricist, writer, and poet. Bimal Roy also utilized Chowdhury's excellent writing skills to make him pen down the screenplay of three great films: *Do Bigha Zameen* (1953), *Parakh* (1960), and *Prem Patra* (1962).

The Reluctant Actor

In Guru Dutt's film *Sahib Bibi Aur Ghulam* (1962), Shashi Kapoor was supposed to play the role of the innocent Bhootnath. But this casting did not happen at the last minute, and Guru Dutt had to play the role reluctantly. We are glad he did!

The Stylish Clapper Boy

Raj Kapoor began as a clapper boy in Bollywood. He would comb his hair and pose before the camera before giving the clap. During the shoot of *Vishkanya* (1943), actor Kidar Sharma was shooting a close-up as the sun set. Raj caught the hero's beard in his clapboard and it came off. He was angrily slapped by Sharma.

The British Indian Actress

Bollywood actress Alia Bhatt is British with Indian descent and holds a British passport. That's because Alia's mother Soni Razdan is of British origin.

Akshay Kumar's Career Graph

Before Akshay Kumar struck gold in Bollywood, he was known as Rajiv Hari Om Bhatia. Prior to his glittering Bollywood career,

Kitne aadmi the?
Hum angrezo ke zamaane ke jailor hain,
ha ha!
Poore pachas hazaar.

Tumhara naam kya hai,
Basanti?

Yeh haath nahin, phansi ka fanda hai!
Basanti! In kutton ke saamne mat nachna!!!

he worked in a travel agency in Calcutta, in a restaurant in Dhaka, as a waiter in Bangkok, and as a jewellery salesman in Delhi.

Rao's Taekwondo Skills

Bollywood actor Rajkummar Rao's real name was Rajkumar Yadav. The actor has some serious martial arts skills, having been formally trained in taekwondo! Here's hoping someone reads this and casts him in an out-and-out action film.

Kareena Kapoor's Unique Name

Kareena Kapoor Khan, who's also known as Bebo in Bollywood circles, was originally named Siddhima. But her mother Babita read the Leo Tolstoy classic *Anna Karenina* when she was pregnant and decided to name her daughter Kareena.

Software Engineer-Turned-Actress

Bollywood actress Taapsee Pannu worked as a software engineer before making her acting debut. She holds a degree in computer science engineering and has also developed an app named 'FontSwap'. Shabash Taapsee!

Katrina's Transition

When she was just fourteen years old, Katrina Kaif won a beauty contest in Hawaii. Then she became a successful model, which opened the doors of Bollywood for this beautiful actress.

Raveena, Kargil War, and the Bomb

In the 1999 Kargil War, some soldiers wrote 'From Raveena Tandon to Nawaz Sharif' on some IAF bombs that were to be used in the war. This was because Sharif had once mentioned in an interview that Raveena was his favourite actress.

His Idol's Slipper

Bollywood actor Pankaj Tripathi worked as a chef at Patna's Hotel Maurya before his eventual struggle and rise in Bollywood.

Once, he met his idol, actor Manoj Bajpayee, there. Tripathi kept the slipper that Bajpayee had forgotten in his hotel room as a souvenir.

Amazing Facts about the Chess Players (*Shatranj Ke Khilari*)

- Satyajit Ray adapted Munshi Premchand's short story for the only Hindi film he made. *Shatranj Ke Khilari* (1977) had stars like Sanjeev Kumar, Saeed Jaffrey, and Shabana Azmi. It also had Amitabh Bachchan doing the narration.
- The film won National Awards for 'Best Feature Film in Hindi' and 'Best Cinematography' (Soumendu Roy). It also won Filmfare Awards for 'Best Director' (Ray), 'Best Supporting Actor' (Saeed Jaffrey), and 'Critics Award for Best Film'.
- The best performance in *Shatranj Ke Khilari* (1977) surprisingly came from Amjad Khan, playing Nawab Wajid Ali Khan to exquisite perfection. It is strange how Ray had visualized Amjad Khan in this role as he was fresh off Gabbar Singh in *Sholay* (1975).
- Shabana Azmi was so thrilled to work with one of her favourite directors that she did not even ask about the script or remuneration. She said, 'If Manik-da had asked me to take a broom and sweep the set from one corner to another, I would have happily done it.'

- Amitabh Bachchan who did the voice-over for the film regrets not getting an opportunity to work with the legend as an actor. But he was proud to be associated with a film by Ray as a voice-over artist.
- The nocturnal Sanjeev Kumar was too busy thinking how to wake up at dawn to shoot for the film to be thinking about anything else. Somehow, he managed to wake up at a time when he normally went to bed. It was a Satyajit Ray movie after all!

Highest-Paid Bollywood Actress

Deepika Padukone is the only actress in Bollywood who has been paid a sum of over ten crore rupees for a film. Apparently, she was paid thirteen crores for *Padmaavat* (2018), which was the highest among the whole cast as she played the titular character. Thanks to her back-to-back hits, Deepika is the highest-paid actress in Bollywood, with a reported net worth of ₹500 crores.

Aishwarya Rai Bachchan

Linguist Beauty

Aishwarya Rai Bachchan can speak as many as six languages, including English and Hindi. The linguist south Indian beauty can fluently speak Tulu and Tamil. She learnt Marathi in school in Bombay and speaks a little Bengali having portrayed Bengali characters in films like *Devdas* (2002), *Chokher Bali* (2003), and *Raincoat* (2004).

Never Give Up

Vidya Balan underwent a lot of struggle to taste success. A Tamil producer rejected her, and Malayalam film *Charam* opposite Mohanlal was shelved. Vidya went through forty screen tests and seventeen make-up shoots before finally being selected for her first film. Today, she's one of the finest in Bollywood.

Lolo

Karisma Kapoor's nickname Lolo is a shortened version of Italian star Gina Lollobrigida's last name. Karisma's mother Babita was a big fan of this Italian actress.

Like Grandfather like Grandson

Ranbir Kapoor shares his grandfather Raj Kapoor's real name (Ranbir) and has a black-and-white picture of Raj Kapoor in his living room. However, Ranbir's favourite actor is Al Pacino, and Ranbir chose to study at the Lee Strasberg Institute only because it was Al Pacino's alma mater.

The First Family of Bollywood

The Kapoors have been the first family of Bollywood for eight decades and four generations. The foundation was laid by Prithviraj Kapoor and continued by Raj, Shammi, and Shashi Kapoor. The third generation featured Raj's sons Randhir, Rajiv, and Rishi. The fourth generation has Randhir's daughters Karisma and Kareena, and Rishi's son Ranbir.

Taxi

In the mid-1970s, Shashi Kapoor signed most films offered to him because he needed money for Prithvi Theatre's stage shows. He had so many films on his plate that he had to shuttle between film sets throughout the day, prompting elder brother Raj Kapoor to give him the nickname 'Taxi.'

Dilip Kumar and Saira Banu

Dilip Kumar was reluctant to have Saira Banu as his co-star because he thought she was too young to be his leading lady. Well, that didn't stop him from marrying her. Dilip Kumar was forty-four and Saira Banu was twenty-two when they got married.

Dilip Kumar's Wedding

Dilip Kumar's wedding was one of the most elaborate and glamorous events of its time in Bollywood. The groom's procession was led by none other than the three stalwarts of Bollywood in those days: Prithviraj Kapoor, Raj Kapoor, and Dev Anand.

The Idea for *Anand*

Hrishikesh Mukherjee got the idea to make his classic film *Anand* (1971) after his dear friend actor-director Raj Kapoor fell seriously ill and he was haunted by the thoughts of his death.

Bobby (1973)

Cinema often borrows from real life, and Bollywood is no exception. In the film *Bobby* the scene where Rishi Kapoor met Dimple Kapadia at her house was inspired by the real-life meeting between Raj Kapoor and Nargis.

Theatre Colleagues

Bollywood actors Shashi Kapoor and Utpal Dutt acted in theatre together. They were part of the theatre group Shakespeareana, run by Shashi's would-be father-in-law Geoffrey Kendal.

Rishi Kapoor's Bollywood Debut

Twenty-one-year-old Rishi Kapoor made his Bollywood debut

Amazing Facts about Shammi Kapoor

- Shammi Kapoor wanted to be an aeronautical engineer before he abandoned the idea to join the theatre and then films.
- He hit jackpot as a hero after shaving off his moustache.
- Shammi Kapoor was a good singer and is also credited as the first dancing hero of Bollywood.

in *Bobby* (1973) only because his father, director Raj Kapoor, was broke at the time after *Mera Naam Joker* (1970) had flopped and could not afford another hero. Over time, twenty new actresses, from Dimple Kapadia to Divya Bharti, made their debuts opposite Rishi Kapoor.

Rishi Faces the Camera as a Toddler

Technically, Rishi Kapoor made his first Bollywood appearance as a toddler in the hit song 'Pyaar Hua Ikrar Hua' from *Shree 420* (1955) along with his brother Randhir and sister Ritu. But Rishi was so small that Nargis had to bribe him with chocolates so that he would shoot properly.

Most Nominations for Best Actor

Actors Dilip Kumar and Shah Rukh Khan have a combined total of eight Filmfare Awards for Best Actor. However, Amitabh Bachchan holds the title for most nominations by being nominated thirty-four times for this Filmfare category.

What's in a Name?

Sridevi was the first female superstar of Bollywood. But her real name was not Sridevi. She was born as Shree Amma Yanger Ayyappan. She had actually adopted the on-screen name Shreedevi, which became Sridevi after a spelling error, which she allowed to continue.

The Great Actor/Director

Utpal Dutt was a great theatre actor and director. He joined English theatre as a student and joined Geoffrey Kendal's Shakespeareana Company later. Soon, he founded the Little Theatre Group, producing English and Bengali plays. Utpal Dutt could speak six languages fluently, including German, Spanish, and Latin, besides English, Hindi, and his mother tongue Bengali.

Amazing Facts about Amitabh Bachchan

- Amitabh Bachchan was the first living Asian celebrity to have a wax model dedicated to him at Madame Tussaud's, London.
- His majestic baritone voice caused his rejection at All India Radio.
- Before entering the film industry, Amitabh worked in Calcutta, first in the coal department of a Calcutta company in 1962 and then as an executive of a British managing agency, Blackers Company, drawing a salary of ₹1,640. His first car was a second-hand Fiat.

Utpal Dutt's Entry into Films

Utpal Dutt's entry into the movies happened when film-maker Madhu Bose came to watch his play *Othello*. He was impressed by Dutt and offered him the lead role in his film based on the life of Michael Madhusudan Dutt. Thus began an impressive career in both Hindi and Bengali films.

Amol Palekar's Bollywood Debut

Bombay-born actor-director Amol Palekar was a banker before he became an actor. Palekar made his acting debut in 1971 with the Marathi film *Shantata! Court Chalu Aahe*. Three years later, he made his Bollywood debut with Basu Chatterjee's *Rajnigandha* (1974), which won the Filmfare Award for Best Film.

The Debut of Two Stars in One Film

Utpal Dutt's debut Hindi film was *Saat Hindustani* (1969), which was also Amitabh Bachchan's first film. Utpal Dutt played a Sikh military man, and the film was based on the liberation of Goa from the Portuguese. The seven ethnic classes depicted in the film symbolized India as a whole.

The Middle-Class Hero

After his successful debut film, Amol Palekar delivered hit after hit. The popular 'slice of life' genre was initiated by his movies like *Chitchor* (1976), *Gharaonda* (1977) and *Gol Maal* (1979), among others. He carved a new identity for himself with a hero-next-door image compared to the larger-than-life image of his contemporary heroes. He was the first hero representing the middle-class.

The Oddball Pair

Amol Palekar and Utpal Dutt formed an oddball pair in Bollywood that was the perfect foil to the angry-young-man movies. The genius of Hrishikesh Mukherjee brought them together in *Gol Maal* (1979) to spark off a unique creative partnership in Hindi comedy movies.

Actor-Turned-Director

Hindi cinema lost the actor Amol Palekar when he decided to concentrate solely on direction. Palekar made his directorial debut in 1981 with the Marathi film *Aakrit.* His Hindi film *Paheli* (2005) received an Oscar nomination, and he has also been appointed the chairman of India's Oscar jury.

Internet-Savvy Hero

The first internet-savvy Bollywood star was Shammi Kapoor who founded the Internet Users Community of India. But rumours that connected him to Yahoo mail (thanks to the 'Chahe Koi Mujhe Junglee Kahe' song where he screams Yahoo!) are absolutely false.

Lucky Mascot

Shammi Kapoor was the lucky mascot for actresses like Asha Parekh, Sharmila Tagore, and Saira Banu, who all made their on-screen Bollywood debuts opposite him in *Dil Deke Dekho* (1959), *Kashmir Ki Kali* (1964), and *Junglee* (1961) respectively and went on to become big stars.

Ambidextrous Big B

Veteran Bollywood star Amitabh Bachchan has a unique talent. Big B is ambidextrous when it comes to writing. That means he can write equally well with both hands.

Naseer Said No to Dumbledore

Bollywood actor Naseeruddin Shah was asked to audition for the role of Albus Dumbledore in the Harry Potter film franchise. But he declined as he was not so keen on doing the role. Wonder if he regrets it now since the movies became so big.

Aamir's Passion

Aamir Khan's parents wanted him to pursue engineering instead of joining Bollywood. They also faced a financial crisis because of the failure of his father's production house. But when Aamir got his first break, he would go for shooting pretending he was going to a hockey match.

And Then One Day

Veteran Bollywood actor Naseeruddin Shah published his autobiography *And Then One Day: A Memoir* in 2014. Interestingly, he had started writing this in diary form as a hobby. It was author/historian Ramachandra Guha who urged him to get it published after reading it.

The Best Bollywood Dancer

Bollywood actress Madhuri Dixit is a trained Kathak dancer. She is the only actress of her times to have been choreographed by the great Kathak exponent Pandit Birju Maharaj. He paid her a compliment saying that she was the best dancer in Bollywood.

Sridevi Declines Hollywood Offer

Sridevi was approached for a small role in acclaimed Hollywood director Steven Spielberg's film *Jurassic Park* (1993). But she had refused as the small role did not do justice to her stature in Indian cinema at the time.

Naseer Loses Out to Ben

Naseeruddin Shah wanted to play the role of Mahatma Gandhi in film-maker Richard Attenborough's international project *Gandhi* (1982). Naseeruddin auditioned for the role, but it went to Ben Kingsley.

Dubbing for Sridevi

During Sridevi's early years in Bollywood, other actresses had to dub for her because she found it tough to speak proper Hindi.

Rekha dubbed for Sridevi in *Aakhree Raasta* (1986) and former actress Naaz dubbed for her in a few movies.

Die-Hard Madhuri Fan

In a crazy incident, a fan of Bollywood actress Madhuri Dixit from Jamshedpur once appealed to the government to declare her birthday a national holiday. He also created a calendar where the new year began with her birthday. That's the Bollywood fan of the decade!

Madhuri Dixit Fast Facts

- Madhuri has a degree in microbiology and had no initial interest in a Bollywood career.
- Her first film was *Abodh* (1984), but she struck gold with *Tezaab* (1988).
- She wore a costume weighing 30 kg for a song in *Devdas* (2002).

Madhuri Dixit Nene

Mammoth *Lagaan*

The Aamir Khan starrer *Lagaan* was one of the highest-grossing Bollywood movies of 2001. But the first cut of the movie was almost seven-and-a-half hours long, and it must have taken a Herculean effort by the editors to cut to its current length on the edit table.

Positive and Negative

Even though Sunil Dutt played the leading man in Bollywood, he also played a Bollywood baddie many times early on in his career. Sunil Dutt has played the role of a dacoit in several Hindi movies.

Suraiya Fan

Bollywood star Dharmendra was such a huge fan of actress Suraiya that he walked miles to watch her film *Dillagi* that released in 1949. Dharmendra watched the movie over more than thirty times.

Choli Ke Peeche

When the Sunjay Dutt–Madhuri Dixit starrer Bollywood movie *Khalnayak* (1993) released, its infamous and controversial song 'Choli Ke Peeche' was protested by as many as forty-two Indian political parties. Despite that, the song and the movie were both superhits.

The Discovery of Smita Patil

Smita Patil was a newsreader on Doordarshan, Pune, and was also an accomplished photographer before being discovered by director Shyam Benegal. She went on to act in over eighty Hindi, Bengali, Gujarati, Malayalam, Marathi, and Kannada and Marathi films in a career that lasted over a decade.

Bhumika

In 1977, Smita Patil won the National Award for Best Actress for *Bhumika* directed by Shyam Benegal. The film was awarded the Golden Plaque in the 1978 Chicago Film Festival. Smita donated the money from her National Award to charity. She was an active feminist and a member of the Women's Centre in Bombay.

The Young Guns of India

Rang De Basanti (2006) took some time before its title was finalized. It was initially named 'Ahuti' and then 'The Young

Guns of India' before the present name was frozen. It took time for A.R. Rehman to compose the music too. He took three years to finish the soundtrack.

Karisma Gets Lucky

Actress Karisma Kapoor got lucky when Aishwarya Rai declined *Raja Hindustani* (1996) opposite Aamir Khan because of her Miss World commitments. Karisma grabbed what was supposed to be Ash's Bollywood debut, which became one of the biggest hits of Karisma's career. Ash went on to win Miss World too.

The Bollywood Soap Collector

Bollywood superstar Salman Khan is a soap collector. His bathroom features a collection of all kinds of herbal and handmade soaps. But Salman's favourite soaps are those made from natural fruit and vegetable extracts. Now we know why Salman likes spending so much time in the shower!

Mogambo Khush Hua

Amrish Puri playing the evil army general Mogambo in *Mr. India* (1987) is one of the most memorable villainous performances in Bollywood history. The catchphrase *'Mogambo khush hua'* is still a rage. To prepare for the role, Puri locked himself in a room for twenty days, where even sunlight couldn't enter.

Indiana Jones and the Temple of Doom (1984)

Amrish Puri in the Temple of Doom

Amrish Puri worked on a Hollywood project to impress one of the greatest film-makers of all time. He played the role of Mola Ram in *Indiana Jones and the Temple of Doom* (1984), impressing director Steven Spielberg so much that he called Puri his favourite villain. Now, that's some compliment!

Jeevan Sangram

In 1914, a ship named Komagata Maru, with more than 375 Indians aboard, was not allowed to enter Canada due to harsh immigration laws. This ship returned to India, where the British police gunned down the Indian passengers. The 1974 film *Jeevan Sangram* was based on this real-life story.

Dilip Kumar's Salary

Devika Rani of Bombay Talkies saw the potential in Dilip Kumar and offered him the job of an actor on a salary of ₹1,250. Initially, Dilip Kumar thought it was his annual salary and was surprised to realize later that it was his monthly salary.

Dil Bhi Tera Hum Bhi Tere

Dharmendra's fee when he made his debut in 1960 in the movie *Dil Bhi Tera Hum Bhi Tere* was only ₹51. We wonder if Dharmendra repeated the title of the movie when he was offered this sum as his salary.

The Poster Boy

Aamir Khan's debut *Qayamat Se Qayamat Tak* (1988) had such a small budget that Aamir Khan and Raj Zutshi had to paste the posters of the film on taxis and autorickshaws themselves to promote it. As he did so, Aamir introduced himself to random strangers as the hero of the film.

The Masala Film Genre

Director–producer Manmohan Desai has been credited for inventing the 'masala film' genre in Bollywood. His biggest hit was *Amar Akbar Anthony* (1977), which was also Desai's first film as producer. *Amar Akbar Anthony* was remade in Telugu as *Ram Robert Rahim* (1980) and in Malayalam as *John Jaffer Janardhanan* (1982).

Amazing *Amar Akbar Anthony* Facts

Mirror, Mirror on the Wall...

During the famous mirror scene, Manmohan Desai was shooting the climax of *Parvarish* (1977) on another floor of the same studio. Amitabh Bachchan shot the scene as he rehearsed in the director's absence. When Manmohan Desai saw the scene later, he became a lifelong fan of Amitabh Bachchan.

Appearances Can Be Deceptive

Flashback to 1972 when Manmohan Desai was introduced to Amitabh Bachchan by Salim–Javed. Desai was unimpressed with what he saw and jokingly remarked, 'The only role I will offer him is a chicken roll.' Five years later, Desai had to eat his words and also the chicken roll.

Big B Big in the West Indies

Amar Akbar Anthony (1977) was the biggest hit in Manmohan Desai's career, and Amitabh received his first Best Actor award. The film was also a massive hit in the Caribbean Islands as Big B became a superstar there. The film ran houseful for months as Indians and non-Indians flocked to the theatres.

Four Legends, One Song

The music of *Amar Akbar and Anthony* (1977) was special. But the song that was super-special was 'Humko Tumse Ho Gaya Hai Pyaar'. It was unique as the musical legends Lata Mangeshkar, Kishore Kumar, Mohammed Rafi, and Mukesh all lent their voices to it. This was the only time when all four legends sang together.

Disraeli Gears

The line spoken by Amitabh – 'sophisticated rhetorician intoxicated with the exuberance of your own verbosity' – is similar to a quotation from a speech given in 1878 by Benjamin Disraeli, former British prime minister. However, Disraeli had used the word 'inebriated' instead of 'intoxicated'.

Jackson's Blues

Unbelievably, Manmohan Desai got the idea for the film while browsing through the newspaper! He read about a drunk named Jackson, who decided to dump his three children in the park. In the beginning of the film, we see Pran's character abandoning his three sons in a park.

The Lonely Hero

Although Vinod Khanna is four years younger than Amitabh Bachchan, he played his elder brother in the film. Khanna's character initially did not have a heroine. But Khanna kept pestering Desai as both Amitabh and Rishi Kapoor had leading ladies. Desai finally gave in and signed Shabana Azmi opposite Vinod Khanna.

My Name is Anthony Gonsalves

The character of Anthony Gonsalves was originally called Anthony Fernandes. But music director Pyarelal decided to pay tribute to his music teacher, a famous arranger and also R.D. Burman's music teacher. Pyarelal suggested the name Anthony Gonsalves, which was accepted. Laxmikant – Pyarelal then composed the song, 'My name is Anthony Gonsalves'.

PK (2014)

Bollywood film *PK* had a paanwala on set every day as long as the shoot commenced. That was because Aamir Khan had to eat 10–15 betel leaves before each shot to get the perfect red colour around his lips as his character demanded.

SRK's Phobia

With *Pathaan* (2023) fever riding high and the Shah Rukh Khan starrer becoming the highest grosser in Bollywood history (until taken over by *Jawan* in 2023 only), an interesting phobia of the star comes to mind. Shah Rukh has a phobia of riding horses. The real Pathaans will be disappointed to hear that as they love riding horses.

Brimful of Asha

Hip-hop group the 'Black Eyed Peas' said that their hit song 'Don't Phunk with My Heart' was inspired by not one but two Bollywood songs: 'Ye Mera Dil Yaar Ka Diwana', (*Don* 1978) and 'Aye Naujawan Hai Sub Kuchh Yaahan' (*Apradh* 1972). Both songs were sung by the great Asha Bhosle.

Bollywood Rocks in Hollywood Land

North America generates 25 per cent of Bollywood's overseas box office revenue, making it a big market for Bollywood. According to Yash Raj Films, one of India's largest production houses and distributors, Bollywood films earn around $100 million annually in America alone.

Chetna (1970)

The film *Chetna* caused instant controversy upon its release as it depicted an alcoholic, foul-mouthed prostitute. It appears that the film was way ahead of its times, and actress Rehana Sultan admitted that the film permanently damaged her image and career.

The Guru of Hindi Cinema

In a significant achievement, actor–director Guru Dutt was ranked No. 73 in Sight and Sound's critics' and directors' poll of the greatest film-makers in the world in 2002.

The Wedding Videographer

Aamir Khan is a good friend of Twinkle Khanna, and the two shared screen space in *Mela* (2000). When Twinkle married Akshay Kumar in a low-key wedding ceremony in 2001, Aamir decided to act as the official videographer for his friend and captured each moment of the ceremony.

Sholay's Run

Sholay (1975) was nominated for nine Filmfare Awards after its release but only managed to win one award. M.S. Shinde won the award for Best Editing. *Sholay* lost out to *Deewar* that was also released in 1975. In Minerva theatre of Bombay, *Sholay* ran uninterrupted for over five years.

Amazing Facts of Sholay

- *Sholay* (1975) was shot in a town called Ramanagara, about 50km from Bangalore. It is still called Ramgarh because *Sholay* was shot there.
- Amitabh Bachchan married Jaya Bhaduri four months before the shoot.
- Sanjeev Kumar proposed marriage to Hema Malini before the shoot, but she married Dharmendra five years after Sholay's release.

A Long Wait

Twenty-two-year-old Amrish Puri started working as a clerk at a government insurance company after he was rejected in an audition. Theatre director Ebrahim Alkazi convinced him to join theatre. Puri was thirty-eight years old when he got his first film break with *Prem Pujari* (1970) and left his government job.

Unlikely Cousins

The iconic singer K.L. Saigal is the first cousin of the legendary Bollywood villain Amrish Puri. K.L. Saigal's mother was the sister of Amrish Puri's father, S. Nihal Singh Puri. The first has inspired countless musicians, and the second has inspired several anti-heroes in Bollywood.

Bollywood's Tryst with Foreign Locations

Hirendra Kumar Basu's *Afreeka Mein Hind/India in Africa* (1939) was the first Indian movie ever to be shot at a foreign location – Africa, in this case. This was followed by S.K. Ojha's

Naaz (1954), starring Ashok Kumar, which was shot in Cairo, Egypt and London, UK.

But it was the Raj Kapoor–Rajendra Kumar–Vyjayanthimala starrer triangular love story *Sangam* (1964) that made shooting at foreign locations a popular trend. It was shot extensively in European locales. The Indian audiences turned up in theatres in large numbers mainly to see the foreign locales in the movie.

India's First Oscar Submission

The epic drama *Mother India* (1957) starring Nargis, Sunil Dutt, and Rajendra Kumar was India's first submission for the Academy Awards in the foreign film category. The movie did not win but earned a place in the final five as the Oscar jury strongly connected with the film.

Do Ankhen Barah Haath (1957)

The first Hindi film to win the prestigious Golden Globe Award was *Do Ankhen Barah Haath* directed by V. Shantaram. It won the Samuel Goldwyn International Film Award for best film produced outside of the United States. It also won a Silver Bear at the 8th Berlin International Film Festival.

From Russia with Love

The most successful foreign film at the Soviet box office was the Hindi film *Shree 420* (1955) starring Raj Kapoor and Nargis. It became the first foreign film to successfully draw an audience of an astonishing thirty-five million viewers at the Soviet box office. The Russians love Raj Kapoor for sure!

Bollywood Music Goes International

'Awaara Hoon' was the first Hindi film song to become an international sensation. The catchy composition from musical duo Shankar–Jaikishan struck an instant chord with global audiences from various classes and backgrounds. In a BBC poll conducted in May 2013, it was rated the second-greatest Bollywood song of all time.

A Rare Pairing

The two greatest performers of their era, Dilip Kumar and Nutan, strangely shared screen space for only one movie. In 1986, they were paired for the first and only time in *Karma*. They had been paired together years ago in a movie called 'Shikwa' but sadly, the project was shelved.

Nutan's Filmfare Fiver

Actress Nutan solely held the record for winning the most Filmfare Awards for Best Actress, until she was joined by Kajol and later, Alia Bhatt. She won the award five times for the movies *Seema* (1955), *Sujata* (1959), *Bandini* (1963), *Milan* (1967), and *Main Tulsi Tere Aangan Ki* (1978).

A New Life Begins at Forty

When Nutan won her fifth Filmfare Award for Best Actress, she created yet another record. She became the oldest winner of the award at forty-two when she won for *Main Tulsi Tere Aangan Ki* (1978).

The First Superstar of Hindi Cinema

Rajesh Khanna was the first superstar in the Hindi film industry and was affectionately called Kaka. Between 1969 and 1971, Rajesh Khanna gave fifteen consecutive solo superhit films. That coined the famous Bollywood saying: 'Upar Aaka aur Niche Kaka' (God rules Heaven and Rajesh Khanna rules Earth).

Hero by Chance

Kumudlal Kunjilal Ganguly became popularly known as Ashok Kumar after he became a movie star totally by accident. He was a lab assistant with Bombay Talkies and got a lucky break as the leading man in *Jeevan Naiya* (1936) when the film's hero Najmul Hassan eloped with heroine Devika Rani.

Struggle in Style

Rajesh Khanna belonged to an affluent family, and a car was always available for him. When owning a car was a dream for actors who were working in films, Rajesh Khanna would travel by car to audition for films and look for work while other actors used public transport.

Two Painful Incidents in Nutan's Life

Two incidents in Nutan's life caused the actress a lot of pain. The first was when she had to drag her own mother to court for mismanaging her funds. It was a difficult decision, but Nutan took it for her family. Thankfully, they patched up after 1983.

The second incident occurred when Nutan slapped Sanjeev Kumar in everyone's presence. Nutan was always careful not to get caught up in any sort of controversy. When she discovered that Sanjeev Kumar was spreading rumours about their alleged affair, she was furious as nothing existed between the two.

Hit Song of *Sholay*

The famous song of *Sholay* (1975) titled 'Yeh Dosti Hum Nahi Todenge' featuring Amitabh Bachchan and Dharmendra as Jai and Veeru took twenty-one days to shoot. Nowadays, some films are shot in that kind of schedule. Good things certainly take time!

Pathaan: Bollywood's 100-Country Release

In 2009, *Jodhaa Akbar* was released in twenty-six countries, which was then the largest Bollywood worldwide release to date. Cut to 25 January 2023 when the SRK starrer *Pathaan* was released in over a hundred countries. Bollywood's come a long way baby!

Bollywood Box Office

In 2009, a comparison of box office collections between Hollywood and Bollywood movies indicated that Bollywood was more popular than Hollywood in terms of theatre collections. Bollywood tickets sold worldwide in 2009 numbered 3.6 billion, while Hollywood movies sold 2.6 billion tickets.

Superstardom

After Rajesh Khanna and Dimple Kapadia got married, a short video of their wedding was shown in theatres across India just before the film *Bobby* started. Strictly for Rajesh Khanna fans of course!

The First Movie to Gross One Crore Rupees

The first anti-hero of Hindi cinema was Ashok Kumar. He played a pickpocket who fell in love in Gyan Mukherjee's *Kismet* (1943). *Kismet* was the first Indian film that grossed one crore rupees at the box office. So technically, Ashok Kumar started the famous 'crore club' of Bollywood.

Pushpaka Vimana

Kamal Hassan starrer *Pushpaka Vimana* or *Pushpak* (1987) was India's first silent full-length feature film in the talkie era. This extremely watchable dark comedy directed by Singeetam Srinivasa Rao has a unique plot featuring an unemployed youth, and is both subtle and intelligent in its treatment.

The First Indian 'Guess Girl'

In 2018, actress Priyanka Chopra created fashion history when she became the first Indian 'Guess Girl' – the only Indian woman to be a brand ambassador for the iconic brand. Guess what? She also joined the legacy of Guess girls like Claudia Schiffer, Adriana Lima, and Anna Nicole Smith.

Gym Star

Bollywood actresses today sweat it out in the gym to get that perfect toned body. But the actress who started the gym trend in Bollywood is Rekha. She is the first actress in Bollywood to have enrolled herself in the basic swimming and exercise class in the gym located at Ramee International Hotel.

Super Singer

The talented actress Rekha loves singing and does a good job of it. In her movie *Khoobsoorat* (1980), she hummed two songs at the request of legendary music director R.D. Burman. Rekha also performed onstage on the reality TV show *The Indian Idol*.

Piggy Chops

Another famous actress who can hum a cool tune is Priyanka Chopra. After winning Miss World and making it big in both Bollywood and Hollywood, Priyanka has also shown her mettle as an international pop star. Shine on you crazy Chopra!

Sanjeev Kumar's Real-Life Love Story

Sanjeev Kumar fell in love with the married Nutan but after being slapped in public, he quickly fell out of love. He fell for Hema Malini next and wanted to marry her. But Hema's mother put her foot down because of his love for drinking and non-veg food. Wonder how she agreed to Hema's marriage with Dharmendra!

Although Sanjeev Kumar lost Hema Malini to Dharmendra, he kept avoiding marriage with the one person who was head over heels in love with him. She was none other than actress Sulakshana Pandit.

The Ruthless Professional

Guru Dutt made extremely sensitive films but was ruthlessly professional. When he was shooting *Baharein Phir Bhi Ayengi* (1966), music director S.D. Burman had a heart attack, and Guru Dutt immediately replaced him with O.P. Nayyar. Dev Anand, who was shooting *Guide* (1965) at the same time, postponed his shoot till S.D. Burman recovered.

R.D. Burman's Debut as Music Director

Legendary Bollywood actor, comedian, director, and producer Mehmood gave another legend his musical break when he signed R.D. Burman as music director for his film *Chhote Nawab* (1961). This led to the development of a close friendship that lasted a lifetime.

From Kollywood to Bollywood to Hollywood

Priyanka Chopra did not make her acting debut in Bollywood. Her debut movie was the 2002 Tamil film *Thamizhan*, co-starring Vijay. Today, she's a global star. Her Hollywood career began with the TV show *Quantico* (2015) and with movies like *Baywatch* (2017) and *Isn't It Romantic* (2019).

Salaam Bombay!

Director Mira Nair's 1988 film *Salaam Bombay!* dealt with the subject of Bombay's street kids and their lives. The film won the Caméra d'Or at the Cannes Film Festival and was also nominated for an Oscar for Best Foreign Language Film.

To Sign Rajesh Khanna

Once, Bollywood superstar Rajesh Khanna was admitted to the hospital for a minor operation. To sign him for their movie whenever the opportunity presented itself, several producers booked rooms around Kaka's hospital room.

The Padukone Factor

Actress Deepika Padukone and director Guru Dutt both hail from Karnataka's Chitrapur Saraswat Brahmin community. The two even share the same surname as Guru Dutt was born Vasanth Kumar Shivsankar Padukone. But his family changed his name to Guru Dutt due to superstition following a childhood accident.

Fast Facts About Sanjeev Kumar

- Sanjeev Kumar's original name was Harihar Jethalal Jariwala. He was popularly known as Haribhai in the Hindi film industry.
- He has acted in regional films in Marathi, Punjabi, Tamil, Telugu, Sindhi, and his mother tongue Gujarati.
- His signature dress was white pants, a white kurta, and matching white chappals.

The Novelization of *Shalimar*

Bollywood film-makers have released successful comic books based on movies like *Krrish* (2006) and *Dhoom* (2004). This was termed as excellent marketing strategy. But it was writer Manohar Malgonkar, who first adapted Krishna Shah's *Shalimar* (1978) into a novel.

Dilip Kumar's Humble Beginnings

Before he became an actor in Hindi movies, Dilip Kumar ran a sandwich stall at the Army Club in Poona. When his contract ended, he returned to Bombay, having saved ₹5000 in the process.

Raj Kapoor in Baku

Raj Kapoor was so popular in Azerbaijan that millions of fans gathered to have a glimpse of their favourite star when he visited the capital Baku in 1956. This is understandable because Azerbaijan was a part of the Soviet Union from 1920 to 1991, where Raj Kapoor's popularity was unparalleled.

Bollywood in Azerbaijan

The name Nargis is most popular for girls in Azerbaijan. Dr Tamerlan Qarayev, ambassador of Azerbaijan, said, 'We have literally grown up watching Hindi movies. Even today Raj Kapoor, Amitabh Bachchan, and Mithun Chakraborty are legends in Azerbaijan. We wholeheartedly accepted the Indian culture as a part of our own.'

Influence of Azerbaijan

Azerbaijan also impacted Bollywood and Indian culture strongly. The popular tale of Laila–Majnu is an Indian rendition of 'Layla and Majnun' written by famous Azerbaijani poet Nizami Ganjavi in the twelfth century.

Dev Anand's Inspiration

Ashok Kumar inspired Dev Anand to become an actor. Dev Anand considered acting as a career after watching *Achhut Kanya* (1936). Ashok Kumar also gave Dev Anand his first movie break. It is said he spotted Dev Anand on the sets and took him in for the Bombay Talkies production *Ziddi* (1948).

Danger Diabolic

When Amitabh Bachchan was struggling in Bombay, Mehmood offered him shelter at his own house. Mehmood also offered Amitabh the hero's role in *Bombay to Goa* (1972). After watching this film Salim–Javed picked Amitabh for *Zanjeer* (1973). Mehmood had an interesting nickname for Amitabh. In an interview, Amitabh admitted that for 'some peculiar reason', Mehmood called him 'Danger Diabolic'.

The Dev Anand–Suraiya Romance

The Dev Anand–Suraiya romance not only lit up the screen with its charm and chemistry but in real life too. Media reports stated that their romance blossomed on the sets of *Vidya* (1948). While shooting a scene on a boat, it capsized, and Dev Anand rescued

Dev Anand

Suraiya in true Bollywood style.

Dev Anand and Suraiya fell in love, and Dev proposed to her on the sets of *Jeet* (1949) with a diamond ring worth ₹3,000 – a huge sum those days. But the marriage could not happen as Suraiya's maternal grandmother strongly opposed the inter-religious match. Suraiya remained unmarried all her life.

Death of an Icon

In 1964, Guru Dutt apparently committed suicide while directing and acting in *Baharen Phir Bhi Ayengi* (1966). Dharmendra replaced Guru Dutt, and the film was eventually released. Sanjeev Kumar replaced Guru Dutt in another incomplete film, *Love and God* (1986). Guru Dutt and Sanjeev Kumar were born on the same day and both died young.

The Death of Sanjeev Kumar

Sanjeev Kumar once revealed that no male member of his family lived beyond fifty. His father and younger brother had died at that age, and his youngest brother had died at thirty-six. It was like predicting his own death as Sanjeev Kumar passed away on 6 November 1985 from a heart attack at the age of just forty-seven!

Dedicated Female Fan Following

Although Rajesh Khanna was a superstar, the songs of music director R.D. Burman and singer Kishore Kumar played a huge part in his success. Rajesh Khanna was so popular among his female fans that he used to receive love letters written in blood. Many had his name tattooed on their body.

Mehmood's Promise to Kishore Kumar

When Mehmood asked good friend Kishore Kumar to recommend him for a role, Kishore Kumar joked, 'How can I give a chance to my competitor?'

Mehmood laughed and replied that he would cast Kishore Kumar when he became a big film-maker. True to his word, Mehmood cast Kishore Kumar in his home production *Padosan* (1968) years later.

Trees as Dancing Props

Bollywood features smart choreography today, and almost all the stars are good dancers. But decades earlier, many Bollywood stars were bad dancers and were made to use trees as a prop when they danced. No wonder we see so much of dancing around trees in the early Bollywood years.

Farooq Shaikh: The Teacher

Farooq Shaikh was a seasoned actor known for memorable roles in movies like *Chashme Buddoor* (1981), *Bazaar* (1982), and *Saath Saath* (1982). He was also known for hosting the talk-show *Jeena Isi Ka Naam Hai*. He and the singer Kavita Krishnamurti both went to St Xavier's College, Mumbai. When Kavita was worried about passing her economics exam, Farooq became her subject teacher and helped her through.

First Indian Woman Cinematographer

In a field dominated by men, B.R. Vijayalakshmi qualified as a cinematographer in 1981. Her first film was Bhagyaraj's *Chinna Veedu* (1985) in Tamil.

Amazing Facts About the Amazing Musical Duo Shankar–Jaikishan

Musical Differences

When the song 'Pyar Hua Ikrar Hua' from *Shree 420* (1955) was being recorded, there were creative differences between the talented musical duo Shankar–Jaikishan. When Shankar wanted to change the antara composed by Jaikishan, there was an argument that led to fisticuffs. Thankfully, other musicians intervened and calmed them down.

The Growing Rift

In the late 1960s, the rift between Shankar and Jaikishan widened mainly because of Shankar's preference for singer Sharda in place of Lata Mangeshkar. Raj Kapoor had to sit to mediate and make peace between the two maestros so that they could compose the music of *Mera Naam Joker* (1970).

Going Solo

Shankar and Jaikishan soon started taking independent contracts as music directors. Surprisingly, each credited the other, and the musical credits still went as Shankar–Jaikishan. In *Andaz* (1971), Jaikishan composed the entire music, but the musical credits went as Shankar–Jaikishan. Sadly, *Andaz* was Jaikishan's last work as he died in 1971.

The End
After Jaikishan's death, Shankar continued composing music under the Shankar–Jaikishan banner. But things were never the same, and the magic was missing without his partner and soulmate Jaikishan. With the exception of *Sanyasi* (1975), Shankar's music was a failure. Shankar passed away in 1987.

Dev Anand's Famous Cap

Dev Anand was arguably Bollywood's first style icon. His style statement included his famous checkered print cap that he wore in *Jewel Thief* (1967). The star bought this stylish cap in Copenhagen, Denmark, while he was shooting for *Pyar Mohabbat* (1966) with Saira Banu there.

Meghe Dhaka Tara (1960)

Legendary Bengali film-maker Ritwik Ghatak's classic film *Meghe Dhaka Tara* found a place in the list of 'The Greatest Films of All Time' by the British Film Institute.

Outbreak of Awards

Shabana Azmi won the National Award for Best Actress in 1974 for her first film *Ankur* (1974). From 1983 to 1985, she won the National Award thrice in a row for her performances in the films *Arth* (1982), *Khandhar* (1984), and *Paar* (1984).

Going International

Shabana Azmi won the Silver Hugo Award for Best Actress at the thirty-second Chicago Film Festival and the Jury Award for Best Actress at Outfest, Los Angeles, for *Fire* (1996). Her impressive list of international films include *Madame Sousatzka*

(1988), *The Bengali Night* (1988), *City of Joy* (1992), *Son of the Pink Panther* (1993), and *In Custody* (1993).

SRK's First Wages

One of the highest paid Bollywood superstars was paid just ₹50 for his first job. Shah Rukh Khan earned this money by being an usher for a Pankaj Udhas concert in Delhi. He utilized his first earnings to buy a train ticket to Agra to see the Taj Mahal.

Tragedy Queen

If Dilip Kumar was known as 'the tragedy king' of Hindi cinema, the term 'tragedy queen' was reserved for Meena Kumari. In the male-dominated industry of the 1950s, the powerful Meena Kumari stood out. Apart from being a great actress, she was also a poet and fashion trendsetter.

The Dragon Lady

The 1908-born Devika Rani was known as the 'Dragon Lady' because she lived life by her own rules. Her film *Karma* (1933) was the first Indian film to have a kissing scene. She eloped with an actor while still married in an era when Indian society was highly conservative.

Thalapathy

The 1994 release *Rasigan* was the Tamil movie that turned Vijay into a superstar and earned him the title of Thalapathy (Commander).

A.R. Rahman, the Musical Genius

A.R. Rahman is one of the greatest Indian composers and has composed music for over 150 films in various languages. His breakthrough moment arrived in 1992 when he composed the music of the Tamil film *Roja* directed by Mani Ratnam. Rahman won his first National Award for Best Music Director.

The Deaths of the Three Musical Legends

The three male Bollywood playback legends – Mohammed Rafi, Kishore Kumar, and Mukesh – lost their lives in their mid-fifties, experiencing a slump in their respective careers. All of them died of heart attack. Mukesh died in 1976 aged fifty-three, Rafi in 1980 aged fifty-five, and Kishore Kumar in 1987 aged fifty-eight.

A.R. Rahman Fast Facts

- A.R. Rahman was born as A.S. Dileep Kumar. He changed his name after converting to Islam.
- He began his music career aged eleven by playing the keyboard for famous south Indian composer Ilaiyaraaja.
- Rahman has won two Academy Awards, two Grammy Awards, a BAFTA Award, a Golden Globe Award, and fifteen Filmfare Awards.

The Last Waltz

Mohammed Rafi, Kishore Kumar, and Mukesh were all waiting for their musical comeback before they died. Ironically, they got the breaks they were looking for just before their deaths – Mukesh through *Kabhi Kabhie* (1976), Rafi through *Karz* (1980), and Kishore Kumar through *Mr India* (1987). Sadly, they did not live to witness their last success.

Mohammed Rafi's Major Break

Mohammed Rafi began his musical career in Hindi cinema as a

chorus singer in the 1940s. After working in several movies for the composer Naushad, Naushad became his mentor. He gave Rafi his major break in 1952 with *Baiju Bawra* that established him as a lead singer.

Exclusive Lyricist

Bollywood music directors R.D. Burman and Laxmikant–Pyarelal worked almost exclusively with lyricist Anand Bakshi in the 1970s and '80s. Anand Bakshi wrote the lyrics for the songs of ninety-nine films where R.D. Burman was the music director and the songs for 302 Laxmikant–Pyarelal films.

Kishore Kumar's Playback Career

The Bollywood music directors of the 1950s and '60s had no faith in Kishore Kumar's singing abilities except for S.D. Burman. Kishore Kumar became the leading playback singer of the industry only after 1969 with *Aradhana,* which proved to be a turning point in his career. Till then, he sang only in his own films and did playback for Dev Anand thanks to S.D. Burman.

R.D. Burman and Kishore Kumar's Partnership

The successful partnership of R.D. Burman's music and Kishore Kumar's singing almost damaged singer Mohammed Rafi's career. But Rafi earned his only National Award for best playback singer because of an R.D. Burman composition, 'Kya Hua Tera Wada'. Strangely, Kishore Kumar never won a National Award.

Kishore Kumar

Tribute to K.L. Saigal

The great K.L. Saigal was Kishore Kumar's idol. When HMV

offered Kishore Kumar the opportunity to sing the cover versions of K.L. Saigal's hit songs, Kishore Kumar declined politely. That was because Kishore Kumar did not want any of his fans to say that his rendition had excelled his guru's work.

The Vampish Nadira

Actress Nadira is remembered for her negative or vampish roles in old Hindi films. Nadira's real name was Florence Ezekiel, and she was born to a Baghdadi Jewish family in Bombay. Nadira was one of the highest-paid actresses of her time and one of the first actresses to own a Rolls Royce.

From Alda to Mala

Actress Mala Sinha hailed from a Nepali Christian family and her real name was Alda Sinha. She decided to change her name as she was often teased as 'Dalda' by her friends. She changed her name to Baby Nazma when she joined the movies as a child artiste and later to Mala Sinha.

REGIONAL CINEMA

After Hindi cinema, the box office revenue has been dominated by the Telugu and Tamil film industries. The Malayalam and Kannada film industries are next. The other prominent industries in Indian cinema are Bengali, Marathi, Gujarati, Punjabi, Bhojpuri, Odia, and Assamese.

South Indian Cinema

South Indian cinema describes the Tamil, Telugu, Kannada, and Malayalam film industries of south India. These four industries collectively produce more than 1,500 films annually, making it the largest film industry in India.

The First South Indian Film

The first south Indian film, *Keechaka Vadham* (1916), was based on an episode from the epic Mahabharata, where the second Pandava Bheema kills Keechaka. It was produced in Tamil Nadu by R. Nataraja Mudaliar.

First Full-Length South Indian Feature

The first full-length south Indian talkie was the Tamil movie *Kalidas* (1931), based on the life of the great ancient Indian poet.

First Telugu Film

The first full-length Telugu film was *Bhishma Pratigna*. It was produced by Raghupathi Venkaiah and released in 1921. Today, Telugu cinema produces more than three hundred films annually and is the second largest film market in India.

The First Kannada Talkie

Movies are classified according to their budgets today. But the first Kannada talkie *Sati Sulochana* that was produced as far back as 1934 only had a budget of ₹40,000.

The Visionaries of Telugu Cinema

Raghupathi Venkaiah Naidu was a film-maker and artiste who was a pioneer in Telugu cinema. Naidu was also the first to build and own cinema halls in Madras (now Chennai), the capital of Madras state (now Tamil Nadu). But Pothina Srinivasarao built the first theatre in Andhra Pradesh called Maruthi Talkies.

Sant Tukaram (1936)

Marathi film *Sant Tukaram* was the first Indian film to be screened at an international film festival. The film found a place at the prestigious Venice Film Festival in 1937 and was judged one of the three best films of the world that year. That's a phenomenal achievement.

Shyamchi Aai

The first movie to win the President's Gold Medal for the 'All India Best Feature Film' at the National Film Awards was legendary Marathi film *Shyamchi Aai* (1953), which was a mother-and-son story.

The Perfect Biopic of Tukaram

The Marathi film *Sant Tukaram* was directed by Sheikh Fattelal and Vishnupant Govind Damle. This biopic of Sant Tukaram (1568–1650), one of the greatest devotees of Vitthal (Lord Vishnu), released in 1936. It is an extraordinary film with the lead character excellently portrayed by theatre actor Vishnupant Pagnis.

The First Multilingual Film Song

Director Bibhuti Mitra's film *Shabnam* released in 1949. S.D. Burman composed possibly the first multilingual film song with stanzas in Bengali, Marathi, and Tamil, which informed the audience that they were all Indians first, and poked mild fun at the associated stereotypes. Indians were just discovering their immense diversity after Independence.

Maya Bazaar

The epic Telugu fantasy film *Maya Bazaar* (1957) was based on the Mahabharata and directed by Kadiri Venkata Reddy. For its time, the technical quotient it displayed was exemplary. It was also the first Telugu movie to be remastered and coloured in 2010.

Swayamvaram

Adoor Gopalakrishnan's directorial debut *Swayamvaram* (1972) pioneered the Malayalam new wave film movement. It was also one of the first Malayalam films to use synchronized sound and outdoor locales.

Ghatashraddha

National Award winner Girish Kasaravalli's film *Ghatashraddha* (1957) marked the entry of Kannada films into India's new-age cinema movement. The unique theme of the film was excommunication in an aristocratic Brahmin society.

Manthan (1976)

The film *Manthan* was directed by Shyam Benegal and produced by 500,000 farmers from the Indian state of Gujarat. The film entered the record books for being funded by the largest number of individuals.

Teenage Screen Mom

Actress Sridevi was only thirteen years old when she played Rajinikanth's stepmother in a Tamil film called *Moondru Mudichu* (1976).

The Biggest Movie Star

Arguably the biggest superstar of south Indian cinema, Rajinikanth is originally from Maharashtra. Born as a Marathi named Sivaji Rao Gaikwad, he moved to south India, where he was launched in Tamil cinema by K. Balachander. Rajinikanth is the most successful Indian movie star. Mind it!

From Movies to Politics

South Indian cinema fans literally worship their movie stars. Because of this adulation, as many as five cinema superstars and people associated with cinema have become the chief ministers of their respective states. They are M.G. Ramachandran (MGR), N.T. Ramarao (NTR), M. Karunanidhi, J. Jayalalithaa, and C.N. Annadurai. While MGR, NTR, and J. Jayalalithaa were actors, M. Karunanidhi and C.N. Anna Durai were scriptwriters.

Moondram Pirai (1982)

Balu Mahendra's romantic drama *Moondram Pirai* became a

cult film in Tamil cinema because of the combination of a unique film-making style and splendid performances by Kamal Haasan and Sridevi. The two leads also featured in the Hindi remake of the same movie named *Sadma* (1983). The pair collaborated for twenty-six movies.

Malayalam Classic

The Malayalam film *Amma Ariyan* (1986) was crowd-funded. Directed by John Abraham, it is the only Malayalam film to feature in the list of British Film Institute's Top 10 Indian Films of All Time. It is also the only south Indian film to share the honours with Indian films like *Pather Panchali* (1955), *Pyaasa* (1957), and *Sholay* (1975).

The Malayali Godfather

The 1991 Siddique–Lal comedy *Godfather* is the Malayalam movie with the longest theatrical run of all time. It ran for 417 days in Sreekumar Theatre in Thiruvananthapuram.

NTR

NTR is still revered as a demigod by many fans of Telugu cinema. His iconic portrayal of Lord Krishna and Lord Rama endeared him to the masses.

Shooting Underwater

Shankar Nag was the first Indian director to film a movie underwater. The Kannada movie was called *Ondu Mutthina Kathe* (1987) with Dr Raj Kumar in the leading role.

Ramoji Film City

Ramoji Film City, Hyderabad, entered the *Guinness Book of World Records* as the largest film production facility in the world. It was built by a Telugu producer named Ramoji Rao.

Mahishasura Mardini (1959)

The Kannada movie *Mahishasura Mardini* was a superhit in every sense of the word. Dubbed and distributed in as many as eight different Indian languages, it was a blockbuster everywhere.

Sridevi's Movie Debut

Legendary actress Sridevi made her debut in a Tamil movie when she was just four years old. The mythological film was *Thunaivan* (1969) in which Sridevi played Lord Murugan.

First Star to be Paid a Crore

Telugu superstar Chiranjeevi is the first Indian actor to receive ₹1 crore as remuneration for a single movie.

Kannada Film Debutants

Many popular artists of regional as well as Hindi cinema made their debut in the Kannada film industry. The impressive list includes Rajinikanth, Mani Ratnam, and Deepika Padukone, among many others.

Kannada Film Industry's Pride

The hugely popular Kannada film *Om* (1995) is the pride of the Kannada film industry. It has been re-released more than five hundred times over the last twenty years which is a record in the history of Indian cinema.

The *Nata Sarvabhouma* of the Kannada Film Industry

Dr Raj Kumar is known as the *Nata Sarvabhouma* of the Kannada film industry. He has received a doctorate for his work as an actor. He is also the only Indian actor to be awarded the prestigious Kentucky Colonel by the American state of Kentucky.

The Power of Rajinikanth

The Rajinikanth starrer *Muthu* (1995) was the first Tamil movie to be dubbed and released in Japan. *Muthu* made Rajini Anna a huge star in Japan. Rajinikanth's *Sivaji: The Boss* (2007) became the first Tamil film to top the box office in the UK and South Africa.

Top Tamil Movie Soundtrack

The soundtrack of Mani Ratnam's Tamil classic *Thalapathi* (1991) has been composed by music maestro Ilaiyaraaja. It is included in the *Guardian's 1000 Albums to Hear Before You Die!*

Acting in a Thousand Films

Renowned Tamil actress Manorama has also earned her place in the *Guinness Book of World Records* by acting in a record one thousand films in her long career. That's the most number of films anyone has done all over the world.

Mohanlal the Wrestler

Before becoming a superstar in Malayalam cinema, Mohanlal was a successful professional wrestler. In fact, he won the state wrestling championship in 1977–78 and was selected for the National Championship in New Delhi. But before he could participate, he got a chance to act, and life changed completely.

Record Sale of Movie Tickets

Kannada film *KGF Chapter 2* (2022) sold about 17.1 million movie tickets through BookMyShow, India's leading online movie booking platform, beating the earlier record on BookMyShow held by Telugu/Tamil movie *Baahubali 2: The Conclusion* (2017).

Superstar Buddies

Mohanlal and Mammootty are the biggest superstars of Malayalam cinema and are also good friends instead of rivals. They have acted together in over fifty films from *Padayottam* (1982) to *Twenty: 20* (2008), and most of these films are blockbusters. United we stand!

Ajantrik (1958)

Director Ritwik Ghatak's debut Bengali classic *Ajantrik* is regarded as India's first science fiction film. It was based on author Subodh Ghosh's short story. A poor taxi driver (Kali Banerjee) discovers that he has a 'living car'. *Ajantrik* received a special screening at the Venice Film Festival in 1959.

The Actor Director

The year 1950 saw the emergence of Partition-centric movies with Nemai Ghosh's *Chinnamul* (The Uprooted). Ritwik Ghatak acted in this movie which Russian film-maker Vsevolod Pudovkin liked so much that he released it in Russia. Encouraged, Ghatak later acted in three of his own films: *Subarnarekha* (1965), *Titas Ekti Nadir Naam* (1973), and *Jukti Takko Aar Gappo* (1974).

Mammootty's Passion

Mammootty's first appearance in Malayalam cinema was in 1971 when he was a teenager. After that, he focused on academics and became a lawyer. But he chose to abandon his successful legal career and returned to his passion, cinema. His fans are grateful for this brave decision.

From a Gurudwara Singer to a Movie Star

Diljit Dosanjh performed kirtans in local gurudwaras till he became a popular Punjabi singer. The hard-working Diljit entered the world of movies and became a star in the Punjabi film industry when his film *Jatt and Juliet 2* (2013) smashed all box office records. Today, he is making a mark in Bollywood.

The First Assamese Film

Jyoti Prasad Agarwala is an Assamese cultural icon and is known as the 'Rupkonwar' of Assamese culture. He is also regarded as the founder of Assamese cinema for his film *Joymoti* (1935).

The Highest-Grossing Marathi Movie

Marathi movie *Sairat* (2016) had a modest budget of ₹4 crore. It became the highest-grossing Marathi movie of all time earning over ₹100 crore worldwide. In the sixty-sixth Berlin International Film Festival, *Sairat* received a standing ovation. The entire cast of *Sairat* was made up of newcomers.

Amazing *Sairat* Facts

- *Sairat* is the first Indian movie to record its music in Hollywood's Sony Scoring Stage, California.
- After the success of this Marathi film, all the on-set employees were paid extra from the profits. The actors received ₹5 crore each.
- *Sairat* was leaked online two days before its release.

Rajinikanth's Escape

Rajinikanth is the only Indian megastar who visits the Himalayan caves after every film! He says that being in the Himalayan caves detoxifies his soul and brings him peace of mind.

The Rise of Rajinikanth

Rajinikanth did several odd jobs as a young man, including that of a coolie (porter).

Before he entered the film industry, he worked as a bus conductor with a salary of around ₹750.

Bairavi (1978), directed by M. Bhaskar, was the first Tamil film to cast Rajinikanth as a solo hero. He earned the sobriquet 'superstar' with this film.

Amazing Facts: *Baahubali 2: The Conclusion* (2017)

- First Indian movie released in 4K High Definition format.
- The filming took almost five years.
- Director S.S. Rajamouli shot four climax sequences in case the movie was leaked online.
- It set the record of the highest ticket prices ever at ₹2,400.
- The VFX team of the movie also worked on *Jurassic World* (2015).

The Telugu Superstar

Telugu movie star Ghattamaneni Mahesh Babu is one of the most popular actor-producers and probably the only star to endorse a national brand. But strangely, he did not learn to read and write Telugu. Mahesh Babu prefers to learn his dialogues by listening to his directors, who narrate them to him.

Guru of Malayalam Cinema

The first Malayalam film that was sent as India's official entry to the Oscars was *Guru* that released in 1997, starring the mighty Mohanlal.

South Indian Superstars Who Worked in Hollywood Projects

- Rajinikanth was part of the 1988 Hollywood film *Bloodstone,* produced by Ashok Amritraj and featuring Brett Stimely and Anna Nicholas in lead roles.

- Rajinikanth's son-in-law Dhanush played the lead in Ken Scott's *The Extraordinary Journey of the Fakir* (2018) and a pivotal role in Netflix's *The Gray Man* (2022), directed by Anthony and Joe Russo (of *Avengers* fame). The film also stars Ryan Gosling and Chris Evans.

- Popular composer-turned-actor G.V. Prakash made his Hollywood debut with *Trap City* (2020). The film stars Brandon T. Jackson and Dennis L.A. White in lead roles.

Lieutenant Colonel Mohanlal

Malayalam superstar Mohanlal is the first Indian actor who has been conferred with the honorary rank of lieutenant colonel in the Territorial Army of India.

Chemmeen

The classic Malayalam film *Chemmeen* (1965) was beautifully cinematographed and focused on the difficult subject of an inter-religious love affair. It was screened at the Cannes Film Festival.

The Arrival of Mani Ratnam

Mani Ratnam made his debut in Tamil cinema with *Pallavi Anu Pallavi* in 1983. But his 1986 film *Mouna Ragam: A Silent Symphony* announced his arrival as a special directorial talent. He has successfully merged his technical expertise with unique themes in many Tamil and Hindi movies.

A Fan of Chicken Biryani

Baahubali (2015) star Prabhas is so fond of food that he wanted to be a hotelier before he decided to pursue an acting career. Chicken biryani is Prabhas's favourite meal, and he reportedly ate fifteen different types of biryanis when he was preparing for his meaty role in the blockbuster *Baahubali*.

Maverick Maestro

Mrinal Sen was one of the pioneers of Indian parallel cinema. He introduced experimental film-making to India and was the first Indian director to use unusual camera movements, montages resembling news reels, and episodic narratives in films. This earned him the title 'Maverick Maestro'.

The First South Indian Star in Hindi Films

Vyjayanthimala is a famous actress in the golden era of Hindi cinema who became the first south Indian to become a star in Hindi films. Being a famous dancer herself, she also introduced classical dance to the industry. Vyjayanthimala was also the first person to refuse a Filmfare Award. She won the Filmfare Award for Best Supporting Actress for *Devdas* (1955). She felt she played a leading role equal to that of Suchitra Sen, her co-star, and could not accept the award for a supporting role.

Vijay's Triple Role

Vijay played a triple role for the first time in his career in the action thriller *Mersal* (2017). The Tamil movie was the highest-grossing film of his career and the most successful at the box office in 2017.

The Talented Mr Dhanush

Tamil movie superstar Dhanush is also a talented songwriter and singer. He wrote the lyrics of the famous song 'Why This Kolaveri Di?' in just six minutes. Reports say that the first recording of the song was ready in thirty-five minutes.

Dhanush's Real Name

Dhanush's real name is Venkatesh Prabhu Kasthuri Raja. When he entered the film industry as a sixteen-year-old, he changed his screen name to Dhanush. That was because his name was similar to established Tamil actors like Ilaya Thilagam Prabhu and Prabhu Deva.

Like Father like Son

Telugu superstar Ram Charan was supported by his father Chiranjeevi during the initial days of his career. Chiranjeevi produced Ram Charan's movies. So, Ram Charan returned the favour by producing his father's comeback film *Khaidi No. 150* (2017). Ram Charan launched his own production house called Konidela Production Company.

PARALLEL CINEMA

Rise of Parallel Cinema

As mainstream Hindi cinema prospered, the growth of parallel/ alternative cinema was observed. These films were socially relevant, realistic, and poetic, steering clear of the typical formulaic narrative. Although parallel cinema's golden age arrived only in the twentieth century, the foundations were laid with *Neecha Nagar* (1946) and *Do Bigha Zamin* (1953).

Parallel Bengali Cinema

Bengali cinema emerged with its own golden era in the early 1950s, earning its rightful place among India's most critically acclaimed regional cinema. The three pillars of Bengali cinema,

Satyajit Ray, Mrinal Sen, and Ritwik Ghatak made their first classics in the Bengali golden era. They are celebrated as world cinema directors today.

Tollywood

Two regional Indian movie industries go by the name Tollywood. Tollygunge, the headquarters of the Bengali film industry in Kolkata has been merged with Hollywood for the Bengali film industry to be termed Tollywood. The Telugu film industry also goes by the same name, merging the words Telugu and Hollywood.

The Father of Bengali Cinema

Dhirendra Nath Ganguly is known as the father of Bengali cinema. Also known as DG, he established the Indo-British Film Co. in 1918, which was the first Bengali-owned production company, and soon became a leading production house in Bengal.

Satyajit Ray

Legendary Bengali film-maker Satyajit Ray is the only Indian director to have received an Oscar. In 1991, he was awarded the Oscar for Lifetime Achievement for a remarkable film career of twenty-nine feature films, five documentaries, and two short films that began with *Pather Panchali* (1955) and ended with *Agantuk* (1991).

First Indian to Receive National Award for Best Actor

Uttam Kumar is regarded as the Mahanayak (Superhero) of Bengali cinema. He was also the first actor to receive the National Film Award for Best Actor for his superlative performance in *Antony Firingee* in 1967.

Shatranj Ke Khilari (1977)

Satyajit Ray's only Hindi movie is *Shatranj Ke Khilari*. It was also the only Indian movie featuring Sir Richard Attenborough as an actor. However, *Sadgati* (1981) was a telefilm featured on DD National that can be considered his second.

The Eternal Pair of Bengali Cinema

Uttam Kumar and Suchitra Sen were the most successful on-screen pair in Bengali cinema. This iconic romantic pair came together for the first time in 1953 in the comedy *Sharey Chuattar* and went on to do thirty films together.

First Facts of Bengali Cinema

- The first feature film produced in Bengali was the silent film *Bilwamangal* in 1919.
- *Jamai Shashthi* (1931) was the first Bengali film with dialogues.
- The first Bengali talkie as a full-length feature film was *Dena Paona* (1931)
- The first coloured Bengali film was *Kanchenjunga* (1962) by Satyajit Ray.

The Journey of *Pather Panchali* to Cannes

Satyajit Ray's first film *Pather Panchali* (1955) was funded by the West Bengal government, which wanted Ray to make changes to the ending to make the film more positive. Ray refused to do this and the film could only make it to the Cannes Film Festival thanks to the intervention of the then prime minister Jawaharlal Nehru.

Ray Bizarre

Indian director Satyajit Ray had other artistic talents apart from film-making. Combining Indian motifs and calligraphy, Ray created four unique Roman fonts. Two of these fonts bear his name and are called Ray Roman and Ray Bizarre. The other two are Daphnis and Holiday Script.

Oxford Honours Ray

Satyajit Ray received an honorary doctorate from Oxford University, becoming only the second film director to be honoured thus at the time. The first recipient of this honorary doctorate was Ray's idol Charlie Chaplin.

Ray of Design

Before becoming a great film-maker, Satyajit Ray designed book covers for Signet Press. Two of his mentionable book covers include Jim Corbett's classic *Man-Eaters of Kumaon* and Jawaharlal Nehru's *Discovery of India*.

Satyajit Ray: Fast Facts

- After 1961, Ray composed the music for all his films and designed their publicity posters.
- Ray described his 1964 film *Charulata* as 'the one film I would make the same way if I had to do it again'.
- *Kanchenjungha* (1962) was his first original screenplay and his first film in colour.

Ray the Music Director

Satyajit Ray had an outstanding sense of music and served as the music director of his own films after his career took off. He was also the music director of the Merchant Ivory production *Shakespeare Wallah* (1965).

Ray's Contribution to Cinematography

Satyajit Ray also influenced cinematography across the world. He was the one who created the effect of daylight on-set, using bounce lighting and photo-negative flashbacks.

Satyajit Ray

The Cowboys of Bollywood: Curry Western Genre

It was in the 1970s that the 'Spaghetti Westerns' from Hollywood were adapted into Bollywood as 'Curry Westerns', which were Westerns, but in the context of India, and with added masala and emotions. Curry Westerns lacked the grimness of Spaghetti Westerns, but they did have a feeling of harshness, treachery, and a demonic enemy who frequently sprang out of thin air. These movies did not focus on themes of territorial rights or the exploitation of nature or the conquering of the wild. Here, kinship, honour, and personal vengeance served as the foundational premise.

Feroz Khan, Dharmendra, and Mithun Chakraborty were the flag-bearers of this genre in Bollywood, all through the 1970s and '80s, playing the quintessential cowboy-like character in various settings, and more often than not, delivering justice.

Most famous movies from this genre include *Khote Sikkay* (1974), *Sholay* (1975), *Kaala Sona* (1975), *Chunaoti* (1980), *Jagir* (1984), *Wanted: Dead or Alive* (1984), *Zalzala* (1988), etc.

Quick Gun Murugan (2009) was a critically acclaimed spoof film on Indian Western or the Curry Western films, including some closely resembling, exaggerated scenes as the classic Jaishankar movies – first Curry Western movies of India from Tamil cinema, including *Kalam Vellum* (1970), *Jakkamma* (1972), *Ganga* (1972), *Enga Pattan Sothu* (1975), etc.

Dil Toh Bachha Hai Jee: Children's Movies in Indian Cinema

Indian cinema has produced some of the most thought-provoking, touching, and relatable movies, when it comes to creating something for the kids. While they might be categorized as children's movies, they are not meant only for children.

Bengali cinema, in particular, has been quite active in this regard and has been at the forefront since the very beginning, producing movies like *Bari Theke Paliye* (1958) by Ritwik Ghatak; *Goopy Gyne Bagha Byne* (1969), *Sonar Kella* (1974), and *Joi Baba Felunath* (1979) from the Feluda series by none other than Satyajit Ray; *Sabuj Dwiper Raja* (1979) by Tapan Sinha; *Damu* (1996) by Raja Sen; and so on.

Bollywood is also not very far behind when it comes to making children's movies. There have been kids-oriented movies since the black-and-white era, and the trend still continues. Noteworthy movies in this context are *Hum Panchhi Ek Daal Ke* (1957), *Nannha Farishta* (1969), *Safed Haathi* (1977), *Aaj Ka Robin Hood* (1988), *Chhota Chetan* (1998) – India's first 3D feature fantasy film, *Jajantaram Mamantaram* (2003) – India's take on *Gulliver's Travels* – *Makdee* (2002), *Iqbal* (2005), *Vaah! Life Ho Toh Aisi!* (2005), *The Blue Umbrella* (2005), *Bhoot Unkle* (2006), *Bhoothnath* (2008), *Jumbo* (2008), *Stanley Ka Dabba* (2011), *Chillar Party* (2011), *Dhanak* (2015), and *Budhia Singh – Born to Run* (2016), among others.

Apart from these movies, there have also been many other movies that were not categorized as children's movies in particular but were and are thoroughly enjoyed by children, nonetheless. This list includes movies like *Mr India* (1987), *Chachi 420* (1997), *Rockford* (1999), *Krrish* series (2003–13), *Bumm Bumm Bole* (2010), *Do Dooni Chaar* (2010), *Ra.One* (2011), *I Am Kalam* (2011), *Gippi* (2013), *Hichki* (2018), etc.

Hindi Hollywood

There are phases in every industry when a certain formula becomes the formula for success and the film industry is no exception to that. Spy thriller movies, biopics, fantasy movies, adventure movies, etc., have all had their phases, and some of them, in particular, seeped their way into Bollywood from Hollywood.

From James Bond (Bond movies) to Ethan Hunt (*Mission Impossible* movies), spy thrillers have always been a popular choice. Bollywood's reply to those movies came in the shape of films like *Surakshaa* (1979) and *Wardat* (1981), where Mithun Chakraborty plays Gopinath/Gunmaster G9; *Agent Vinod* (1977), which was reprised in 2012 with the same name but with a different storyline; *Farz* (1967), where Jeetendra played Gopal Kishan Pandey aka Agent 116, which was later played by Dharmendra as well in *Keemat* (1973); *The Great Gambler* (1979), with Amitabh Bachchan's double-role fiasco in an espionage setting; and *Akayla* (1991), among others.

In the action-adventure genre, there are a bunch of movies (more than fifty) in Hollywood based on the character 'Tarzan', created by Edgar Rice Burroughs. Naturally, such a successful character was adapted in Bollywood too. The first Indian Tarzan film was *Toofani Tarzan* (1937) by Wadia Movietone, starring John Cawas as Tarzan. Next came *Zimbo* (1958), made by Homi Wadia with an Indian version of Tarzan, played by Azad. This set up the pace for the Tarzan movies in the 1960s, with movies like *Tarzan aur Jadugar* (1963), *Tarzan aur Jalpari* (1964), and *Tarzan and Delilah* (1964). Then in 1965, Dara Singh played Tarzan in three films with Mumtaz as the leading lady. Many more Tarzan movies came after that with different leads, like *Tarzan in Fairyland* (1968) and *Tarzan 303* (1970). The Tarzan trend started fading after that and made a comeback years later in the Hemant Birje and Kimi Katkar starrer *Adventures of Tarzan* (1985), and then came its sequel, *Tarzan Ki Beti* (2002).

Notable Bollywood Movies with Amazing Prosthetic Make-Up

When it comes to the use of prosthetic make-up to make the movies more interesting, Bollywood is not very far behind the global cinema, having presented some really good movies with convincing prosthetic work. Prime examples include:

- ***Hindustani/Indian* (1996)**
  Kamal Haasan in dual role as Senapathy and Chandra Bose.

- ***Chachi 420* (1997)**
  Kamal Haasan again in a dual role, as Jai Prakash Paswan and the Indian Mrs Doubtfire, Laxmi Godbole.

- ***Dhoom 2* (2006)**
  Hrithik Roshan as the thief Mr A/Aryan, donning several get-ups for his stealing quests, including that of the royal queen, an old man, and a dwarf, among others.

- ***Paa* (2009)**
  Amitabh Bachchan as a twelve-year-old kid Auro, who suffers from a rare genetic disorder, progeria.

- ***Fan* (2016)**
  Shah Rukh Khan in a dual role, as superstar Aryan Khanna and his obsessive fan Gaurav Chandna, who looks somewhat like him.

- ***Tumbbad* (2018)**
  Harsh K. as the cursed demigod Hastar.

- ***Chhapaak* (2020)**
  Deepika Padukone as the acid-attack survivor Malti Agarwal (based on Laxmi Agarwal).

- ***83* (2021)**
  Ranveer Singh as the 1983 Indian cricket team captain Kapil Dev.

Bollywood Movies with Laughable Prosthetic Make-Up

- ***Action Replayy* (2010)**
  Akshay Kumar as the buck-toothed Kishen Chopra.

- ***Haseena Parkar* (2017)**
  Shraddha Kapoor as underworld don Dawood's sister, Haseena Parkar.

- ***Chhichhore* (2019)**
  The entire cast including Sushant Singh Rajput and Shraddha Kapoor in their older versions.

- ***PM Narendra Modi* (2019)**
  Vivek Oberoi as Prime Minister Narendra Modi.

And Then There Were the Ramsay Brothers...

Think of the horror movies from the 1970s and '80s Bollywood, and what pops in your mind at once is the name Ramsay Brothers! They can be credited with bringing the genre to the forefront in Indian cinema, by making tight-budget, edgy but nevertheless scary movies. But those movies have not aged well. Though they are still considered cult classics in a way, the films definitely didn't have the most convincing appearances of ghosts, monsters, demons, or spirits – thanks to their prosthetic make-up. The must-watch ones from the Ramsay repertoire are *Do Gaz Zameen Ke Neeche* (1972), *Purana Mandir* (1984) – with Anirudh Agarwal as the famous monster-demon Saamri, who has a recurring role in other Ramsay movies as well; *Tahkhana* (1986), *Veerana* (1988), *Purani Haveli* (1989), *Shaitani Ilaka* (1990), and *Bandh Darwaza* (1990), among others.

Shyam Ramsay

Ek Chatur Naarrr...
Aapne toh humse humaara guroor hee chheen liya!
Hi, I'm Chitti the Robot. Speed 1 terahertz, memory 1 zettabyte.
Kuch kuch hota hai, tum nahi samjhogi.

Naatu Naatu...
Waise bhi perfection ko improve karna mushkil hota hai.
Wonderful, wonderful!!!
Saheb-e-Alam

National Film Awards 2023 to Honour Best Films in Indian Cinema for 2021–2022

Best Feature Film	*Rocketry: The Nambi Effect* (2022) by R. Madhavan
Best Children's Film	*Gandhi & Co.* (2022) by Manish Saini
Best Debut Film of a Director	*Meppadiyan* (2022) by Vishnu Mohan
Best Director	*Godavari* (2021) by Nikhil Mahajan
Best Popular Film Providing Wholesome Entertainment	*RRR* (2022) by S.S. Rajamouli
Nargis Dutt Award for Best Feature Film on National Integration	*The Kashmir Files* (2022) by Vivek Agnihotri
Best Actor	*Pushpa: The Rise – Part 1* (2021) by Allu Arjun
Best Actress	*Gangubai Kathiawadi* (2022) by Alia Bhatt and *Mimi* (2021) by Kriti Sanon

5

BLOODLINE

EVERY FIELD OF WORK HAS SOME DOMINATING NAMES RULING THE INDUSTRY, AND THE FILM INDUSTRY IS NO EXCEPTION TO IT. IT BEGINS WITH CERTAIN PIONEERS WHO ARE JOINED BY THEIR FAMILIES IN THE SAME FIELD IN WHICH THEY HAVE TASTED SUCCESS. THE COPPOLAS, MAYERS, WARNER BROTHERS, KAPOORS, KHANS, BACHCHANS, ETC., ARE ALL SUCH FAMILIES WHOSE GENERATIONS HAVE BEEN AND ARE DOMINATING THE FILM INDUSTRY.

Famous Hollywood Families

In Hollywood, film familes have made a significant contribution to the growth of the movie industry.

David O. Selznick and Louis B. Mayer

The year 1930 witnessed the greatest union of Hollywood families when producer Lewis Selznick's son David O. Selznick married Louis B. Mayer's daughter Irene. Selznick worked as vice-president at MGM with his father-in-law and formed the Academy of Motion Picture Arts and Sciences in 1927 with thirty-six other founders of the film industry. In 1935, Selznick left MGM to set up Selznick International Pictures, which produced the highest-grossing film of all time, *Gone with the Wind* (1939).

The Coppolas

Francis Ford Coppola is at the helm of the Coppola family, having directed iconic films like *The Godfather* (1972) and *Apocalypse Now* (1979), among others. In 1969, Coppola co-founded American Zoetrope studio with George Lucas with an aim to find creative, fast, and economic approaches to film-making.

Francis Ford Coppola's daughter Sofia Coppola was also a successful film-maker and won an Oscar for writing her second film, *Lost in Translation* (2003). Coppola's son Roman Coppola has won the Golden Globe for direction, and his other son Gian-Carlo Coppola is a successful film producer. Gian-Carlo's daughter Gia Coppola is a successful director, and the Oscar-winning star Nicholas Cage is Coppola's nephew through his father.

Warner Brothers

Harry, Albert, Sam, and Jack Warner built one of the heavyweight Hollywood studios, Warner Brothers, in 1923. They released the first 'talkie', *The Jazz Singer* (1927) and went on to produce iconic classics like *Casablanca* (1942), *A Streetcar Named Desire* (1951), *My Fair Lady* (1964), and *Bonnie and Clyde* (1967).

The Marx Brothers

Even before the inception of Hollywood, the five Marx brothers were superstars in their own right. Groucho, Chico, Harpo, Zeppo, and Gummo became Broadway stars in the early 1900s, and created three iconic comedy movies of all time with Paramount in *Monkey Business* (1931), *Horse Feathers* (1932), and *Duck Soup* (1933). They have inspired and continue to inspire every generation of comedians in film history.

The Barrymores

In 1875, Maurice Barrymore shifted from England to New York City to make his Broadway debut. His three children – Lionel, Ethel, and John Barrymore – tasted success in Hollywood and theatre. John's son, John Drew Barrymore, was also an actor. Today, the Barrymore family legacy is carried on by John Drew Barrymore's daughter Drew Barrymore, a successful actress, producer, and director with her production company named Flower Films.

The Fondas

Henry Fonda made his Hollywood debut in 1935 and acted in over eighty movies, cementing his position as the perfect American leading man. He received his first Academy Award for Best Actor only when he was seventy-six years old for *On Golden Pond* (1981), and this was special as his daughter Jane starred in the movie too. Jane Fonda went on to become a leading Hollywood actress, bagging two Oscars for *Klute* (1971) and *Coming Home* (1978). Jane's brother Peter was a successful writer, producer, and actor. His daughter Bridget Fonda and Jane's son Troy Garity carry the Fonda family legacy into a third generation.

The Murdochs

After dominating print and broadcast media in Australia and Britain, Rupert Murdoch made his entry into Hollywood in 1985 by acquiring a struggling 20th Century Fox. Murdoch made the studio churn out two of the biggest Hollywood blockbusters in history in *Titanic* (1997) and *Avatar* (2009). His sons, Lachlan and James Murdoch, work closely with their father, while the former is currently the CEO.

Bollywood Filmy Families

The Kapoors

The legacy of the oldest family in Bollywood was begun by Prithviraj Kapoor, one of the founding members of the Hindi film industry. His son, actor-producer-director Raj Kapoor took the family to new heights by forming R.K. Studios in 1948. Raj's younger brothers Shashi Kapoor and Shammi Kapoor, and his sons Randhir Kapoor, Rajiv Kapoor, and Rishi Kapoor, are all celebrated stars in Hindi cinema. The current Kapoor generation is spearheaded by Randhir's daughters, Kareena and Karisma, and Rishi's son Ranbir Kapoor.

The Bachchans

The Bachchans are a successful family of actors beginning with Big B or Amitabh Bachchan, his wife Jaya Bachchan, son Abhishek Bachchan, and daughter-in-law Aishwarya Rai Bachchan. Now, Abhishek's nephew Agastya Nanda has also made his Bollywood debut.

Abhishek Bachchan and Aishwarya Rai Bachchan

The Second Kapoor Family

The second Kapoor family in Bollywood features three brothers in producer Boney Kapoor and actors Anil Kapoor and Sanjay Kapoor. The late actress Sridevi was married to Boney Kapoor, and their daughter Janhvi Kapoor is a successful actress. The other actors in the second generation include Arjun Kapoor, Sonam Kapoor, and Harsh Varrdhan Kapoor.

The Third Kapoor Family

From megaserials on television to movies on the big screen

and OTT platforms, Ekta Kapoor has done them all thanks to the support of her parents, former actor Jeetendra and Shobha Kapoor. Ekta's brother Tusshar Kapoor has made a unique comic presence in his films.

The Chopra–Johar family

Producer brothers B.R. Chopra and Yash Chopra have contributed immensely to Hindi cinema, and Aditya Chopra, son of Yash Chopra has carried forward his uncle and father's legacy with aplomb. Aditya's cousin Karan Johar, son of producer Yash Johar, has also made a mark in Hollywood with his brand of films.

The Khan-daan

Bollywood superstar Salman Khan's family is one of the most powerful families of Bollywood currently. Salman's father Salim Khan is a veteran screenplay writer. Salman's brothers Arbaaz Khan and Sohail Khan are actors, directors, and producers for Salman Khan's films.

The Pataudis

Former actress Sharmila Tagore became the begum of the Nawab of Pataudi, Mansoor Ali Khan. Their son Saif Ali Khan is a Bollywood star and their daughter Soha Ali Khan is an actress. Saif's daughter Sara Ali Khan, from his first wife Amrita Singh, is also a successful Bollywood actress. Presently, he is married to actress Kareena Kapoor, and they have two sons, Taimur and Jeh.

The Bhatts

The Bhatt family is a unique mix of film-makers and actors. Mahesh Bhatt is a reputed film-maker, and his daughters Pooja and Alia Bhatt have made their mark in Bollywood. Mahesh Bhatt's younger brother Mukesh Bhatt is a producer along with his son Vishesh Bhatt.

Index

A

A Matter of Life and Death 5
Academy Award 19, 20, 21, 24, 35, 37, 38, 41, 50, 53, 54, 59, 64, 68, 77, 78, 79, 120, 121, 171, 172, 179, 269
Academy of Motion Picture 5, 267
Academy of Motion Picture Arts and Sciences 5, 267
Academy Ratio 5
Action 151, 262
Actor 11, 21, 39, 40, 45, 59, 60, 64, 68, 76, 79, 80, 93, 99, 103, 108, 109, 111, 112, 113, 120, 121, 129, 134, 146, 164, 179, 189, 194, 196, 200, 201, 203, 207, 211, 212, 214, 247, 253, 266, 269
Actress 21, 38, 59, 68, 76, 79, 80, 111, 114, 115, 120, 134, 140, 166, 167, 180, 181, 203, 206, 207, 217, 226, 230, 236, 240, 243, 251, 266
Aerial Shot 15
African Cinema 51
AI 89, 90, 96, 97
Alam Ara 174
Alberini, Filoteo 3
Almodovar, Pedro 20
Anand, Dev 173, 188, 189, 190, 196, 210, 229, 232, 233, 236, 239
Animation 5, 24, 50, 72
Anime 46
Arts and Sciences 5, 267
Aspect Ratio 4, 5
Australian Cinema 56
Australian Film 7, 58, 64
Author 33, 60, 78, 84, 85, 140, 149, 152, 189, 201, 215, 246
Azmi, Shabana 207, 221, 236

B

B. Cecil 73, 156
Bachchan, Amitabh 181, 182, 187, 190, 192, 193, 195, 196, 198, 200, 207, 208, 211, 212, 213, 214, 220, 221, 224, 227, 232, 259, 261, 270
Bardot, Brigitte 30
Belgian Cinema 35
Bengali Cinema 252, 253, 254
Bergman, Ingmar 18, 34, 43, 156
Bergman, Ingrid 18, 132
Berlin International Film Festival 30, 247
Big Five 30, 76
Billy The Kid 10, 141
Bollywood 82, 173, 175, 176, 178, 179, 180, 181, 182, 183, 185, 186, 187, 188, 191, 195, 200, 201, 202, 203, 206, 207, 208, 209, 210, 211, 213, 214, 215, 216, 217, 218, 219, 222,

223, 224, 225, 226, 227, 228, 229, 230, 231, 232, 233, 234, 236, 237, 238, 239, 247, 257, 258, 259, 260, 261, 262, 263, 270, 271
Brando, Marlon 118, 132, 146, 148, 170
British Cinema 31
British Film 6, 32, 51, 66
Broadway 8, 142, 268, 269
Buffalo Bill Cody 10
Burman, R.d. 222, 229, 230, 233, 239
Butch Cassidy and the Sundance Kid 78

C
California 72, 74, 139, 140, 143, 156, 248
Camera 2, 3, 6, 7, 8, 14, 18, 20, 21, 27, 28, 35, 40, 42, 47, 50, 107, 142, 143, 150, 151, 158, 159, 162, 163, 190, 203, 251
Camera Angles 13
Cameron, James 150, 151, 153, 155, 156
Canada 30, 71, 218
Cannes Film Festival 30, 35, 50, 230, 250, 254
Casablanca 18, 132, 268
Casting 16, 120, 154, 203
Chan, Jackie 118, 119, 121, 124, 125, 126, 139
Chaplin, Charlie 31, 34, 44, 73, 113, 114, 124, 125, 128, 129, 137, 255
Chekhov Technique 12
Chekhov, Michael 12
Children's Movies 258
Chopra, B.r. 185, 271
Chopra, Priyanka 228, 229, 230
Chopra, Yash 198, 199, 271
Cinema 1, 3, 4, 5, 6, 8, 17, 19, 20, 25, 43, 46, 51, 52, 70, 156, 173, 174, 175, 177, 194, 210, 223, 226, 240, 241, 249, 252, 253, 254, 258, 266
Cinema Halls 6, 241
Cinema Lumière 3, 4
Cinematographer 77
Citizen Kane 81, 82, 149, 162
Cleopatra 109, 110, 146
Colour 3, 4, 58
Contract 27, 30, 83, 231
Cross-Cut 13
Cruise, Tom 82, 88, 118, 142, 147, 172, 180
Cuarón, Alfonso 53
Cumberbatch, Benedict 33, 34
Curtis, Richard 32
Curry Western 257

D
Danish Cinema 19
Depp, Johnny 90, 107, 122, 138
Dey, Manna 195

Dharmendra 185, 195, 216, 217, 219, 227, 229, 233, 257, 259
Dicaprio, Leonardo 76, 98, 99, 102, 111, 15
Dialogue 5, 60, 139, 180,
Digital Light Processing (Dlp) 7
Disney 42, 44, 52, 80, 81, 85, 88, 138
Dissolve 11, 66, 169
Dixit, Madhuri 215, 216, 217
Dogme 95 6, 17, 20
Dollars Trilogy 40
Double Exposure 10
Dr No 33, 134
Dressing Room 10
Drive-In Movie Theatre 9
Dutt, Guru 173, 188, 189, 190, 193, 194, 201, 203, 223, 229, 230, 231, 233

E

Eastern Cinema 44
Edison, Thomas 4, 8, 72
Effects 72, 78, 93
Einstein, Albert 31
Eisenstein Sergei 42, 44, 50
Entertainment 31, 56, 71, 73, 85, 95, 187
European Cinema 17
European Film Award 19
Eye-Level Shot 13

F

Famous 27, 94, 236, 267
Father of Hollywood 71
Feature-Length Film 7
Federal Bureau of Investigation (FBI) 75
Felliniesque 39
Fiction 6, 8, 150, 201, 246
Film 3, 6, 7, 8, 10, 19, 20, 22, 23, 24, 26, 27, 30, 32, 35, 39, 41, 43, 46, 48, 49, 50, 51, 53, 54, 55, 57, 59, 60, 66, 75, 76, 81, 84, 132, 152, 158, 163, 164, 167, 175, 176, 178, 184, 191, 201, 207, 213, 217, 219, 230, 236, 240, 241, 242, 244, 245, 247, 250, 253, 254, 266,
Film Festival 175, 241
Film Industry 3, 19, 32, 34, 36, 46, 51, 52, 53, 57, 70, 73, 173, 178, 180, 184, 185, 202, 212, 226, 231, 240, 245, 247, 248, 252, 253, 259, 267, 270
Filming 7, 18, 27, 28, 34, 35, 47, 48, 57, 59, 82, 83, 84, 88, 103, 107, 108, 109, 113, 114, 115, 118, 122, 128, 129, 134, 135, 136, 149, 156, 157, 163, 185, 196, 249
Film-Maker 10, 12, 18, 20, 22, 23, 24, 28, 35, 36, 48, 49, 50, 51, 52, 53, 55, 67, 82, 156, 157, 177, 212, 215, 234, 236, 241, 247, 253, 255, 268, 271

Film-Making 4, 7, 17, 20, 25, 30, 41, 47, 50, 71, 72, 86, 174, 177, 191, 243, 251, 255
Fleming, Ian 33
Ford, Harrison 82, 91, 110, 111
Four Weddings and a Funeral 32
French Cinema 25
French Film 9, 10, 23, 25, 26
French New Wave 17, 25, 26, 40, 52
Frozen 80, 81

G

Genre 219, 257
German Cinema 22
German Expressionism 17
Germany 24, 30, 75, 132, 177, 200
Godard, Jean-Luc 25, 27, 28
Golden Age 25, 73, 148
Golden Era 173, 175, 251, 252, 253
Golden Globe 19, 35, 50, 54, 225, 238, 268
Gone with the Wind 5, 11, 76, 77, 86, 268
Great Depression 9
Griffith, D. W. 72
Ground-Level Shot 14

H

Hanaway, Frank 10
Hays, Will H. 9
High/Top-Angle Shot 14
Hindi Cinema 173, 194, 223, 226
Hip-Level Shot 14
Hitchcock, Alfred 10, 34, 87, 149, 163, 164
Hollywood 5, 8, 19, 20, 21, 22, 23, 30, 36, 41, 42, 44, 51, 53, 55, 58, 70, 71, 72, 73, 74, 75, 76, 77, 78, 79, 80, 82, 83, 84, 85, 86, 87, 88, 89, 92, 93, 94, 96, 108, 109, 110, 112, 113, 119, 120, 124, 128, 132, 133, 134, 136, 137, 139, 140, 141, 142, 143, 146, 149, 151, 156, 157, 158, 160, 164, 165, 167, 170, 178, 182, 187, 192, 193, 200, 215, 218, 223, 228, 229, 230, 248, 250, 253, 257, 259, 260, 267, 268, 269, 271
Hollywood Boulevard 74
Hollywood Walk of Fame 72, 73, 74, 124
Holmes, Sherlock 78
Hypocrites 8

I

Image 133, 155, 213, 223
In Old California 72
In the Mood for Love 45
Indian Cinema 174, 175, 177, 240, 258, 266
Intertitles 9
Invention 7, 17
Irwin, May 8
Italian Cinema 3, 36, 40, 71

Italian Neorealism 17
Italy 3, 30, 36, 38, 161

J
J Cut 13
Jaws 79
Jump Cut 12
Jump Cuts 18
Jurassic Park 77, 215

K
Kapoor, Anil 181, 196, 199, 270
Kapoor, Kareena 180, 206, 271
Kapoor, Raj 173, 174, 181, 182, 192, 193, 199, 202, 203, 209, 210, 211, 225, 231, 232, 235, 270
Kapoor, Shammi 202, 210, 214, 270
Kapoor, Shashi 182, 197, 203, 209, 211, 270
Kar-Wai, Wong 45, 47, 49
Khan, Saif Ali 180, 199, 271
Khan, Salman 185, 218, 271
Khan, Shah Rukh 179, 180, 183, 184, 197, 199, 201, 202, 211, 222, 237, 261
Khanna, Rajesh 194, 195, 202, 226, 227, 228, 230, 233, 234
Kinetoscope 1, 4
King, Stephen 78
Knee-Level Shot 14
Kubrick, Stanley 34, 48, 149, 150, 155, 161, 163
Kumar, Ashok 182, 188, 225, 226, 228, 232
Kumar, Dilip 173, 174, 178, 185, 188, 189, 192, 193, 209, 210, 211, 219, 226, 231, 237
Kumar, Kishore 175, 188, 190, 191, 196, 198, 199, 221, 233, 234, 238, 239, 240
Kumar, Manoj 183
Kumar, Rajendra 184, 225
Kumari, Meena 173, 183, 194, 237
Kurosawa, Akira 44, 46, 47, 48, 49, 50

L
L Cut 13
L'arroseur Arrose 6
La Presa Di Roma 3
La Sortie Des Ouvriers De L'usine Lumière 8
Lee, Bruce 128, 132, 135, 137, 138, 139, 141, 143
London 8, 32, 52, 64, 86, 87, 94, 102, 147, 163, 171, 197, 212, 225
Los Angeles 32, 72, 86, 99, 120, 161, 184, 236
Low-Angle Shot 14
Luhrmann, Baz 82
Lumière Brothers 2
Lyricist 239

M
Madhubala 173, 174, 176, 180, 181, 185, 196
Mamet, David 12
Mangeshkar, Lata 175, 187, 189, 221, 235
Matches: An Appeal 6
Matrix 69, 76, 157
Mcdaniel, Hattie 11
Media 81, 269
Meisner, Sandford 11
Meisner Technique 11
Méliès, Georges 10
Method Acting 11, 98
Method Acting Technique 11
Metro-Goldwyn-Mayer (MGM) 30, 79
Mifune, Toshiro 44
Mikkelsen, Mads 19
Mission: Impossible 259
Monroe, Marilyn 136, 146
Montage Cut 13
Mother India 179, 184, 225
Motion Picture Producers and Distributors of America (MPPDA) 9
Motion Picture Rating System 10
Moulin Rouge! 69, 82, 98, 107
Movie 4, 7, 8, 10, 30, 45, 60, 65, 68, 85, 95, 119, 120, 136, 146, 157, 158, 173, 178, 185, 202, 228, 243, 245, 246, 247
Movietone 5, 59, 174
Moving Picture 1, 6, 173
Music 5, 76, 83, 175, 191, 225, 230, 237, 256
Musical 5, 36, 82, 175, 193, 221, 225, 230, 235, 238
Muybridge, Eadweard 6

N
Nargis 173, 179, 184, 192, 199, 211, 225, 232, 266
Narrative Fiction 8
National Award 217, 236, 237, 239, 242, 253
Nau Do Gyarah 190
Naushad 175, 184, 191, 238
Neecha Nagar 175, 252
New Jersey 8, 9, 71, 72
Newsreels 5
Nickelodeon 8
Nolan, Christopher 64, 148, 152, 153
Nollywood 51
Nomination 41, 50, 77, 79, 184, 214
Non-Linear Narratives 18
Nutan 173, 226, 227, 229

O
Oscar 8, 11, 21, 34, 38, 39, 40, 46, 49, 50, 54, 58, 59, 62, 77, 81, 86, 93, 95, 99, 102, 114, 119, 120, 121, 137, 140, 146, 163, 165, 166, 167, 172, 179, 184, 214, 225, 230, 253, 268

P
Pacino, Al 91, 97, 119, 122, 123, 125, 127, 128, 157, 209
Padukone, Deepika 187, 207, 230, 245, 262
Palekar, Amol 213, 214
Palme D'or 35, 49, 50, 175
Panorama Shot 7
Parasite 46, 49, 50
Paris 2, 3, 7, 10, 29, 36, 56, 66, 179, 184
Phalke, Dadasaheb 175
Picture 1, 5, 9, 10, 34, 46, 53, 59, 78, 85, 86, 87, 93, 175, 267
Pierini, Professor Pietro 4
Pinocchio 52, 160, 161
Pirates of the Caribbean: On Stranger Tides 75
Pixar Animation Studios 72
Polish Cinema 24
Popcorn 9
Pope 4
Portman, Natalie 79, 102, 112, 123
Potter, Harry 54, 81, 92, 94, 112, 135, 140, 141, 214
Primetime Emmy 19
Prince, Louis Le 1
Producer 198, 219, 271
Prosthetic Makeup 261, 262
Puri, Amrish 195, 218, 224

R
Rafi, Mohammed 175, 193, 221, 238, 239
Rahman, A.r. 237, 238
Raja Harishchandra 173, 175
Rajamouli, S.S. 249
Rajinikanth 243, 245, 248, 250
Rani, Devika 174, 177, 181, 219, 227, 237
Ratnam, Mani 237, 245, 251
Ray, Satyajit 187, 207, 208, 253, 254, 255, 256, 258
Record 187, 201, 202, 246
Reeves, Keanu 103, 111, 122
Regent Street Cinema 8
Rehman 173, 180, 181, 194, 217
Rehman, Waheeda 173, 181, 194
Reporter 79
Rice, John 8
Ritchie, Guy 35
Role 21, 140, 251
Roshan, Hrithik 182, 261
Roundhay Garden Scene 1
Rowling, J.k. 33, 81
RRR 182, 197, 266
Russell, Ken 8
Russian Cinema 41

S
Sadhana 173
Saigal, K.l. 224, 239
Schindler's List 77, 154, 158
Schwarzenegger, Arnold 84, 99, 106, 115, 118, 140, 141, 143
Scorsese, Martin 76, 108, 151, 157, 158, 159, 160, 164

Screen 67, 96, 137, 243
Screenplay 37, 53, 60, 76
Seven Samurai 46, 47, 50
Shakespeare 47, 128, 133, 201, 256
Shatranj Ke Khilari 207, 253
Sholay 179, 185, 190, 197, 202, 207, 223, 224, 227, 244, 257
Shot 7, 8, 9, 13, 14, 15, 22, 25, 27, 29, 41, 45, 47, 59, 64, 72, 84, 103, 107, 110, 111, 123, 149, 155, 162, 163, 174, 179, 181, 186, 190, 220, 222, 224, 225, 227, 249
Shoulder-Level Shot 14
Singin' in the Rain 5
Skyfall 32
Slumdog Millionaire 82, 150
Smith, George Albert 3
Song 49, 182, 184, 186, 227, 242
Sound 4, 5, 9, 32, 48, 76, 223
South American and Mexican Cinema 52
South Indian Cinema 240
Spaghetti Western 40
Spanish Cinema 20
Spielberg, Steven 77, 79, 151, 156, 157, 158, 159, 160, 163, 215, 218
Split Screen 11
Sridevi 211, 215, 243, 245, 270
Stallone, Sylvester 84, 99, 139, 140, 141, 182
Standard Cut 12
Stanislavski Method 11
Stanislavski, Konstantin 11
Star 44, 55, 88, 91, 102, 113, 119, 120, 140, 146, 158, 159, 182, 183, 197, 199, 228, 243, 245, 247, 251
Story 7, 47, 48, 57, 66, 73, 93, 163, 177, 179, 229
Strasberg, Lee 11, 209
Studios 6, 19, 79, 268
Stuntman 10, 149
Sundance Film Festival In Park City 30
Superstar 184, 185, 202, 211, 218, 220, 226, 230, 233, 237, 243, 245, 246, 250, 252, 261, 271
Suraiya 216, 232, 233

T

Tarantino, Quentin 35, 98, 108, 152, 158
Tarkovsky, Andrei 43, 44
Taxi Driver 78, 108, 159
Technicolor 4
Terminator 99, 106, 115, 118, 151, 153
The Big Five 76
The Conqueror 72
The Count of Monte Cristo 72
The Godfather 118, 124, 125, 136, 146, 148, 170, 268
The Great Train Robbery 8, 10
The Hays Code 9
The Horse In Motion 6

The Jazz Singer 5, 84, 93, 268
The Kiss 8
The Lion King 80, 81
The Shawshank Redemption 155
The Silence of The Lambs 76, 78
The Sound of Music 76
The Squaw Man 73
The Story of The Kelly Gang 57
The Wizard of Oz 5, 80, 86, 115, 167
The Wolf of Wall Street 69, 76, 77, 111
Theatre 2, 3, 4, 8, 9, 21, 23, 31, 39, 56, 63, 85, 86, 162, 164, 175, 179, 209, 210, 211, 212, 223, 224, 228, 241, 242, 167
Tinseltown Iii, 71
Titanic 75, 119, 150, 155, 156, 269
Toronto International Film Festival 30
Toy Story 73
Trier, Lars von 6
Tripod 7
Truffaut, François 25, 27
TV 79, 141, 196, 229, 230

U

Un Chien Andalou 28, 29

V

Vague, Nouvelle 25
Venice Film Festival 24, 30, 43, 241, 247
Vinterberg, Thomas 6, 19, 20
Vyjayanthimala 173, 185, 251

W

Warner Brothers 5, 73, 80, 81, 92, 267, 268
Weber, Lois 8
Western 10, 40, 78, 141, 194, 257
Whitley, H. J. 71
Who's Afraid of Virginia Woolf? 10, 81
Wings 22, 64, 78, 93
Wives Beware 9
World Cinema 17
World War I 3, 19, 71

Z

Zorro 21

Image Copyright Information

Images from Shutterstock.com:

Pages – 04, 19, 21, 31, 36, 46, 50, 55, 58, 74, 85, 88, 99, 101, 104, 105, 112, 116, 123, 126, 130, 131, 138, 145, 147, 159, 163, 168, 175, 178, 184, 198, 204, 205, 208, 216, 218, 233, 239, 256, 264, 265, 270, 282

Images from Wikimedia.org:

Page 127 – CCA 2.0 Generic
https://commons.wikimedia.org/wiki/File:Alfredo_James_Pacino.jpg by Peter Martorano

Page 263 – CCA SA 3.0 Unported
https://commons.wikimedia.org/wiki/File:Shyam_Ramsay_in_a_contemplative_mood.jpg by Durlov

The End